SEAN SCULLY

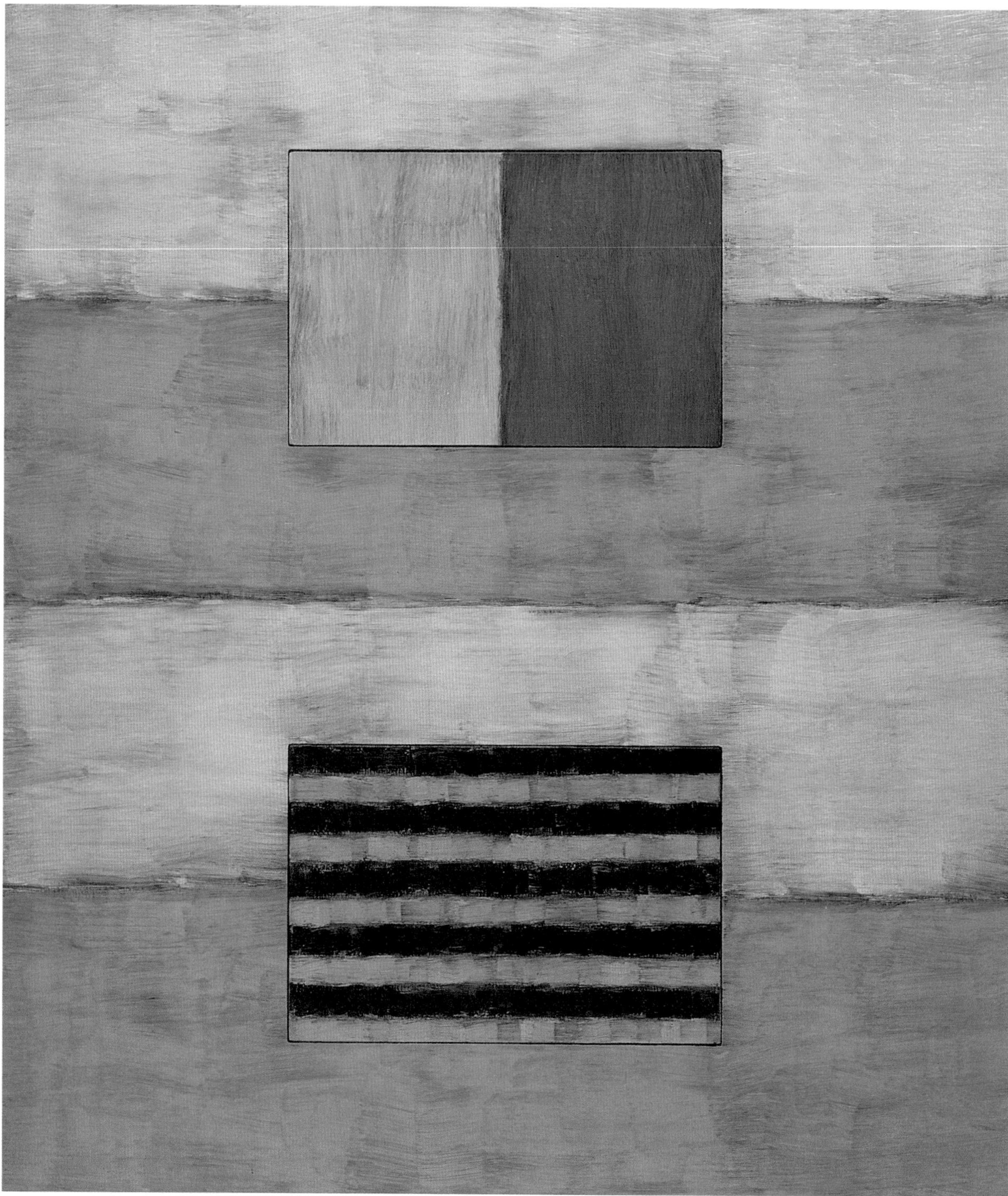

SEAN SCULLY

RESISTANCE AND PERSISTENCE: SELECTED WRITINGS

Edited by Florence Ingleby

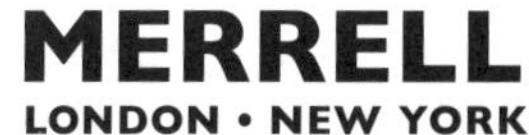

First published 2006 by Merrell Publishers Limited

Head office:
81 Southwark Street
London SE1 0HX

New York office:
49 West 24th Street, 8th Floor
New York, NY 10010

merrellpublishers.com

PUBLISHER Hugh Merrell
EDITORIAL DIRECTOR Julian Honer
US DIRECTOR Joan Brookbank
SALES AND MARKETING MANAGER Kim Cope
SALES AND MARKETING EXECUTIVE Amina Arab
CO-EDITIONS MANAGER Anne Le Moigne
ASSOCIATE MANAGER, US SALES AND MARKETING Elizabeth Choi
MANAGING EDITOR Anthea Snow
PROJECT EDITORS Claire Chandler and Rosanna Fairhead
EDITOR Helen Miles
ART DIRECTOR Nicola Bailey
DESIGNER Paul Shinn
PRODUCTION MANAGER Michelle Draycott
PRODUCTION CONTROLLER Sadie Butler

British Library Cataloguing-in-Publication Data:
Scully, Sean, 1945–
Sean Scully : resistance and persistence : selected writings
1. Scully, Sean, 1945– – Themes, motives 2. Art – Philosophy
I. Title
759.1'3
ISBN-13: 978-18589-4351-0
ISBN-10: 1-8589-4351-5

Produced by Merrell Publishers Limited
Designed by Maggi Smith
Copy-edited by Matthew Taylor
Proof-read by Helen Maxey
Indexed by Hilary Bird

Printed and bound in Spain

Jacket front and back
FOUR DAYS 1990 (detail)
Oil on canvas
274.3 × 365.8 cm (108 × 144 in.)
Private collection

Frontispiece
MAGDALENA 1993
Oil on canvas
203.2 × 177.8 cm (80 × 70 in.)
Private collection

CONTENTS

Art does not need to make sense or to function or to demonstrate any particular idea. It testifies to the beauty of imperfect human thought and action muddled up with feeling.

Sean Scully
Barcelona, August 2002

As an artist, one of the foremost abstract painters of our time, Sean Scully needs no introduction. But as a writer and commentator a few introductory words may be helpful.

One evening, a few years ago, I attended a lecture given by Scully after the formal opening of his *Wall of Light* sculpture at the University of Limerick in southern Ireland. I was struck then by the similarity between the way that he spoke about art, especially his own, and the way in which his paintings work their magic on the eye and mind. His paintings, when first encountered, look very simple: these bricks of colour, which seem so effortlessly built, offer an unsettlingly complex emotional potential, with an almost physical depth of possibility. Similarly, in the lecture theatre his delivery and the deadpan manner in which his ideas were phrased somehow married the skills of philosopher and comedian. He created a smokescreen, but behind the illusion of simply stated ideas lurked flashes of a frighteningly aggressive intellect and a profound understanding of the nature of painting and his place as an artist in the twenty-first century.

The origin of this book of Scully's selected writings is in a small publication made to coincide with an exhibition of his paintings at the Ingleby Gallery in Edinburgh, in the summer of 2005. That book printed the text of a single lecture given at the Institut Valencia d'Art Modern in May 2004 and led to conversations with Sean about his writing in general. He began to send us essays, lectures and assorted musings, most of which appear here in print for the first time.

The title, *Resistance and Persistence*, is taken from his essay on the twentieth-century Italian painter Giorgio Morandi, but it also seems to sum up Scully's position, and approach. These writings deal with his own work over a period of nearly forty years and with a life lived between London, New York, Barcelona and, more recently, Munich. Included are his thoughts on such heavyweights as Van Gogh, Matisse, Rothko and Pollock, but also on lesser-known figures: Liliane Tomasko, for example, or the essay on Ian Stephenson, which is not just a tribute to a fellow painter but a poignant memoir of Scully's own art school years and what it means to be inspired by another human being.

Sean Scully has himself been an inspiration for another generation of artists, and with *Resistance and Persistence* he presents, in his own voice, a glimpse of where his ideas, and above all where his powerful paintings, come from. It is a pleasure and privilege to have played a small part in bringing his words into print.

Florence Ingleby, 2006

Giorgio Morandi was born in Bologna in 1890. He studied art at the Accademia di Belle Arti there from 1907 to 1915.

He lived all his life with his three sisters, Anna, Dina and Maria Teresa. From the age of twenty until his death he lived in a flat at Via Fordazza 36, Bologna, and in the family country house in Grizzana in the mountains 35 kilometres away. He travelled to Venice, where he saw Monet and Cézanne, but throughout his life he moved very little, being content to live and work in his simple rooms in Bologna and his home in Grizzana. And it was only in 1956, at the age of sixty-six, that Morandi made his one and only trip abroad, which was to attend an opening of an exhibition he had in Winterthur. He died in Bologna in 1964.

Crucially, Morandi never visited Paris, the centre of art in the first half of the twentieth century, which is like not visiting New York or London now. When I was a student passing through the halls of the Tate Gallery in London, looking for role models, I would consistently pass a typically small painting by Morandi. It seemed to upset and disturb everything else that was going on. It was as if it was participating in the Modernist dialogue, since its spirit was twentieth-century, and clearly painted after the discovery of abstraction but, then again, stubbornly refusing to participate with appropriate enthusiasm. It seemed to be permanently hung on a short wall. So you saw it between seeing other paintings that were, of course, always bigger. Everything, it seemed, was bigger than the Morandi. Nothing else was as self-effacing. And nothing else was so awkwardly sealed. So you'd see Morandi after you'd looked at one painting, and you turned your body and your head to look at the next, and as you were leaving one room to go into another room you'd see the Morandi again. Not fitting in. Not playing the game. Being a part of it and not being a part of it, so therefore in the margin of the communal conversation, the common consensus built by the surrounding works. Imagine one sees, for example, a short wall, between big walls that occupy major spaces, as the margin of the architecture, or the transition between one major event and the next; this is where Morandi lived in the museum. Not exactly an event, but a tap on the back of the head. An appeal to the conscience, one might say. A worrying doubt, made by a doubter who raises the disturbing possibility that the Modernist juggernaut that we were so happy about might one day crash and burn.

And then there would be this small painting that says, "yes". This kind of thing can happen. And it has happened before. Rome was for around a thousand years the centre of the universe known to man. And it is therefore very Italian to know that the favours of history can wash in and then wash out, leaving empty buildings and unfortunately located agendas.

One day I'd see it and I'd think, this is great. It's really weird. And then another day I'd see it and I'd think to myself that he was an idiot. And so was the Tate for putting it up all the time. And then another day I'd see it, and I just didn't know what to think. It wasn't exciting, yet it was exciting. Exciting in its resistance, in its subversiveness. Someone asked me once if abstraction was subversive. I did not think so. And I don't think so now. It's subversive in the sense that it makes or helps people to think freely. But it's not trying to bring some other structure down to be seen. It makes its own space or has invented its own space. A space that didn't previously exist. This, coincidentally, Morandi did. This small painting used a space that was not used before, or could not usefully be used by anything else. The architecture of the idea was to say, "Yes. Correct. But what about this? That was big; this is small. That was a statement, this is a state." That Morandi was making an art of figuration during an epoch characterized by a wholesale march towards abstraction was in itself an act of defiance. However, in his case the defiance was wrapped in a cloak made of humble subversion. His paintings were not merely opposite in subject. His 'opposite' subject was painted apparently meekly in colours that were pale and seemingly tired, as if defeated at the outset of their contest with international abstraction. Like a boxer who fights each round without getting up from his seat in the corner of the ring. As if, in a sense, to make a demonstration of rising for the contest would be far too conformist and compromising. Morandi paints in pale, nearly dead colour, which itself cannot or will not rise to full spectrum. It will not reach across space to communicate visual power, but makes you reach across space towards it. We do the walking. The painting does the waiting. It lets you, in fact it invites you to walk past it and ignore it: it is only after you have seen many other paintings that you return to it, with your doubt. Morandi embodies the patience and the diffidence of history.

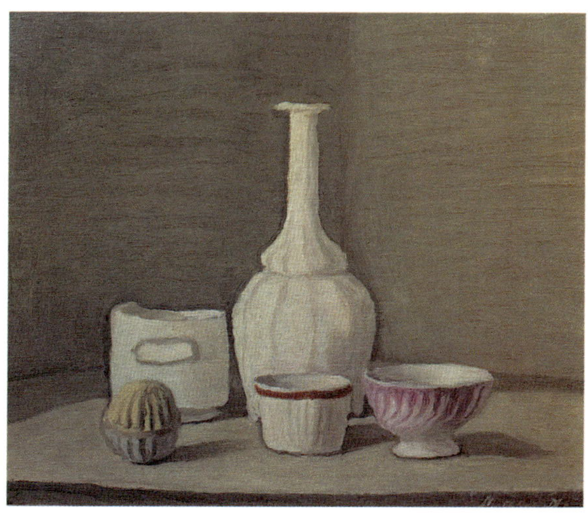

Giorgio Morandi (1890–1964)
Still Life, 1946
Oil on canvas
53.3 x 61.3 cm (21 x 24 in.)
London, Tate

The undersized painting that is pallid at birth doesn't need to be defeated by time and by its offspring, history. Morandi, who is full of history, understands it can begin in life that way. As if it has already been weakened by time as it is being made.

Morandi, the priest of subversion and reverence, sits in his small room stroking his humble surfaces with a vibrating acceptance of the impossibilities and necessity of resistance. Resistance to the majority and resistance to progress. When Fascism was rising in Europe like a galloping fire, Giorgio Morandi was a young man at art school and trying to articulate his place in the contemporary world.

He began his public life as an artist with an active dialogue with the visual ideas of his day, the most dominant of which was Cubism. His landscape and still-life paintings from around 1913 and 1914 demonstrate a willingness to do what all young artists must do, which is to learn the lessons of recent art. However, in Morandi's case this dialogue is short-lived, and his rejection of internationalism is born of a deeply felt negative reaction to war and its consequences. Thus he began his unique journey by travelling in the opposite direction to his contemporaries.

THE ACT OF LOOKING with Cézanne

To see and to work. To paint in a way that was predetermined and to paint a subject that was always virtually the same. Thus simultaneously to liberate the painting style which represented the subject without prejudice, as I would call it, and to read that subject as space, light, colour and form. Morandi paints things that exist, though they are stripped of all burdensome references to social function and history or political contexts. His discreetly expressive painting style is in concert with a subject that is also discrete, in the sense that they are vessels and containers whose meaning is open and exists outside clear political or functional reference. We are free to enjoy them and feel them as we might an abstract painting, yet they are faithful and mysterious representations of objects that were there. Huddled together in familial dependencies. So that their edges touch, and the bodily group-ings and their contact enables them to stand humble yet noble on their simple shelf. They stand for themselves, but they don't articulate exactly what that is.

The sameness of his subject amplifies the imaginative response. He has learned the lessons of abstraction. He has understood how powerfully repetition, and visiting the same or similar motif again and again, can open up emotional depth and interpretive range. Abstraction abstracted reality to reach the non-objective shore of new experience. Morandi reverses this journey and returns this possibility to simple observed reality. In this he is very different from Cézanne, his great example. Cézanne never knew abstraction until he was an old man, even though he pioneered it by making painting systematic. Yet in his way he overcame appearance with structure. This Morandi did not have to do, since the appearances of things in the world had already been conquered by abstraction.

I once watched a film of Cézanne painting. He moved as a bird moves, and his head was rapidly inclined toward the subject, the canvas, the subject and the canvas. Back and forth in a triangular relationship between the painter, the subject and the painting. This Morandi did also, since he was painting his jars or the view out of his window in Grizzana. Always in a triangle. When I paint, I look at the canvas on the wall, and I paint it. I move back and forth, between my seat and the painting, in a straight line, between me and the work. The painting being the subject and the object, all in one. There is no triangle. Everything I need to make the painting is in me when I start. And this difference is crucial. There are similarities, but the difference is profound.

Robert Irwin has described Morandi as making a unique kind of Abstract Expressionism. While being able to identify with this generous view, and being as much in favour of Morandi's work as Irwin, I would describe Morandi oppositely. The Abstract Expressionists worked in an atmosphere that benefited from group support, and furthermore their position in world culture was advanced from being in the right place at the right time. The various group photographs that were taken of De Kooning, Pollock, Krasner, Motherwell, Newman *et al.* testify to the cultural momentum of which they were the positive recipients. The Abstract Expressionists were working harmoniously with contemporary cultural history, and their careers were enlarged accordingly. They were working on the back of European art, as exemplified by Surrealism and geometric abstraction, whilst rejecting and improving it in favour of a new 'heroic' American art. They had the writers, such as [Clement] Greenberg, [Irving] Sandler and [Thomas] Hess, and the moneyed patrons such as Peggy Guggenheim, as well as the construction of new art palaces in America to contextualize critically, to buy and exhibit, these powerful new works.

The simple fact that Morandi, even today, still represents a 'cause' that other artists feel obliged to assist shows how resistible the work of Morandi was. Morandi's paintings were not really collected, because they simply didn't fit. Because when the great collections of America and Europe were being assembled in the 1950s and '60s, what largely 'fitted' was major abstraction.

Many painters like to argue that the 'subject' of Morandi is not important, and that one can ignore the figuration in his work, in order to enjoy the abstraction. However, Morandi's work was ignored by the major institutions for good reason. And simply put, it is not abstract. And it therefore cannot even legitimately be seen as a form of Abstract Expressionism. It should be read as figuratively based.

As a counterweight to the dominance of American painting of the 1950s, Morandi holds a position that cannot be challenged and today seems to yield an array of possible influences and examples for young painters. Morandi's work doesn't negotiate with Abstract Expressionism, as does, say, the work of the important French artist Yves Klein, who competes with America for scale and conceptual directness, or like other Europeans such as [Pierre] Soulages, [Emil] Schumacher and [Antoni] Tapies, who worked on a similarly large scale. Morandi's extreme originality is achieved as a counterpoint to all this. He is the authentic opposite. He doesn't attempt to compete with American art: he does the contrary, which is what American art cannot do since no culture can effectively represent the opposite of itself.

I was talking to a friend once on the 'phone about a painting I had just finished. The painting is called *Wall of Light Sky*. She was asking me to describe it. After a few minutes I said, "Look, I can describe it to you, by describing something that can't really exist." I told her, since it was made of many greys that were mixed in with pink and red and blue, that it was maybe like a Morandi on a giant scale that was drawn on a broken grid. So I was talking of the way a simple subject could be given a compressed complex history, by being overpainted in uncertain colours. This made everything clear to her, even though I had described the impossible, since a giant Morandi is the opposite of what a Morandi is. What its sense of being is, and what it registers itself as in the world of art.

Morandi is the opposite of heroic-scale abstraction in every way. That Morandi worked in isolation is part of the central meaning of his work. He chose to resist Modernism in a way that Jackson Pollock did not and did not have to. Pollock, for example, was working in a rising culture that had just won a world war, and played a major role in defeating Fascism. The USA had been flooded with grateful, eager-to-be-patriotic immigrants after the Second World War, and it was glowing with self-belief. New York represented openness and freedom and, importantly, wealth. There was no reason why its artists should resist its direction. They were, after all, the equivalent of Masaccio working in Florence in the fifteenth century. New York was the new Florence and was a golden gate to a future of freedom and wealth.

Morandi's world was very different. His world was not big, in the sense that it was expanding into light. It was small, in the sense that in the midst of personal crisis, Fascism and impending darkness, Morandi had to paint in a corner out of 'what was left'. What he could salvage. Not what was possible, in terms of invention, growth and freedom, but what he could hold on to, as a human being, in a context of failed hope and danger.

In 1915, when Italy entered the First World War, Morandi was conscripted into the Italian army. This event caused him to suffer a nervous breakdown.

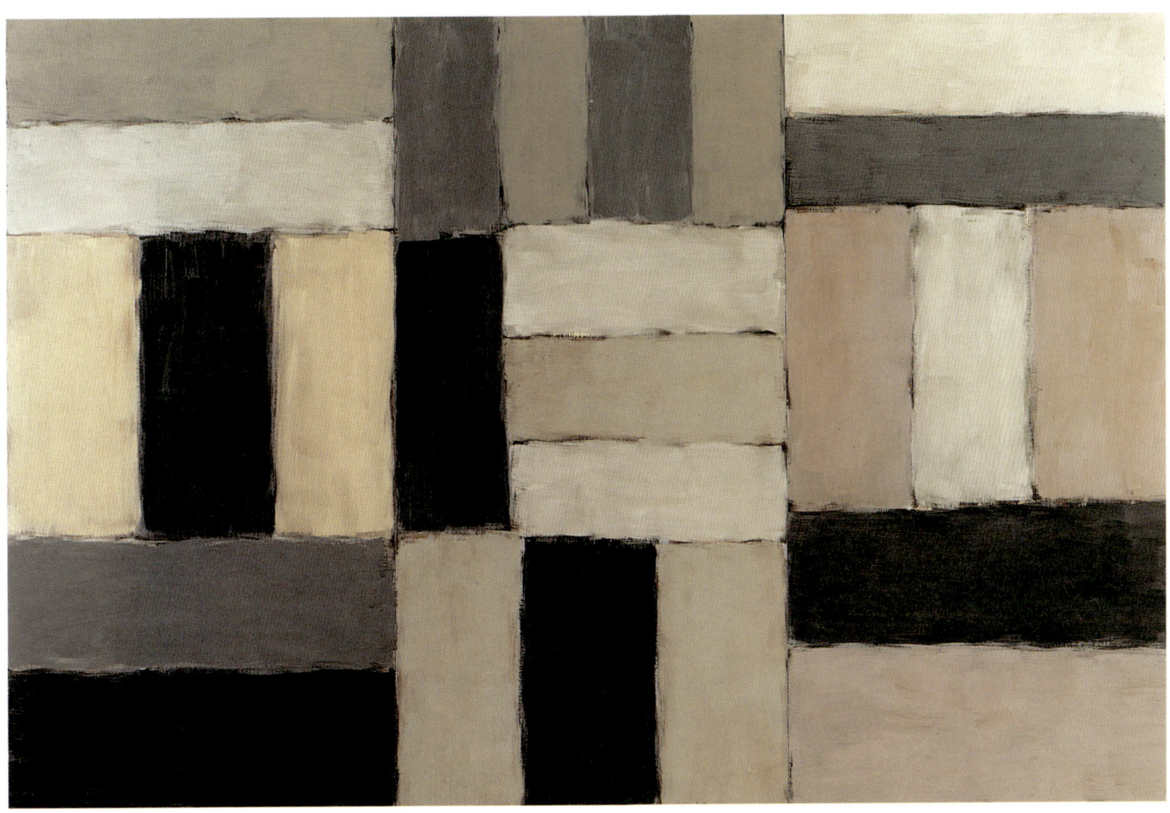

It is also the case that, politically speaking, Modernism, as exemplified by Futurism in Italy, had been on occasions loosely connected with Fascism. After his breakdown Morandi withdrew into a quiet life of teaching. There he could create a distance from the polarized world of political extremes, war and the Italian avant-garde. This is, I believe, when Morandi began actively to separate himself from the international community of artists, to create his own private space populated by his mute, hand-size, familiar figures. The subject of his intimate-scale vases and boxes and jars gave him stability and the peace vital for his mental well-being. With this extremely unique subject he was able to rebuild himself emotionally and begin the gradual formulation of a great understated body of work that was a return to small-scale painting in the tradition of Chardin and Manet.

His personal crisis in the face of the non-negotiable image of progress, as widely understood in 1915 Italy, is what forced him to turn away from Modernism. His escape and his solution are what have made him into a great artist for us today. We still revere the Modernist masters of the twentieth century, though now they seem as if they are from another age. However, Morandi sits more comfortably and truthfully for us, on our highway of doubt. His alternative to Modernism corresponds with the temperature of our own time, precisely because it is anti-heroic and therefore the opposite of Abstract Expressionism.

During the years immediately after his breakdown Morandi was still engaged in a Modernism of sorts: though now it was Pittura Metafisica. In reality this meant he was gradually moving away from internationalism and the influence of Cubism towards a national style. It is symbolically important that in his Pittura Metafisica period Morandi painted a form of construction or still life that was contained within its own box. Cubism broke up the solidity of the object, fractured it and spread it out over the picture plane. Pittura Metafisica, as exemplified by Morandi's painting *Still Life with a Ball* (1918), established a dream world where objects sit silently and in a protected context. They are secure and framed inside the picture and therefore, metaphorically and symbolically, not in direct contact with the outside world. By 1920 Morandi had positioned himself in his own box, which was his modest studio, where he began to paint his 'still-life' paintings in solitude. This represents a journey away from international engagement through a national engagement and ultimately into a private world where he stayed for the rest of his working life.

Modernism, represented by the Futurists Boccioni, Severini and Balla, stood for progress in the painting world of Italy in 1913. The interaction with the machine and its dynamic movement was reflected powerfully in their paintings. Their engagement with the machine world was responsible for their force since they fed off the juggernaut of progress. However, like those of the Suprematists and the Constructivists in Russia, the paintings of the Futurists lacked sensibility. One only has to look at the paintings of Rosanova and Malevich to see that they are painted with a kind of generic neutrality. To find a profoundly personal painting style for the Suprematists or the Futurists was not the point of their work or of their mission, which was to represent in paint an international idea. The representation of movement in, for example, *Dynamism of a Dog on a Leash* by Giacomo Balla (1912, Buffalo, Albright-Knox Gallery) is dynamic, but it is also mechanical in style. This undoubtedly was the point, since an overly subjective or personal world-view would have appeared anti-progressive and bourgeois.

It is against this backdrop of Fascism, Modernism and its opposition to a personal and private sense of poetry that Morandi made his small revolution. This radical resistance, a stand for the individual as a spiritual being, made with humble work in a small room in Bologna, should not be underestimated. By slowly withdrawing into his own private box, Morandi constructed a reality that gave him time

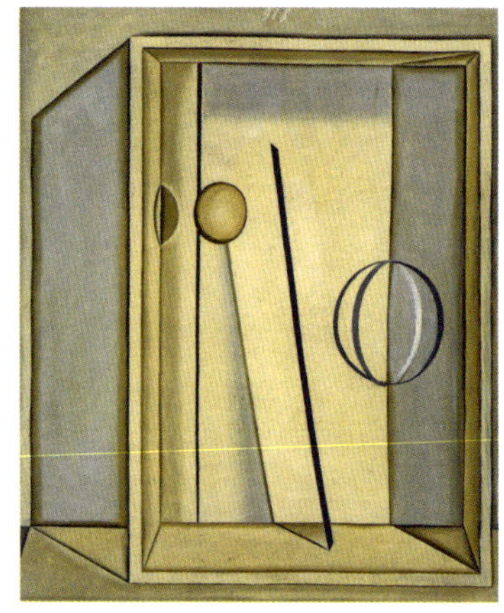

Giorgio Morandi (1890–1964)
Still Life with a Ball, 1918
Oil on canvas
65 x 55 cm (25½ x 21½ in.)
Milan, Italy, Civico Museo d'Arte
Contemporanea, Jucker Collection

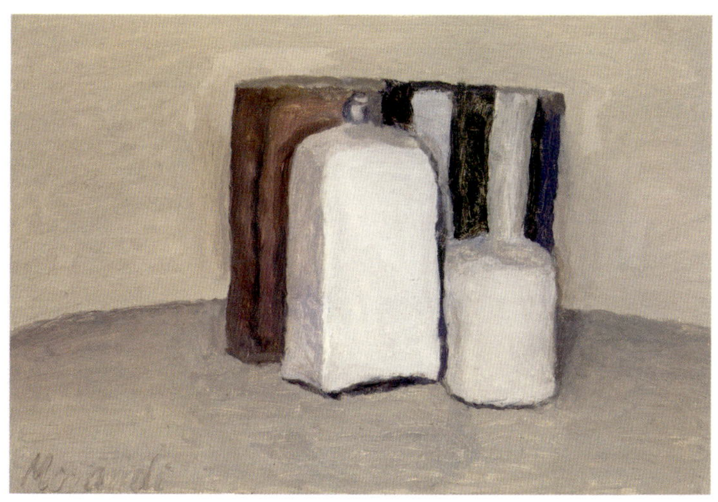

Giorgio Morandi (1890–1964)
Still Life, c. 1957
Oil on canvas
25.4 x 40.6 cm (10 x 16 in.)
Iowa City, IA, University of Iowa Museum of Art,
Gift of Owen and Leone Elliott·

to think and work against the way large masses of Europe were moving. Morandi worked in the shadows of his studio, for the existential position, to feel as an individual. This is fundamental to the gradual formulation of a masterful sensibility.

Morandi paints like no other, before or since. His brushstroke is in complete philosophical agreement with the subject, the scale and the colour of his paintings. It is expressive, though it is modest, and not so expressionistic as to disturb the sense of meditative silence that inhabits all his works.

Still Life (c. 1957) carries a signature in the lower left corner that is huge in relation to the size of the painting. The signature stands for the individual as author. And for the uniqueness of touch that runs through the painting. As is typical of Morandi, the colour is pale and profoundly gentle. Two jars and two boxes, huddling together, their vertical bashful shapes partially hidden by the bodies of familial, neighbourly objects. All the figures close the space between them, and all the figures contain space within their bodies. The absence of earth colour gives the two front figures weight and absence of weight simultaneously, so they appear lit up. The two boxes behind them make a backdrop that has sculptural force. The central figure is compressed, pushed into the position of being protected and captive. This quiet drama takes place on a grey, bent interior horizon which gives the centralized composition its place and its insecurity. Morandi's hand is everywhere, dominating the weak colour, yet allowing the whole composition to pulsate evenly. Even the shadows running around the figures as a dark grey collar lock them into place, and the light from the back of the surface is allowed to leak out through the laconic brushstrokes of the painter. He is timeless yet vital, timorous and seemingly threatened by something outside, yet determined and stoic in his will to be. To be human. To stand noble, modest and resistant to the violence of the world.

Formentera, May 2005

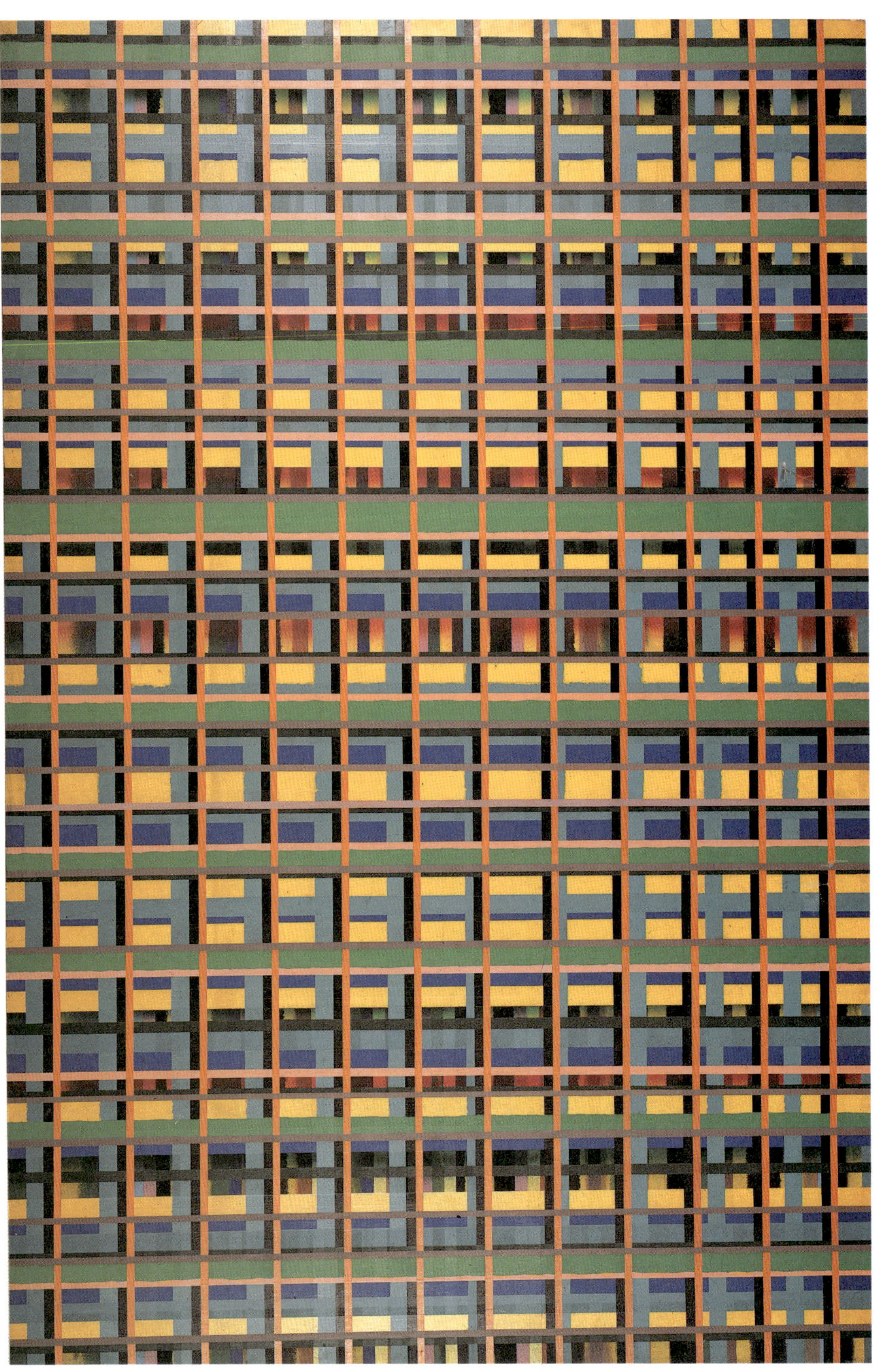

opposite
BRIDGE 1970
Acrylic on canvas
274.3 × 152.4 cm (108 × 60 in.)
Private collection

BACKCLOTH 1970
Acrylic on canvas
198.1 × 304.8 cm (78 × 120 in.)
Private collection

I would like to begin by discussing my geographical roots, as I think they have some bearing on my work; actually, they're intertwined with it. What I would like to do today is concentrate on two phases of my work that connect very well. In fact, I have recently completed what I consider to be a kind of circle. And I would like to give this lecture a title: "High and Low, or the Sublime and the Ordinary".

These are two paintings from 1970; *Backcloth* is 10 feet wide, and *Bridge* is 9 feet high. It is very important when one is looking at my work or relating my work to other people's work to bear in mind that I do come from Europe, which gives my

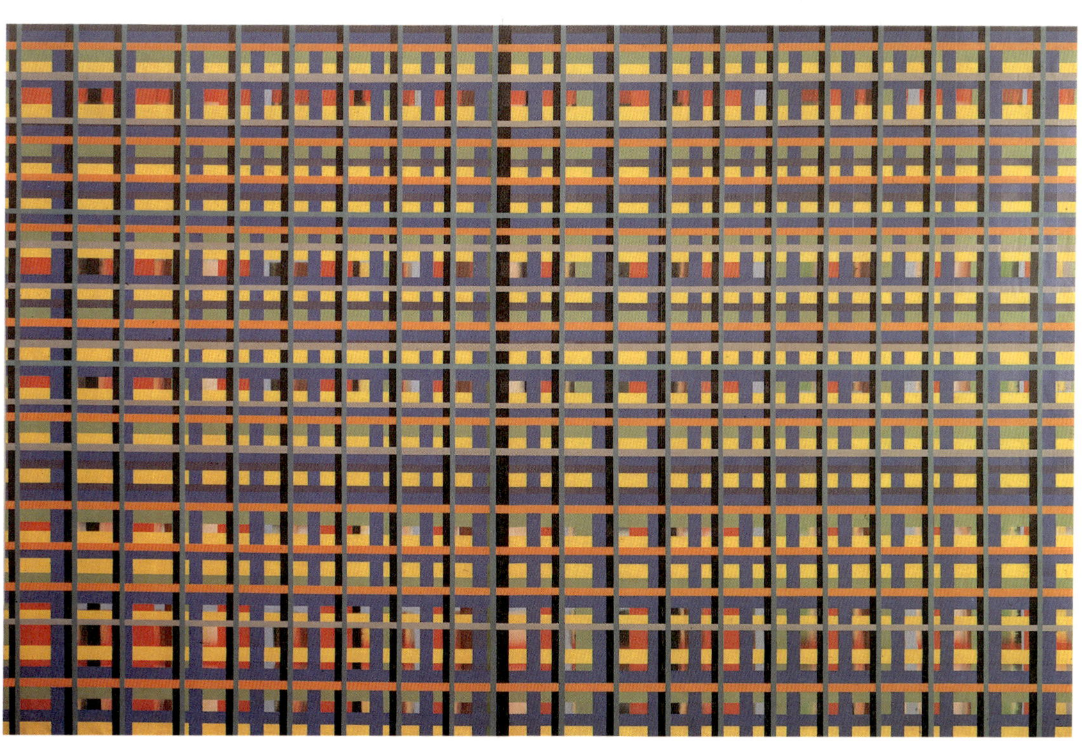

evolution its own particular character. And my work, for a very long time, has been based on the grid: the interaction of the horizontal with the vertical and the vertical with the horizontal. And I use those two forms, those primary directions that we can describe. When I made these paintings, I was trying to resolve two very important influences. On one hand, I was powerfully impressed by the work of Mondrian. To me he represented the Old World and the aspirations of an artist trying to make work that is spiritual and profound through the use of the horizontal and the vertical. On the other hand, there was another artist that I was very impressed by, and that was Jackson Pollock. Pollock represented the New World and a kind of freedom. I knew he came from Wyoming, and it seemed to me that all the cowboy movies I had ever seen and everything that I had up to that point found out about art somehow intersected in the work of Jackson Pollock. So I tried, in a single work, to locate myself in relation to these two artists.

It might be worth mentioning at this point that when I made these paintings I lived in Newcastle, which is a shipbuilding town dissected by a river. The river is crossed by nine bridges made up of overlapping steel girders, and as you look out you see overlapping grids as you go across. Another, though secondary, influence on my work at this point was Bridget Riley, who did paintings that have a low optical hum to them.

The primary issue for me with these paintings, as I said, was in resolving Mondrian and Pollock. Mondrian, as mentioned, represented the values, the conscience and the integrity of the Old World (Europe) as opposed to the New World (America), whose values have been expressed in loud, brash terms. There was a kind of materialism, a literalism, about American art that very often led to an excess of scale and spatial light effects. However, the work of each of these two artists contains a

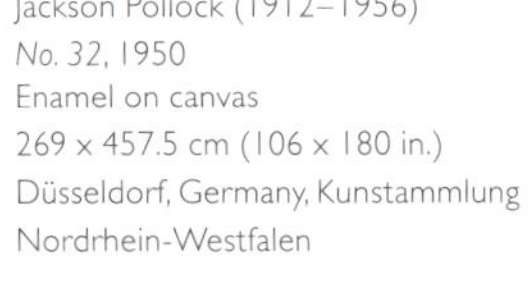

Jackson Pollock (1912–1956)
No. 32, 1950
Enamel on canvas
269 x 457.5 cm (106 x 180 in.)
Düsseldorf, Germany, Kunstammlung
Nordrhein-Westfalen

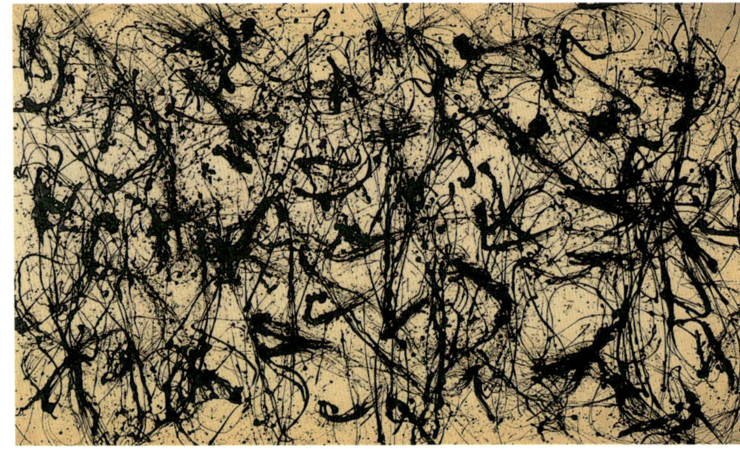

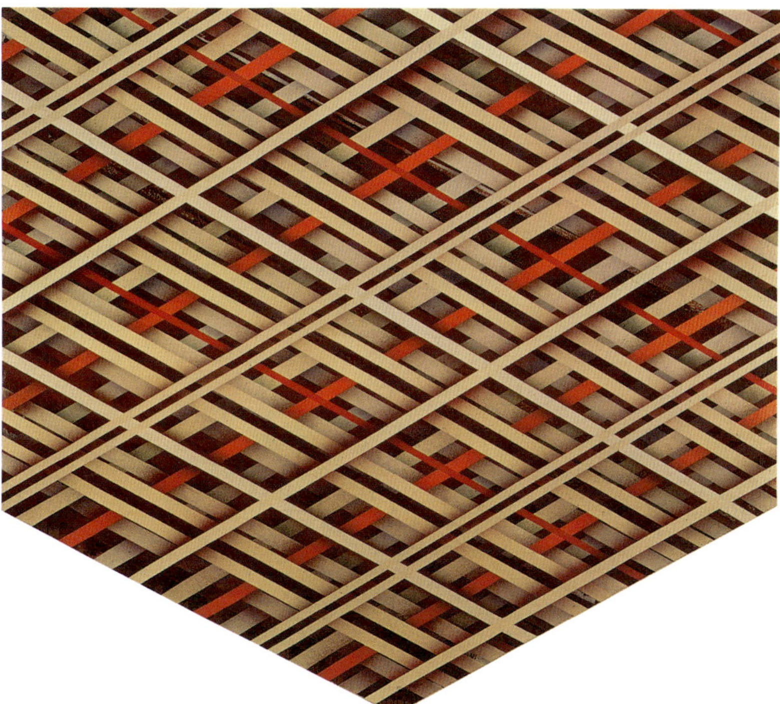

contradiction inherent in itself. Mondrian's paintings appear to be compositional, but when one looks at his relentless façade there is no possibility for spatial hierarchy. So in a sense, the composition in his work is levelled out by the power of the surface. Now, Jackson Pollock represented all-over-ness, and what this was about was a kind of anarchy, or levelling of order, knocking down hierarchies, knocking down the values of the Old World where I lived. The contradiction in Pollock's work is that it resolves itself into an even harmony, as they are very calm works despite the anarchy. Even though the chaos is very apparent in the method, the overall effect is one of sublime harmony. In any case, at this point I sensed the thrill of a dangerous truth, and that truth turned out, of course, to be my truth, my own, the thrill of me confronting what would become the base and foundation of my own work. These paintings are frankly illusionistic. And like Pollock's, they are built up in layers; but like Mondrian's, they are strictly geometric, only horizontals and verticals.

I cut the corners from the bottoms of some of these paintings because I wanted the structures of the paintings to relate to the picture edge. I did a number of paintings like *East Coast Light #2* (1973). That's a very important impulse in my work. It is something I've never given up – that is, to always work from the literal fact of the picture edge, to always relate to it. I did do some of these paintings as

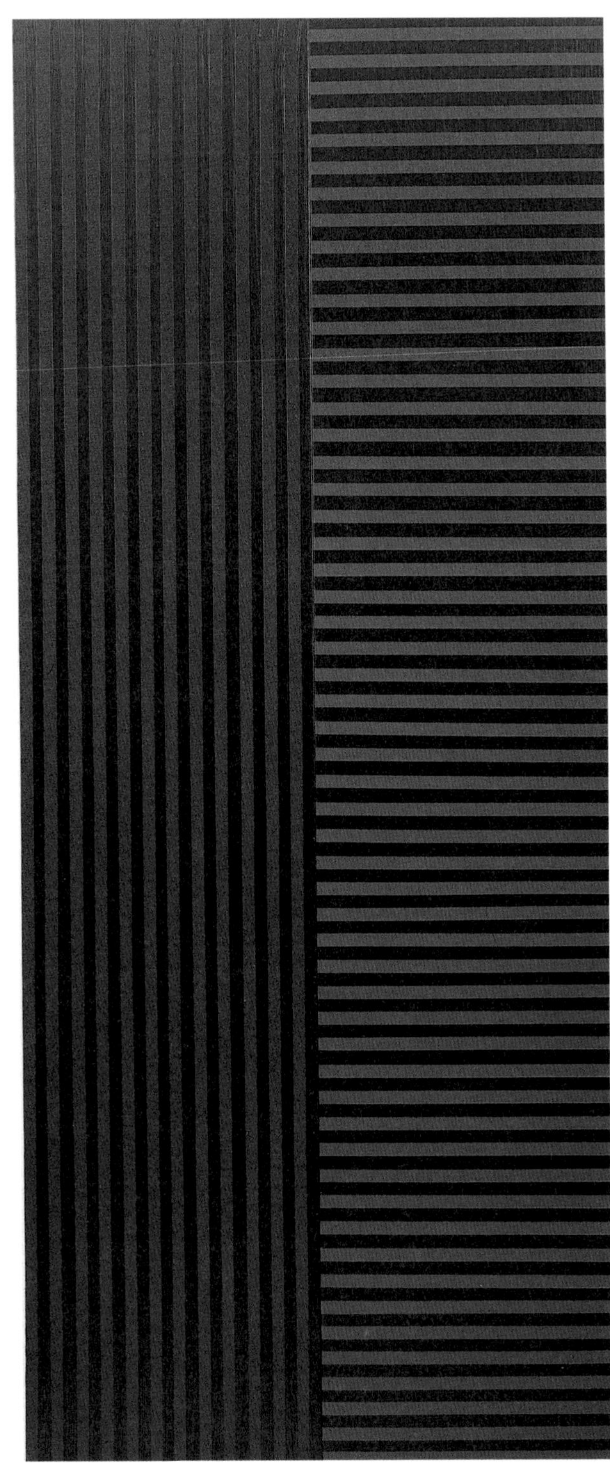

CATHERINE 1980
Oil on board
213.4 x 91.4 cm (84 x 36 in.)
Private collection

squares (e.g., *Overlay I*, 1973, page 162), and although they were not less satisfactory to me as paintings, they were further from the most serious impulse, the closest impulse to me. These paintings jump forward! The last painting you saw was from 1973, and now we go up to 1980–81. The first is *Heart of Darkness* (12 feet wide and 8 feet high; page 48), and the second is called *Catherine* (1980; 8 feet wide and 9 feet high). They're oil paintings, made up of three panels each, and flat.

I should say something here about abstraction, about why I make abstract paintings. I agree with Kandinsky's view that the depiction of the appearance of the real world somehow obstructs access to the spiritual domain. And it is that domain that I am trying to gain access to with my paintings. That is what I am always trying to address. And that's why I paint abstractly. A second reason is that abstraction has become the basis for other art forms. Carter Ratcliff, a very fine critic, just wrote an essay on my work in which he said that the reason that I chose to paint abstractly is because I wanted to work on the foundation on art. And that's true. I wanted to work on its primary structure, its primary emotions, and I wanted to get as deep into its heart-centre as I could. And that's why I've never done anything but abstract paintings since I began to paint them, even though I started out as a figurative painter.

In regard to Kandinsky, however, I agree with [Clement] Greenberg's view that the depiction of space in abstraction leads to a kind of illustration. The overt depiction of picture space, to my mind, gets in the way of the high ideals of abstraction, which has to be realized more frontally, more physically. I see Kandinsky and Mondrian as presenting the two dynamic possibilities from which abstract painting has developed up until the present time. And because of that I have always related to Mondrian. Mondrian's façades are greatly preferable to me over Kandinsky's spatial compositions, though I consider Kandinsky's theories on the spiritual in art profoundly important.

There are some paintings – *Installation, Maestà* (page 96), *Blame* and *Come In* (page 49), of 1982 – that have projections. The reason that I make a painting project is because I want it to have more physical mass. I want the paintings to be more *real*, as objects. At the time I made these there was a lot of painting being shown in New York that was called 'Neo-Expressionist'. Neo-Expressionism was a resurgence of large-scale graphic figurative and expressionistic painting. And I found it very, very good for abstraction. It gave abstract painting a kick in the pants, which it needed. And abstraction is now giving figuration a good kick in the pants. But that's the way it goes; that's how we keep ourselves alive in art.

So, what I did at this time was to violate the picture plane – that sacred picture plane which led to the problem in the first place. I'll talk about that a bit later, how it has something to do with Greenberg's formalism. Anyway, I wanted these paintings to have a physical bulk, so that they could be viewed like the sides of buildings.

It might also be helpful now if I explained why I have painted with stripes for twenty years up to this point – in ten years it will probably be thirty years. I think that it is because I am an obsessive artist, not a formalist. By that I mean that I am interested in content, or depth, subject-matter rather than experimentation – which means I would like to follow the examples set by Rothko and Mondrian. Even though my paintings have changed, the changes have come from a desire to address my views on content and subject-matter. Changes have never come about because of play or from pure experimentation; I am not particularly interested in that. What I've done with the stripe is to reinterpret it over and over and over again. Yet I don't work automatically. I don't accept my obsession with a particular form without subjecting it to a lot of criticism. Thus I don't paint over and over again in the same way for many years without making radical changes (as somebody like Agnes Martin did). I try to subject my obsessive nature to a criticality so that I am always questioning it; and by doing that I force myself to constantly re-establish my relationship with the work. In other words, I have a scepticism about that obsessiveness that results in formal change, rather than being an interest in pure experimentation. And I think in the main that there are two kinds of abstract painter. One can have a varying amount of one kind or the other in oneself; I'm not saying you're either this or that. But the two extremes are, on the one hand, the kind of abstract painter who looks for composition and new forms, and on the other, the kind who looks for content.

The painting titled *Angel* (page 58) is made of two panels, one painted heavily with thick oil paint and the other flat and white, with black lines drawn on it. I wanted to paint a picture that was very light and airy. I actually thought of this painting while I was on an aeroplane, and then I just went back to the studio and painted it. It was a very easy painting to make because the idea for the painting was so clear: it was about the contrast between being clothed and being naked, or between body and spirit. I wanted to make a painting that involved a suspension of meaning, where neither the left side nor the right side of the painting provided a static truth. The painting is always in flux since both sides are presented with equal force.

The painting on the right is much longer – it is 12 feet long and called *By Night and By Day*. Sometimes I give my paintings longer titles. The reason I would do that is because I see the painting as a kind of narrative, travelling from left to right and back again; so then I will give the work a title that takes longer to read. That's also a flat painting. The painting called *Maestà* (page 96) is a homage to Duccio's

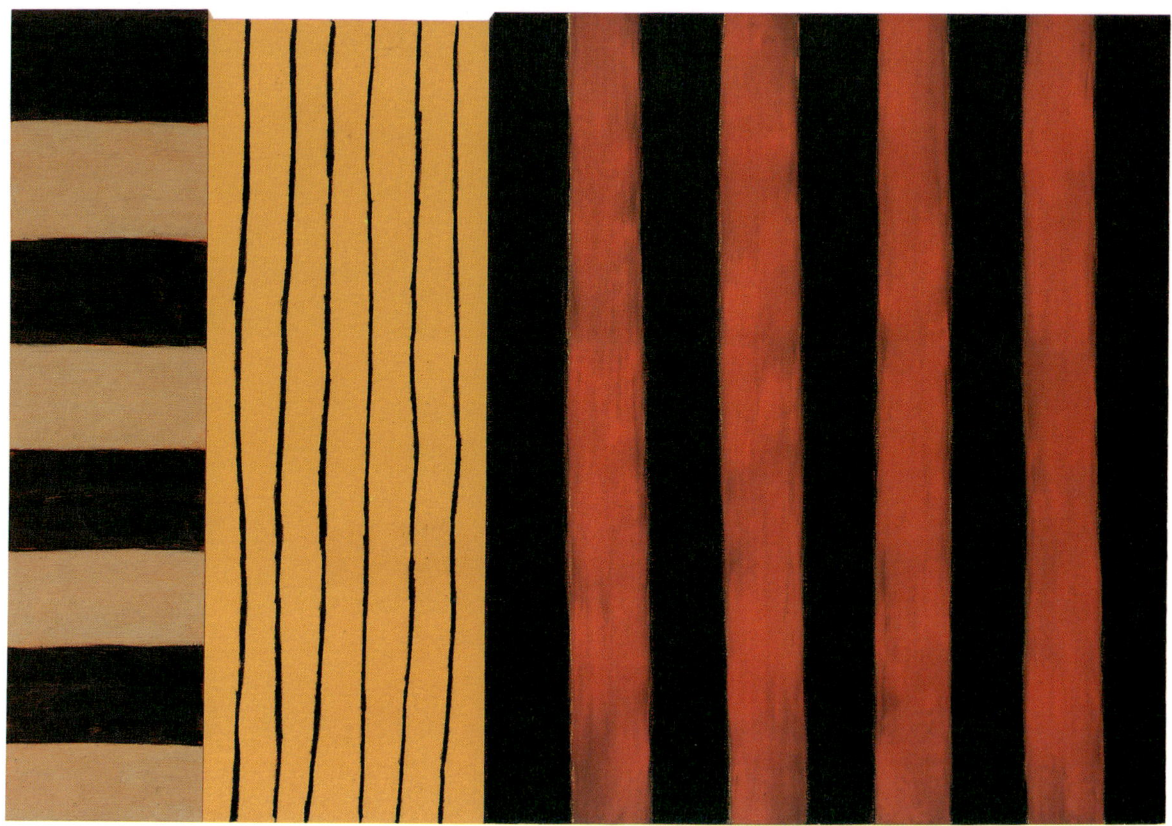

painting of the same name. The central panel, the panel that juts forward and has physical bulk, is the panel that has a lot of colour in it. It is red and blue. The surrounding panels are black and white – opposite, of course, in their orientation, vertical and horizontal. They hold in the central panel, or they represent a grounding for it, which in this painting represents body. The other panels are more empty of colour and, I think, make an allusion to the world of the spirit.

To quote again from Carter Ratcliff's article: he says that my paintings are not compositions that are messages to decipher. That's right; that's not the right way to look at them. A more helpful way to look at them would be to try and see them as personalities – the way you might see a personality or a person that needs to be understood in conflicting ways. I'm not trying to make paintings that are decipherable and 'understood', because I don't think that is what is needed; that becomes a dead thing. I try to make paintings that are not conquerable, that can be reused over and over again, that are not merely designs – which brings me to this painting called *Tiger* (page 24). The part that sticks out at the top makes it look very top-heavy and dangerous. In fact, this painting jumped on him. In fact, I had to put the top panel on to make the painting more physically aggressive.

Following from what I just said about paintings being decipherable, it might be interesting now to talk about imperfection in my work and about surface and emotion. Going back just momentarily to Mondrian: Mondrian's bridge to spirituality is a bridge that is about near-perfection. Things aren't actually perfect, but they are about near-perfection. Mine are not. My paintings are about flaws and about life (street life). There's an interesting line for me that has a strong relationship to this painting and runs between Jasper Johns' 'flag' paintings, which are very object-orientated (as my paintings are), rather than spatially orientated. Of particular help to me with Johns' flag paintings (in relation to this objectness) was the brushstroke. The irrefutable object in Minimalist painting very quickly became, for me, the inert object, the lifeless object. The tautology in Johns' painting, was, however, that it alleviated the tedium of the 'objectness' of the painting and the banality of the image (through the surface, through connecting the painting to the history of painting), so in that sense they go back to European painting because of that very beautiful brushstroked structure.

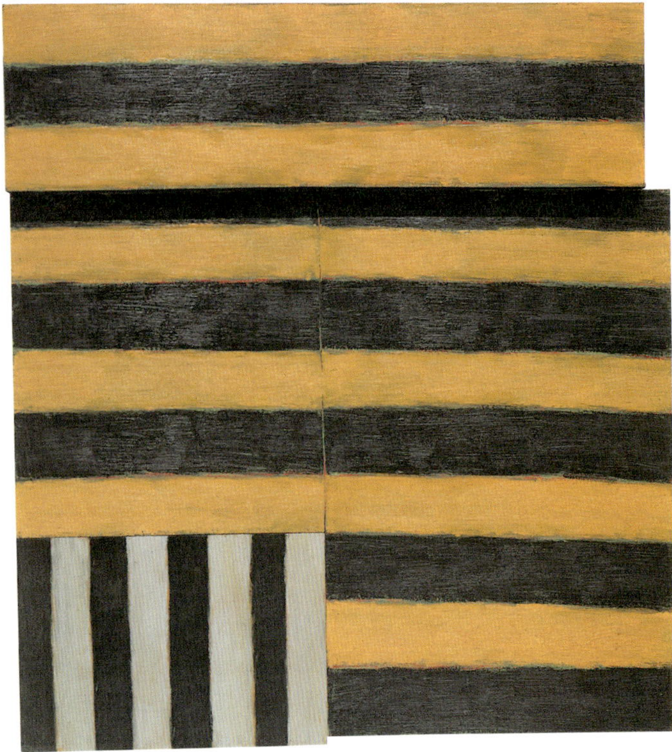

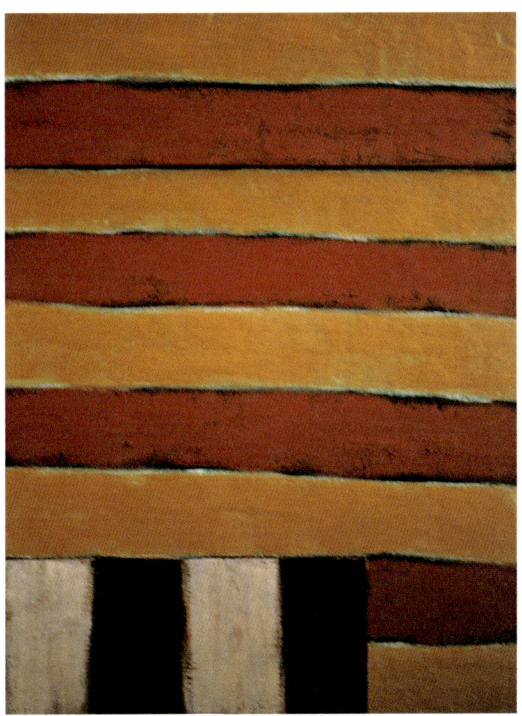

CRADLE 1984
Oil on linen
162.5 x 122 cm (64 x 48 in.)
Private collection

This is called *Cradle*. Now, paint strokes are very crucial to an understanding of my work. The paint strokes do a number of things, but they do not simply describe the form in my work: they affirm the human spirit, the involvement of the human spirit. What is particularly moving to me about this idea, and what is also very dynamic about it, is that a paint stroke that describes a form *also* describes a gesture. That means that it stands outside technological development and can never be subjected to mechanization or technology. It is always about renewing the primitive impulse in order to make the gesture. I find it very powerful in relation to the rest of the world. Obviously, if one is going to be an artist, one has to try to find how to make one's particular art form, whatever it is, relevant or necessary in its own time. I think that this relationship can make painting a very powerful and humanizing art form right now. That means that one has to then deal with the issue of style, which is of course a real problem. What you have to do is find a way of painting something that embodies all of your aspirations – which is why painting is so difficult, because it is a very narrow art form. My painting style, of course, is based on a very simple form: my painting doesn't go across, against the form, but goes with it and can be seen differently as individual strokes. So that while making a pictorial structure, a surface structure, they also follow the direction of the form, which means that the band has a kind of speed to it that varies from painting to painting.

I think it is also helpful at this point to mention that the reason I always use separate panels in my work is because I don't like to paint the ends of the stripe. Now, that's a funny thing to say, but it is also a serious thing to say, and it has a lot to do with (again) the same issue: with style and with reality. The reason I don't like to paint the end of the stripe is because I don't like to be in a position where I feel that I am describing something, where I have to take into account things that might somehow interfere with the velocity of the painting of the form. What I do is to let the stripe, or rather the way it is painted, go off the end of one panel, and I abut that with the end of the band or stripe that goes off from another panel. So there's a collision. Joe Masheck of ArtLife calls it "car crashes" in my work. The surfaces crash into each other because I don't slow down when I get to the end of the stripe; I just paint right off. So they have the immediacy of sculpture whether they're in relief or not (that doesn't matter). The fact that they're on separate panels connects them to the real world and also gives them a physical urgency. That's why I paint that way.

I'll show you how this painting was made. And just to say something about my own art-historical tradition: I would say that Velázquez, obviously Duccio and Giotto, figure in it very strongly. Flat painters figure strongly, surface painters. But Velázquez is a painter that I greatly admire because his work has a dignity and a very beautiful narrative surface structure. That is, if you look at a Velázquez painting, you will see that its different parts are painted in different ways. The brushstrokes are always very evident, and those of course led to a lot of things that Manet did in his paintings. The surfaces are very subjective and intense – all the way through a Velázquez painting – and with that one can follow a kind of story, an essential narrative. It's picked up again very explosively in Van Gogh's paintings and again in Mondrian. It is clear that Van Gogh leads to Mondrian's early work.

To the right (*Ridge*) is a little painting on wood, two pieces of wood. I did a number of these. I would paint them and then slap them together. They're very small, 12 inches or 15 inches.

Now, I'd like to address the title of this lecture, "High and Low, or the Sublime and the Ordinary". This means that when one is dealing with the domain of the spirit, with lofty ideas, one is dealing with High Art. The danger here, not just with abstraction but with any idealistic art, is that you get further away from life. The 'higher' the art, the further away from life you get. What I've tried to do with my work is to keep a line open, or rather to make a line between the ordinary and the sublime. John Caldwell wrote an essay on my work and said that in the tradition of the sublime it is very unusual for paintings to be so overtly physical, because most paintings that aspire to the sublime are very discreet physically – like Rothko, one of

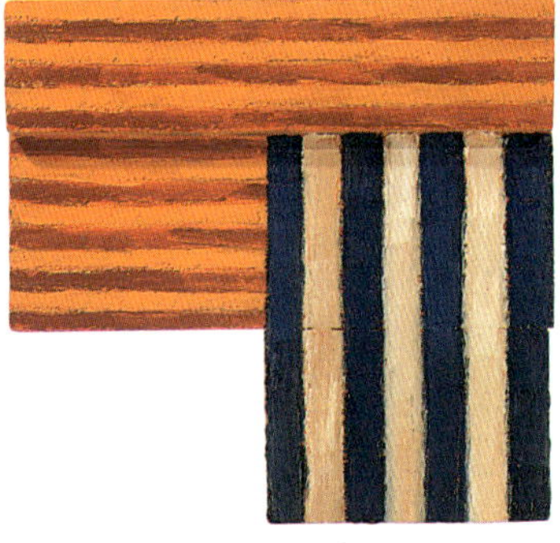

RIDGE 1982
Oil on board
38.1 × 40.6 cm (15 × 16 in.)
Private collection

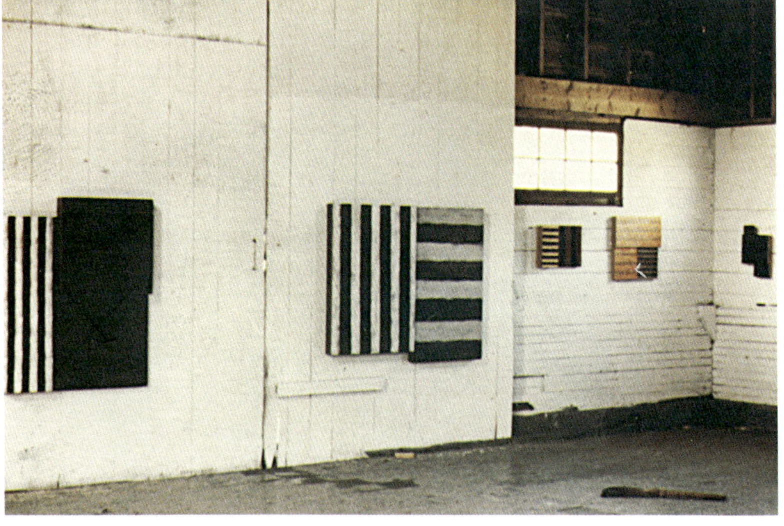

Montauk, Edward F. Albee Foundation
'The Barn', Long Island, New York
Photograph by Sean Scully, 1982

my favourite artists. Even though his paintings are huge, they are very discreet, very physically on the surface; and they are very thin. However, I think that it is physicality in art that keeps it connected, affirms its connection and its dependence on the real world, on life, on ordinary life. I have chosen to confront two traditions in my work: the tradition of the sublime and the tradition of objects, which has a lot to do, of course, with Minimalism. And it is because of this belief that I feel that the physicality of the surface is so crucial to the life of the painting, to the accountability of the painting; the painting can be used to constantly reaffirm that connection. That's why I won't let go of that.

This photograph (opposite) is very nice because it shows that there really isn't a whole lot of difference between my paintings and that wall. The difference, of course, is that some of the things that exist on that wall unconsciously exist in my paintings consciously. That's one of the differences. On this issue I take it that people know what formalism is, by which I mean Greenberg and formalism. The problem with that was that, instead of the high feeding on the low, it was the high feeding on the high; and so it was a dead end, and that's not good. It became a kind

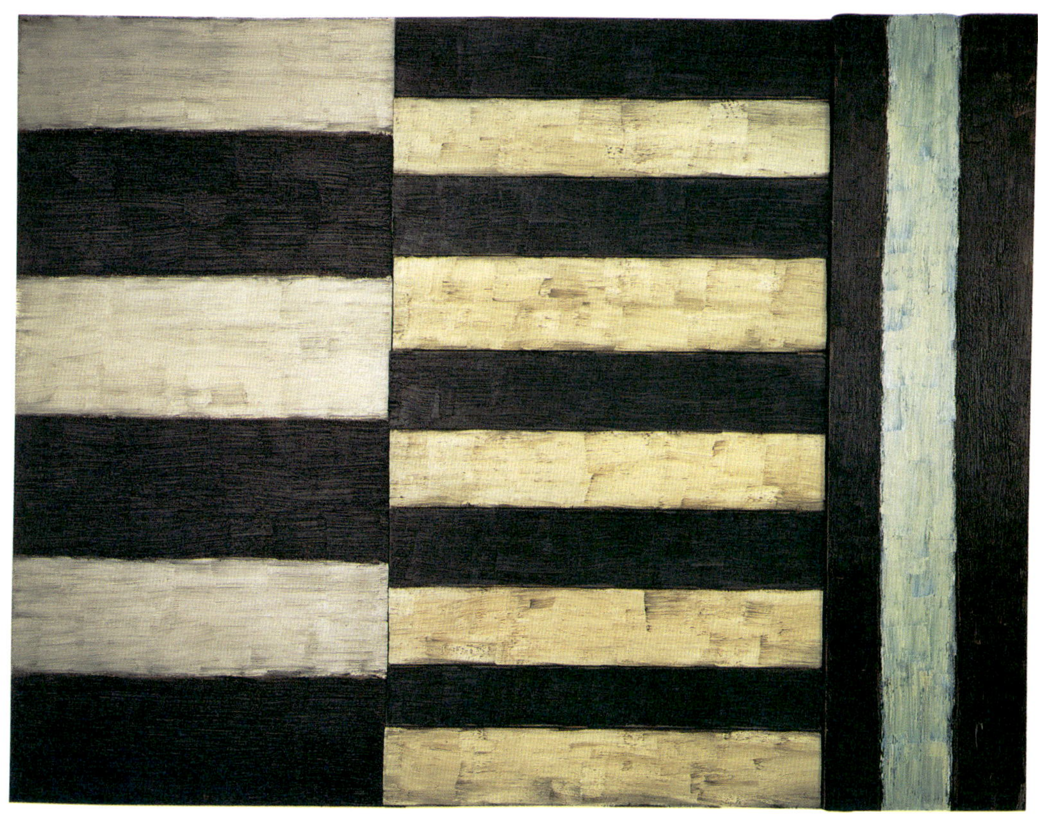

of academy, and so the paintings lacked life. What they were really about was rules. They seem to me to be dead now, those pictures …

Long Night (1985; previous page) has a middle panel made up of wooden boards (they're real stripes), and I painted over the boards. It has some relief with that very large piece that comes forward just for the width of the board, no more. It makes a point of the material, of the fact that they are boards. I constantly try to bring my paintings back to reality, and then I try to make them soar through the use of colour – overlaying the colour and the emotive painting itself. So the paintings are based on a number of contradictions: like the opposition of horizontal and vertical, the opposition of the banality of the subject-matter (stripes) and the lofty claims that I make for the paintings (my intentions). The gesture in the surface constantly affirms and insists on the human presence.

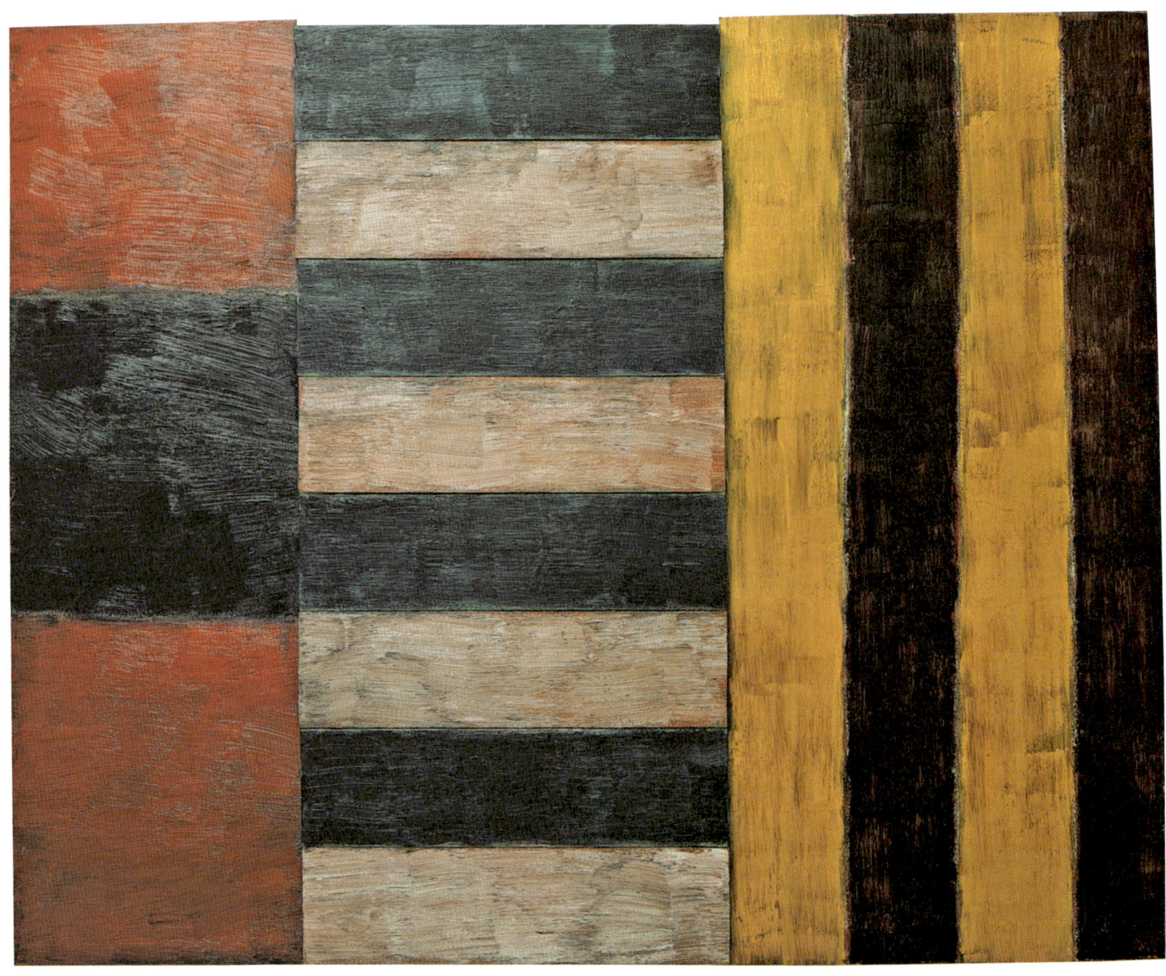

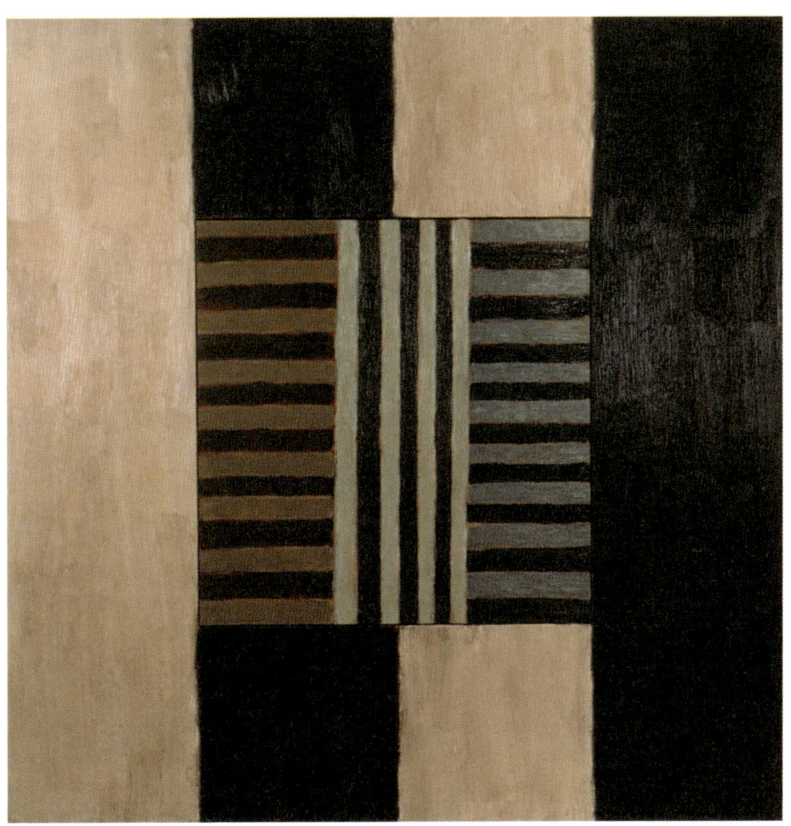

The painting on the left (*Round and Round*, 1984) is another with painted boards in the middle. I found that interesting. It was in an exhibition in Düsseldorf, the Schmela Gallery. The gallery is very rough and is all concrete and brick walls. I liked the idea of showing the paintings in a very rough environment. It makes that connection very strong. *Any Questions* (1984; page 56) is a painting I did about three or four years ago, in which I tried to break up the perfection of the form that I used. On the left side I reduced the colour to black and white, and I saw that as a figure, like the eternal figure. And on the right side of the painting I painted the form as if that side had fallen apart and then had to be put back together again. It is very schizophrenic between one side and the other. The left side projects, and so the sides have a strangely competitive physicality. The black-and-white side has the advantage of being projected forward, but the other side has the advantage of being a number of panels bolted together with a piece out.

Here is a 6-foot-square painting called *Vice*. There is an inset in the middle on which, in fact, the ends of the stripes are painted: here and on the separate panel,

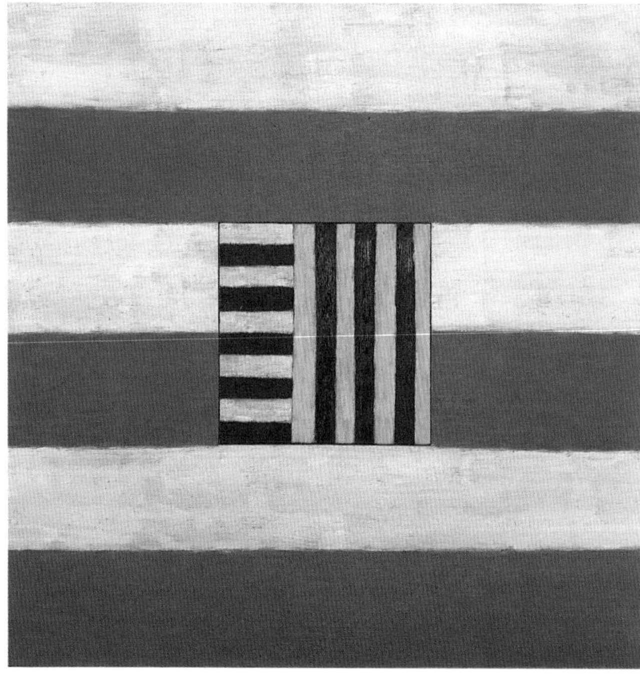

there and on the separate square. So it's really like a square with an inset that is physically pushed in, causing a great pressure. It is very important to mention that I painted them separately. I don't paint them together; I paint them apart, and then I put them together afterwards. This painting is about painting things, for want of a better phrase, in a traditional sense by painting the ends of the stripes and so on and then sticking it in. *Precious* is another painting with a square put into the middle.

The painting opposite is called *Dreamland*. It is an interesting painting, formally, for me. It comes quite close to the possibility of getting rid of repetition. It flirts with that. However, the panel, the inset that drops in at the top, reaffirms it. The areas in my paintings are all, of course, 'all-over' paintings. They're like bits of all-over paintings that are put together in competition with each other or in harmony with each other or in discord with each other. I don't necessarily try to harmonize the panels, or the areas, in my work. All the areas are made up of repeated imagery. They are compositional paintings that are made up of all-over paintings. There's another contradiction for you.

Also opposite is a painting that I thought of as either a barred window or as a figure-ground painting. It's called *Nostromo*, after Joseph Conrad's novel. The yellow panel set into the painting is painted in a very dry way, while the rest is painted heavily and very physically. I was interested in the fragility of that relationship, that

DREAMLAND 1987
Oil on canvas
228.6 × 297.2 cm (90 × 117 in.)
Private collection

NOSTROMO 1987
Oil on canvas
228 × 375.9 cm (90 × 148 in.)
Private collection

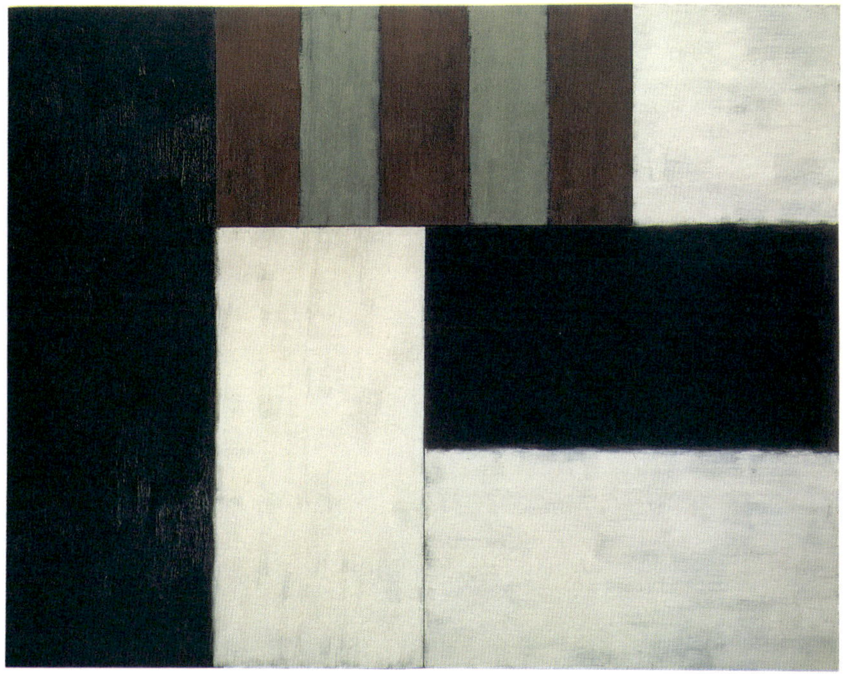

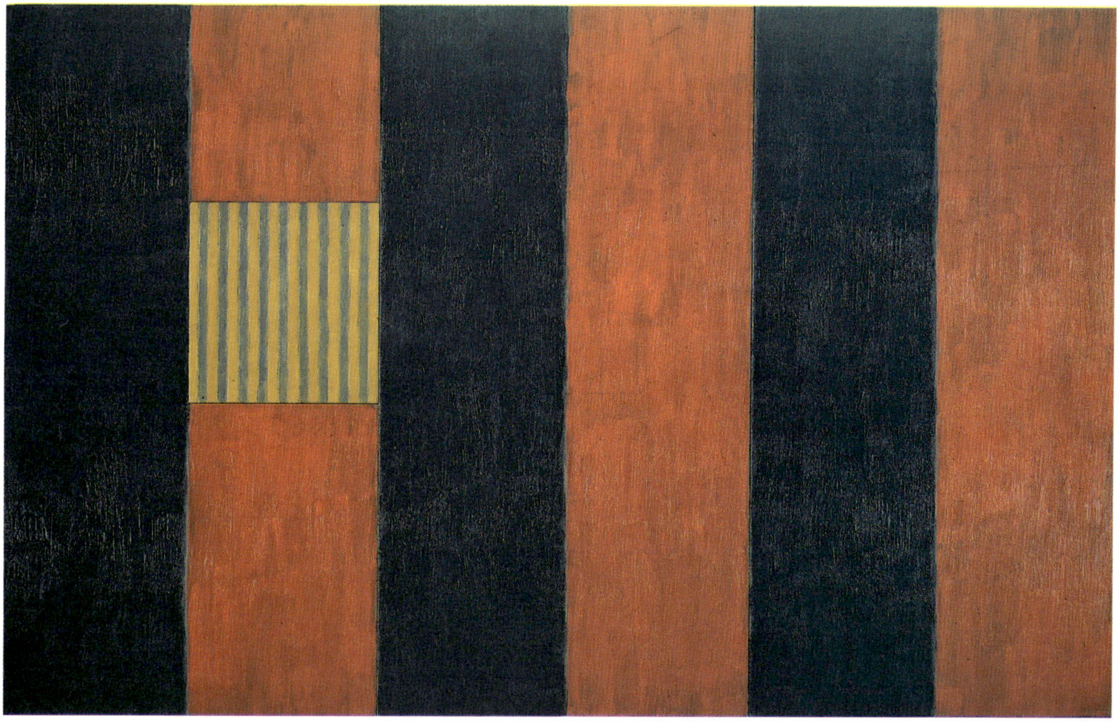

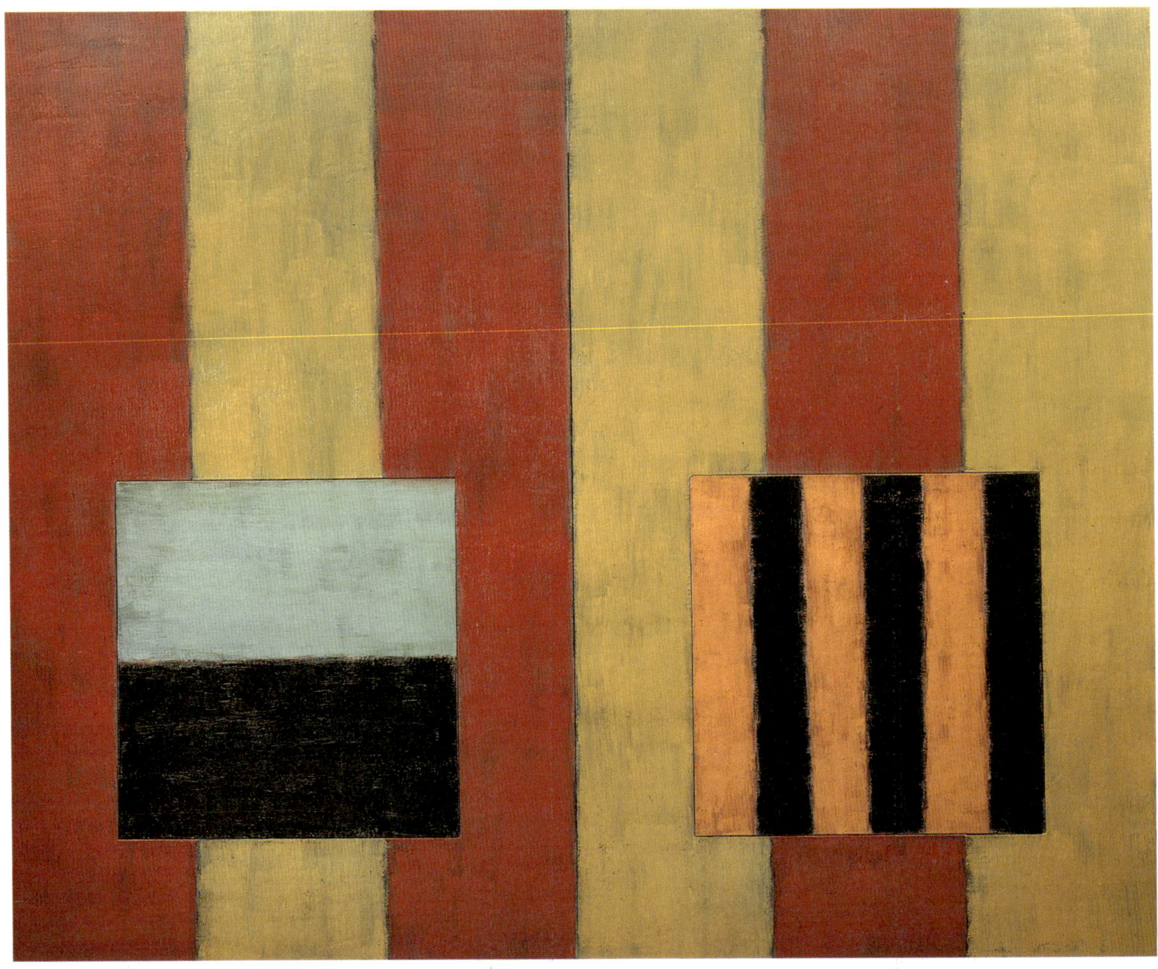

CATHERINE 1987
Oil on canvas
243.8 x 304.8 cm (96 x 120 in.)
Fort Worth, TX, Modern Art Museum

the outside of the painting swamped the inset, the smaller panel, which is more intimate. This introduces another point that is interesting to me: how to make paintings functional on a number of different levels, from far away as signs (or emblems) and close up. I try to humanize my paintings through the physical layering of colour, which can add surface complexity and mystery to a painting that has enormous size and bulk. Up close, I would like the painting to be felt poetically and intimately.

This is a painting called *Catherine* (1987). Here I think that the issue of the wall is very clearly expressed. The painting is flat, about $8^{1}/_{2}$ feet high and very roughly painted. It has a calmness about it, but it also has a manual quality that undermines, works against, subverts its austerity.

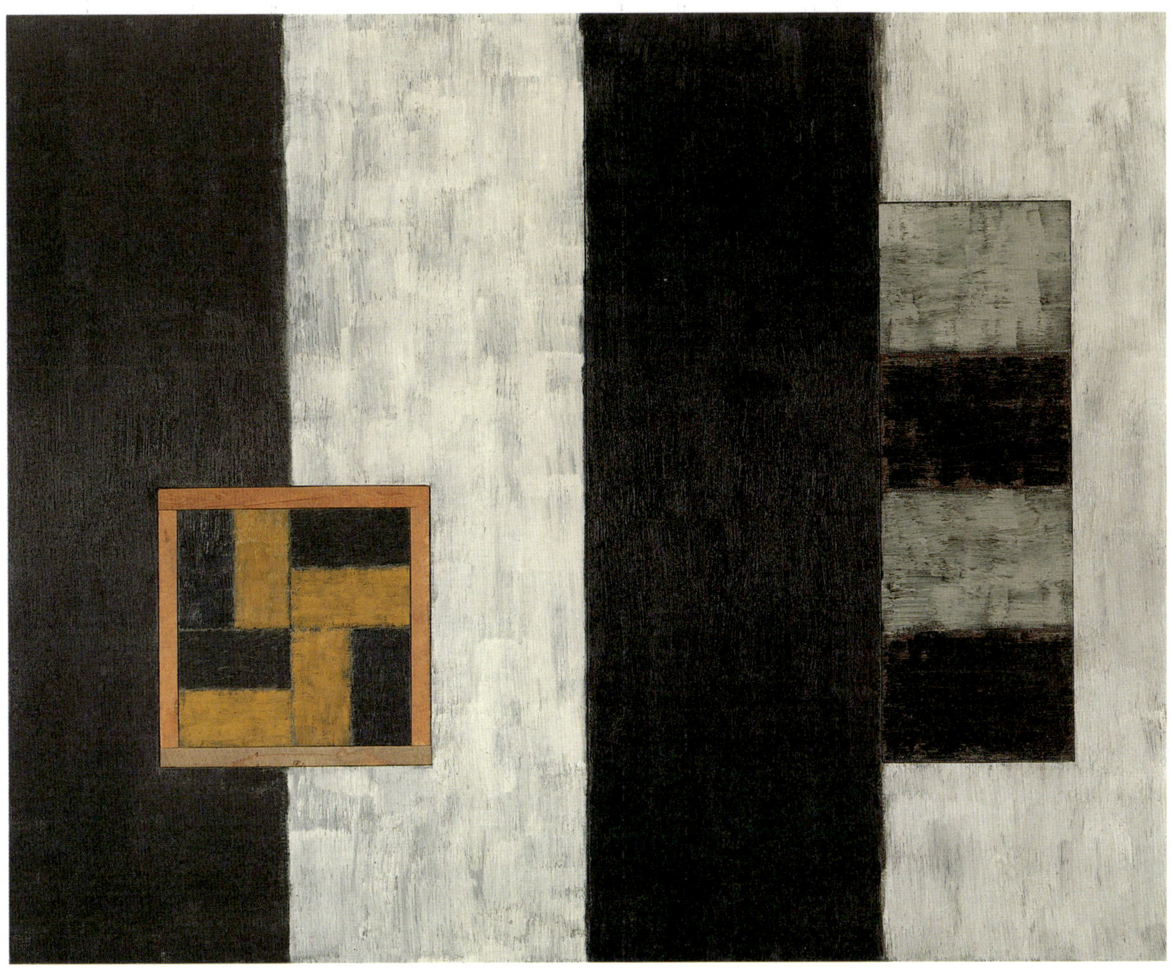

The painting above is called *Between You and Me*. The inset on the left is surrounded by a very rough wooden frame. The inset on the right is not; it is scraped out and fits very flatly within the painting. The wide vertical bands are all painted differently, by the way. It's not just a black-and-white painting; there are greys such that each band evolved very slowly and with great difficulty. The inset has a kind of isolated quality. I thought of this painting as being about that kind of situation where something is cut off from something else. And by framing it in wood it becomes very emphatically isolated. It also goes around and in on itself. As you can see, I can extrapolate from these paintings a kind of narrative.

This painting (page 34) is called *White Window*. It is very important to me that it is a window. The windows in my recent paintings are something that I am very

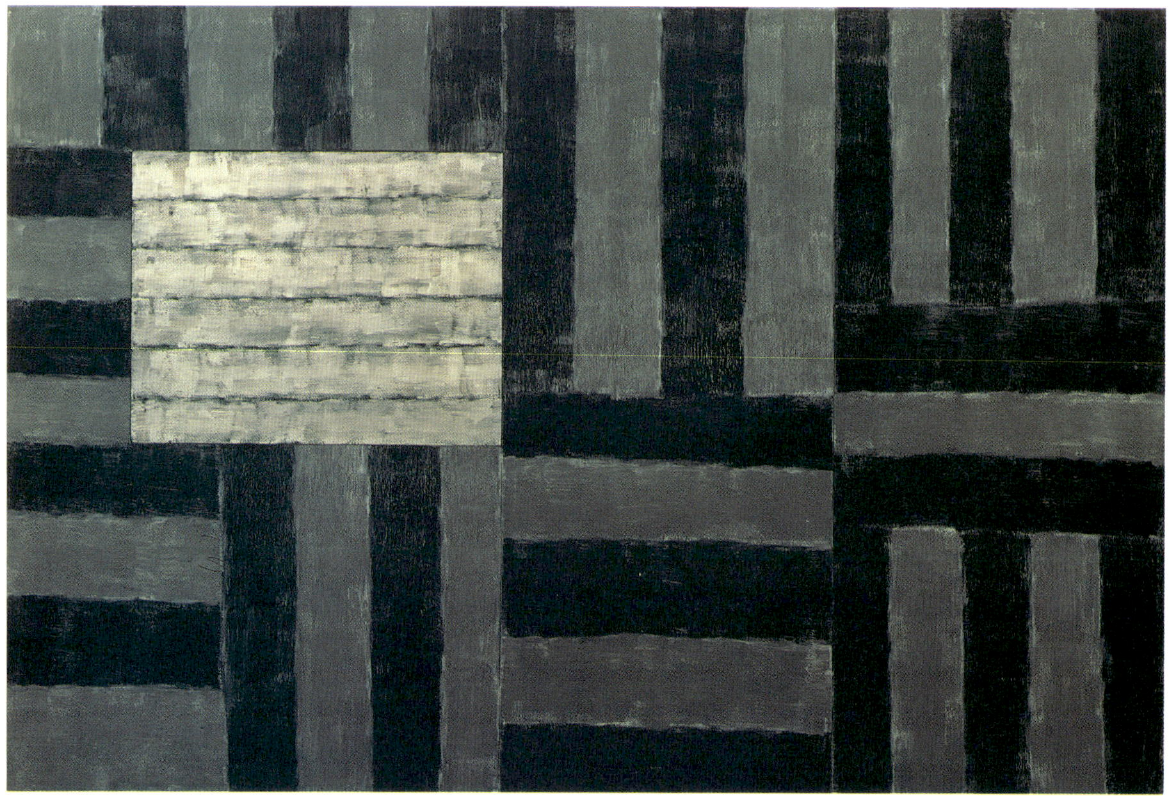

excited about: they are not an illusion, and they're not necessarily an allusion to another space, a physical space, as they might be if the paintings were to be interpreted literally or materially. They function as metaphors for either hope or disturbance, or for another kind of reality in what is an otherwise obsessive field. What I'm saying is that the paintings of the last seven years never give in to the impulse to paint automatically. They beg the question, or they set it up so that the paintings could go that way, but there's always that fight for the reaffirmation of something else. This is my way of making the paintings human. The outside, as you can see, is made up of three panels, and they're huge – very aggressively painted black and grey bars that don't quite comfortably fit with each other.

Why and What (Yellow) is the last painting I want to talk about. It is very interesting in relation to the first paintings that I spoke about because it seems that I've come, after all this time, full circle: still interested in Mondrian and Jackson Pollock. However, the paintings, instead of being illusionistic, are now much more physically overt. The panel on the left is a steel plate, and the panel on the right is a painting. So, it is a painting-in-a-painting, which, of course, engages another

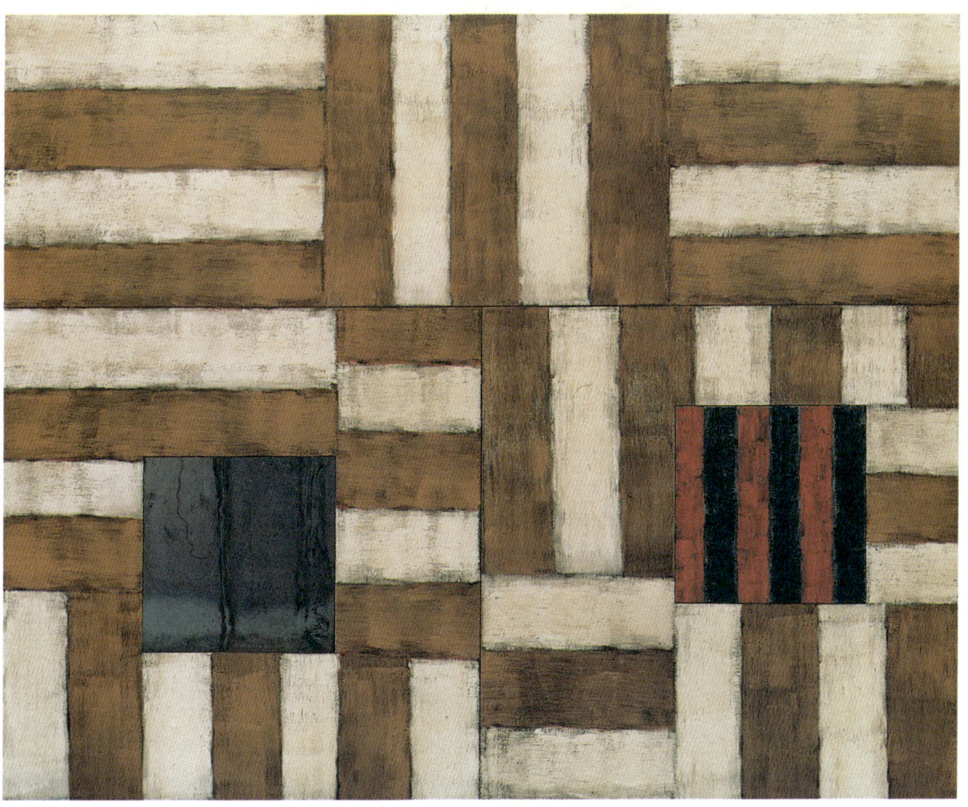

tradition in art: the painting-in-a-painting, one that Velázquez dealt with very often. The metal plate is not just a colour; it is a thing, another relationship with the paint surface. I didn't talk about the paint surface as flesh in this lecture, but it represents the flesh of the body, the skin of the painting. And that refers back through the tradition of painting: in itself a very delicate, fragile thing that always seems to be under threat. The metal plate is something that is made up of the same material as it is just untreated steel, as are buildings and tanks. So it has a very threatening relationship with the painting. But then, on the other hand, the panel on the right affirms colour and the tradition of painting and so is a complex painting in the way it can be experienced. I think of my paintings as being hopeful, not pessimistic, not ironical or cynical. And I am particularly interested in the metaphor of the window right now. That for me, as I said before, is a metaphor for hope.

<u>ON COLOUR</u>

Thinking about the colour in my work, and its darkness ... I often think about how the light in my work – the light produced by this colour, which is so emphatically attached to its own body weight, its own gravity – has a tendency to fall back into the painting. The painting has to be opened up.

The colour, of course, could be opened up. Red could be bright red. Yellow could be the colour of flowers. And green could be leaf green. This would make the painting more immediate, more obviously communicative, more readily available ... and less burdened by the issue of interior content.

My painting, however, is a compression: a compression of form, edge, weight. And colour participates in this density. The painting is immediate since it is painted aggressively, by hand; yet it is difficult because it is compressed. The light in the painting has to be opened up, pulled out.

And it is exactly this difficulty that gives the work its interior life. It is an incarnation, not an explanation.

Mooseurach, May 2004

Something that's fascinating fascinates. It holds your attention, because it's somehow right and somehow not right. It communicates without explaining, without justifying. And this contradiction, this confliction, this confusion – like putting a building on top of a pinhead – fascinates. And what fascinates goes the distance.

New York, January 2006

Sometimes my joy, the thrill of painting, deserts me. Then I'm left with my theories, my issues, my ideas about right and wrong – as if art were a problem instead of an affirmation. I have to live through this and wait patiently for another angel to tap me on the shoulder.

New York, November 1983

I went to the studio in Barcelona. I was tired and I was getting ill, and I didn't want to work at all. I had no energy and I had a headache. I started working on the painting I had abandoned a couple of weeks before because it was my least favourite – it was the 'abandoned one' left standing up against the wall. So I reluctantly put it on the painting wall and started working. Then something happened, and I painted as if I couldn't make a mistake. Three hours later it was finished, and it was the most beautiful painting in the room. That's painting. You never know. You never know what you will get when you start.

Barcelona, February 2002

Van Gogh's paintings not only anticipate the collapse of the rural age, but they are composed in a way that anticipates snapshots in photography. As a framed-art section of life, that is so specific in its choice of subject matter and formal arrangement, it speaks only of itself and testifies only to that, excluding other possibilities. Van Gogh's focus was so intense within the boundary of each painting that, cumulatively, his works not only make a symphony of colour and linear rhythm but also move profoundly to isolation. The very intensity of these paintings is what cuts them off and cuts them out of the world.

The physically and optically manifested passion and focus of each work would have made it impossible for Van Gogh to join them all together. They shine brilliantly but in isolation to each other.

In a painting by Van Gogh, there is no retreat, no pause, and no reflective or intermediary space. Van Gogh painted everything as something. Thus there is no air or space between events, as there was in other landscape or interior paintings; in Van Gogh everything is an event. Even the sky or the view out of the window is painted with a pulsating frontality. Thus there is nowhere to rest, because there is no in-between. The sense of rhythmic, violent claustrophobia adds tremendously to a sense of surface desperation. He wants to make everything real. So even the clouds in the sky become solidified into concrete objects with rhythm. While making movement, he gives the colour a brutal weight and forcefully squeezes out of the surface anything that might be a negotiator or bridge between objects. The rhythmic objectness of these deeply committed works is what impressed me so. I took this idea to an extreme, so that in an abstract painting, everything was something, in the sense that it had the force of an object.

This is not to say that a big Van Gogh exhibition is not more symphonic than the experience of seeing a simple painting by him. It certainly is, and the rhythm and habitual colour of the artist's palette (especially yellow) will set any room trembling with the rhythm of love and life and the love of life. However, the paintings can be felt as visual explorations, and each exploration is in a sense indifferent to

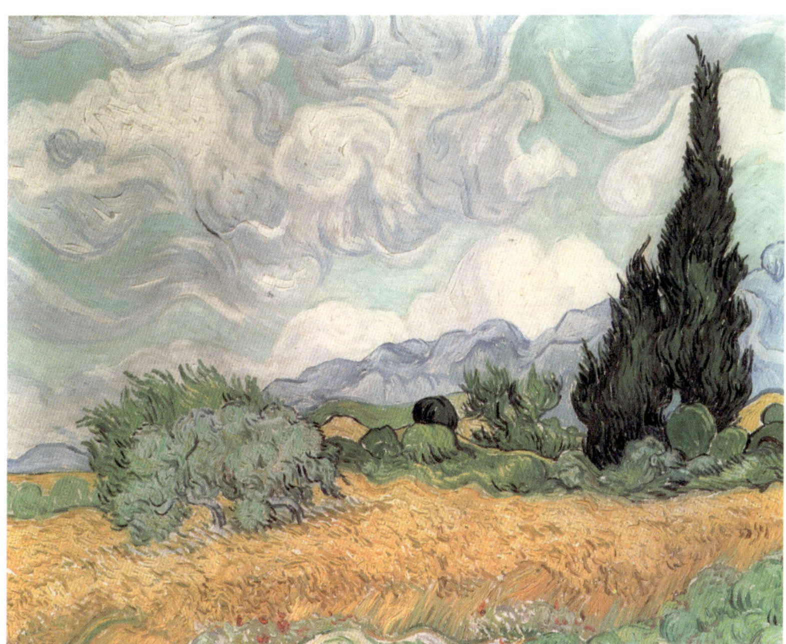

the others. Their claustrophobic and blinkered intensity would have meant that these works took without mercy everything that their creator had to give them, leaving him exhausted and without the ability to join them together. Just as a contemporary snapshot is isolated and independent from every other contemporary snapshot, so too Van Gogh's paintings registered the alienation that was just beginning to make its appearance on our cultural horizon. For others it was out of focus, but Van Gogh gripped it and was gripped by it in return. His tragedy and his paintings (unlike modern photography) demanded a visceral kind of self-sacrificing love in order to be made. His power and problem was that he used a nineteenth-century medium to express a twentieth-century anxiety. And since the medium of painting is by definition extremely personal, in his hands it became extremely dangerous. The casualty felt among painters of the twentieth century is something Van Gogh began. Photography in particular is an art form that came along exactly at the right cultural–historical moment to put some distance between us and what we were doing to our world.

As I impact with the painting and as I hope others impact with the painting, so too will the divisions within the painting impact and form relations with each other. The moment of us coming together with the painting (as the painting remakes its relationships with its own borders) is meant to be a moment of emotion. It's active.

New York, December 2002

Thinking about colour and what I said earlier, that it has to be opened up, reminded me of a conversation I had with Bob Hughes once. He asked me what a painting was like. I said it was like a book. You know my brother was a bookbinder, and I was a typesetter. So I always loved books. When you see a book on a shelf, it's a sculpture, because you see the spine facing out to you carrying the title. But when you open it, it is like holding wings. The object is opened up and you can decode it. Painting is like this. Like a closed book that becomes an open book. It always needs to be decoded and opened up. Then it shows itself, though it doesn't explain itself. Paintings that can go the distance are like this. They are not graphic, so they don't give everything up at a glance, but they give enough to provoke you to open them up.

Zurich, March 2005

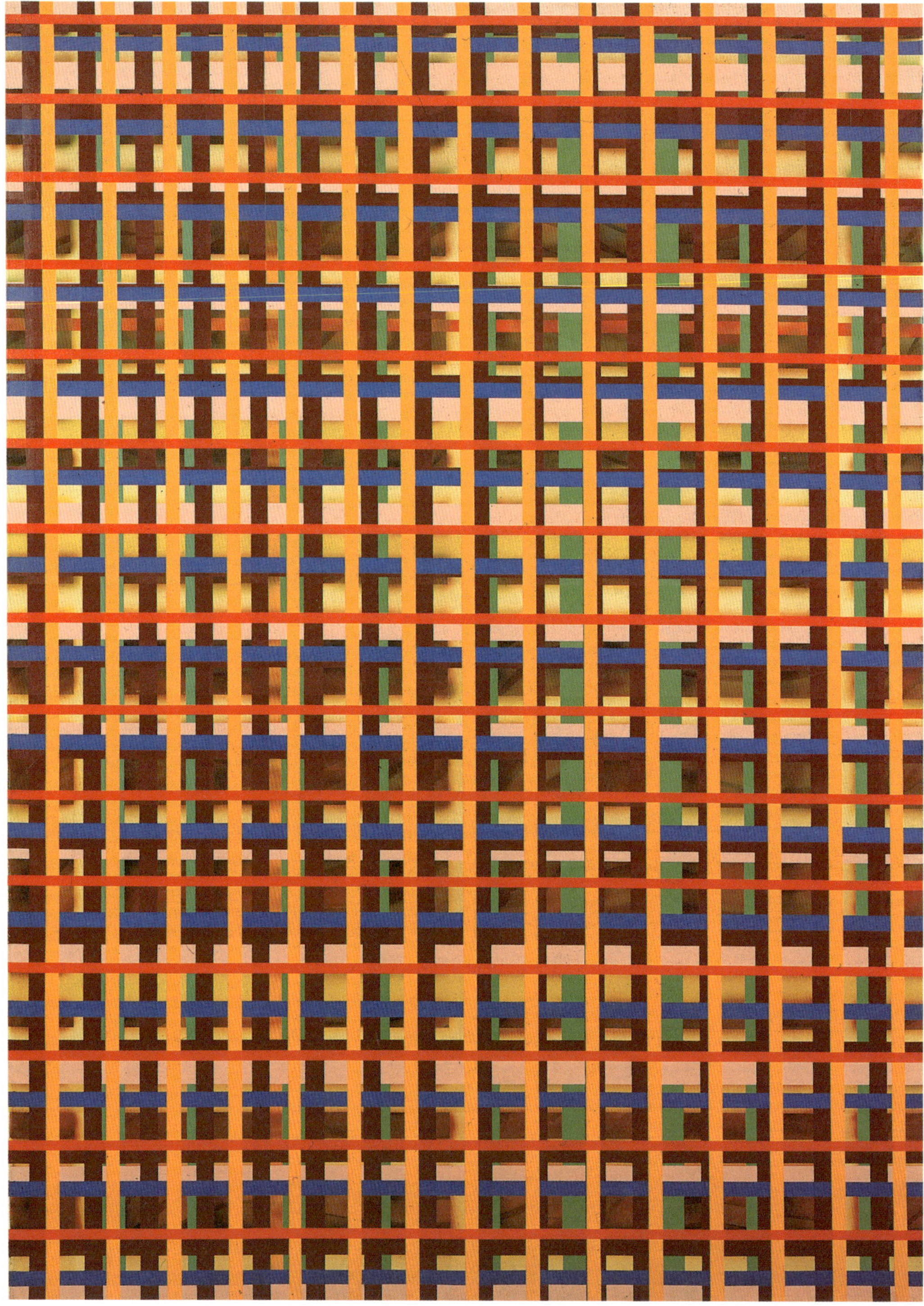

The way I talk is, I don't work from notes, so I tend to search for words. It probably isn't a good deal for you, but it is more interesting for me. It's like my work – I try to make it somewhat experimental. There is a consistency to it. I do believe the things I believe, and I say generally the same kind of things. But I try and set it up in one way or another that makes it interesting for me – so that during the course of the lecture I might find something that I didn't know when I walked into the room. It's experimental and a little bit rough. I hope you will bear with me.

What I have done today [in showing these images side by side] is set up a diptych, which is something that I am always doing in my paintings. I'll talk about that more in depth as I go along. This will be reflective of the way I work; I tend to work in pairs or to make two things and put them together. These two paintings [*Backcloth* (page 17) and *Red Light*] were made in the early 1970s. The idea was to try and reconcile two major examples: one, Jackson Pollock, and the other, Mondrian. Pollock represented for me a kind of desire and freedom, sensuality and sexuality. Mondrian represented conscious structure and morality and the way that they can be impacted into a very intensely layered, worked surface, where an extreme kind of modesty is also at work, where the expressionism at work is repressed. And those two aspects or possibilities of human nature I tend to try to work with – both of them – all the time.

These paintings are made by overlaying systems which are measured off differently. They are vertical and horizontal, and layered and layered, until I got to the point where I didn't think I could put anything else on without losing all the moves I had made. There is a reference all the way back to the start of the painting. *Backcloth* started as a loose, gestural kind of painting. Recently I walked into a gallery in New York, and I remember I saw a painting by a young New York painter that I thought was one of my paintings. I think his name is Gary Lang. Of course I liked it, but when I looked at it closely it wasn't the same as mine – his reasons for doing it and mine were different. Even though the experience of the painting is related, his painting is not as systematic as mine. In other words, the grids weren't always tremendously even; he would put one or two lines placed strategically. I would never have done that because behind my work was a kind of driven, manic, moral imperative. But the fact that the paintings looked somewhat similar in a strange way made the difference between them even greater. It also reminded me how inexhaustible the enterprise is. People keep managing to turn the stone in a different way.

I went to New York in 1975, and this [below] was the kind of work that I was doing when I was there. There is a tremendous break between the spatial illusionism and the almost catatonic visual effects that I was working with when I left. The colour was reduced right down. What I did when I went there was really to strip myself right down to nothing, basically – as far down as I could go without having a thing. I didn't want to take anything with me. It was really an extreme action – personally quite dangerous, I think – and it was something I did with my entire being; there was a real sense of existential danger when I moved to New York. What I wanted to do was engage the aspects of art that I considered important. There were two artists: [Ad] Reinhardt and [Robert] Ryman. Both purists

BLACK ON BLACK 1978–79
Oil and acrylic on canvas
213.4 x 213.4 cm (84 x 84 in.)
Madrid, Museo Nacional Centro de Arte
Reina Sophía

in their own way. One more quirky than the other, but both very puritanical. The colour I was dealing with was the colour of night, and relates to Reinhardt.

This painting is *Red Yellow Blue Triptych*, a triptych made up of stripes. At this time every surface that I made was divided exactly in two: it was split (i.e., the colour on the top edge would alternate on the bottom edge), and that was in every single painting that I did during that period. Every surface was democratically split between two colours, almost all horizontally. At the top you would have, let's say, brown-grey-black and, at the bottom, let's say, blue-black, and these would set up a kind of colour vibration. This made a nocturnal light, or cushion of light, that existed in front of the painting. It's interesting the way this structural idea relates to the notion of the diptych. Even the surfaces themselves were diptychs. It wasn't just one surface. I hadn't just mixed up the colours and put them down. Everything was split. In a strange way, psychologically I think, I was back to the split between my desire to embrace sexuality and morality all at the same time. *Red Yellow Blue Triptych* is three surfaces making up one work; it stands in relation to what I subsequently did, in that the surfaces are separated. By pushing the viewer to the edge of the surface, to the left and to the right in a constant and repetitive way, one is forcing the details of the painting out. The way the painting relates to the environment becomes very strong. I felt at this time that I wanted to make my work as morally severe as I could. I was very interested in Reinhardt's list of things he couldn't do, rather than things he could do. I think it's interesting ethically to talk about things you can't do. Ryman, by leaving out colour completely, achieved a kind of historical status in painting where, by not concerning himself with metaphorical content and by isolating the way material was put down, he did two things. One was that he moved the situation forward, and his work was able to have a dialogue with other kinds of art, Minimal and Neo-Conceptual art;

and at the same time he held the line and his paintings referred back to other paintings. In fact, some people talked about them in relation to Piero della Francesca, though they are more related to the materialism of [Piero] Manzoni [1933–1963].

This was a very interesting period for me. I felt that I was looking at two kinds of formalism when I was in America. The kind of work that I am interested in is mainly manifested in painting. I don't think it is possible to overestimate the importance of Clement Greenberg. There was one word that Greenberg used in all of this that bothered me a lot. That was 'taste'. It seems to me that 'taste' somehow symbolizes the difference between the Post-Minimalists and Minimalists and the Colour Field painters. I felt the drive towards a kind of purism was manifested much more clearly by the Minimalists than the other people. It has something to do with this word 'taste'. When I was teaching at Princeton, Clement Greenberg came out to talk. There was a man there called Sam Hunter, an art historian, and he took me under his wing. On the evening that Greenberg came to talk, Sam had a party in his house afterwards (and I remember it was a small house), and after the talk I refused to speak to him [Greenberg]. It wasn't a question of me being aggressive; I was afraid of him. It was a sign of my respect for his intellect. It hinges on this word 'taste', so it seemed to me that perhaps he was this purist, who secretly liked [François] Boucher. And I bet he had the Boucher in his toilet – which only he was allowed to use.

There was another secret agenda going on. I thought the Post-Minimalists, Ryman in particular, manifested close to point zero much more clearly, much more honestly. This party was a disaster, as you can imagine. I sat in one room, and lots of people sat in the other, and in our room was the bar, and every time Greenberg came in to get a drink I had to look the other way. I was really quite afraid of him! I thought he was quite a despot. He would kind of give you an invitation to join his club, but I felt that the price was your independence. With this word 'taste', it meant that something else would come into the work that seemed arbitrary to me. My works were very relentless – very driven – but they had that kind of fury that was systematic. There was a profundity that I was after that I think this issue of 'taste' somehow subverted.

The question for me was: what was I going to do now? Was I going to move away from painting to extend my ideas or make more paintings? When you start breaking things apart, the implications are quite sculptural. You are dealing with environmental issues. I had a lot of ideas to do with environmental issues. I was building lofts (construction work), and I really liked it. I liked putting things up

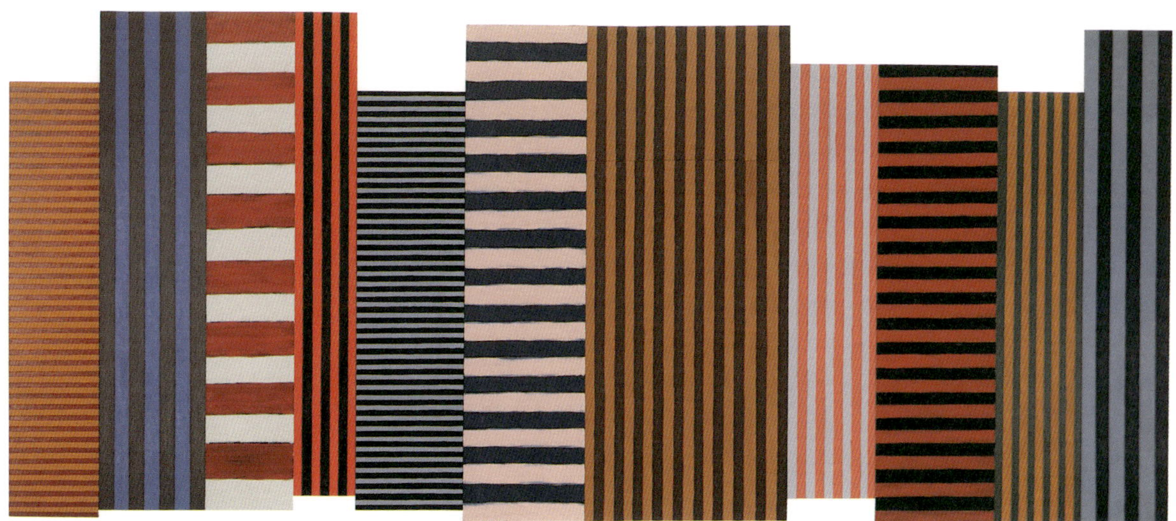

and leaving strange architectural additions. I had a lot of ideas at that time about that. In the end, my extremely passionate love of painting won; and I decided that the model that had been used up to that point would lead to the death of painting. And that's where it was headed. I decided to put back into painting all the things that had been left out. So again, there is another rupture in my work. In the first place I took everything out, and then I went to New York and after about five years put everything back in again. But of course, I couldn't put it back in the same way again because I had learned something.

The painting above is called *Backs and Fronts* (1981). At that point the title itself said something about my intention: I was thinking about people standing in a long line. Making a reference to people, they are all about the size of human beings apart from that one in the middle – that is really a big person. There were eleven panels here. I painted them all – all separately, all over the place – and when I had finished painting them, I just stuck them together. There was a show out of PS1 [Institute for Art and Urban Resources, New York] called *Critical Perspectives*. Six art critics had a room, and I was in Joe Masheck's room. At that time, 1980, there was a lot of punk energy in New York, and the punk people liked mine the best. I felt that there was a lot of anarchistic, unreasonable energy in the relationships that I was making in this painting, *Backs and Fronts*. And I had decided that what had been stripped out of painting – i.e., the ability to make relationships, to be metaphorical and referential, spiritual, poetic, all those things and aspects of human nature – had to be put back in if painting was to go forward.

The painting below is called *Heart of Darkness*. I was reading [Joseph Conrad's] *Heart of Darkness* at the time. Recently I decided that triptychs should have titles with three words. They are, in a sense, narrative. I was reading that novella at the time I was painting, and it influenced my personality. I tend to read quite often, and books are like my soul partner. I find the right novel, and it is my friend whilst I am working and thinking. I think they seep into my work. The panel on the left – it is interesting the way I resolved it. It says something about the way I work, which is rather urban. I couldn't get the painting to work out at all. (By the way, the middle panel on here was from another painting.) Things get moved around like sculpture. Real time was involved in my work. I would deliberately paint something in one room and leave it there and not look at it and paint something in another room from a memory that I would have about the first painting. My memory of the sensation.

In the 1970s my involvement with Minimalism and Post-Minimalism was obviously informed by a puritanical zeal. Here, I am putting back all the shit that I took out. I was walking up to the art shop and I passed the back of the post office, on Lispenard Street, and there were some beautiful yellow and black stripes, painted so the trucks wouldn't hit the wall. They were painted by someone

Oil on canvas
243.8 × 365.8 cm (96 × 144 in.)
The Art Institute of Chicago

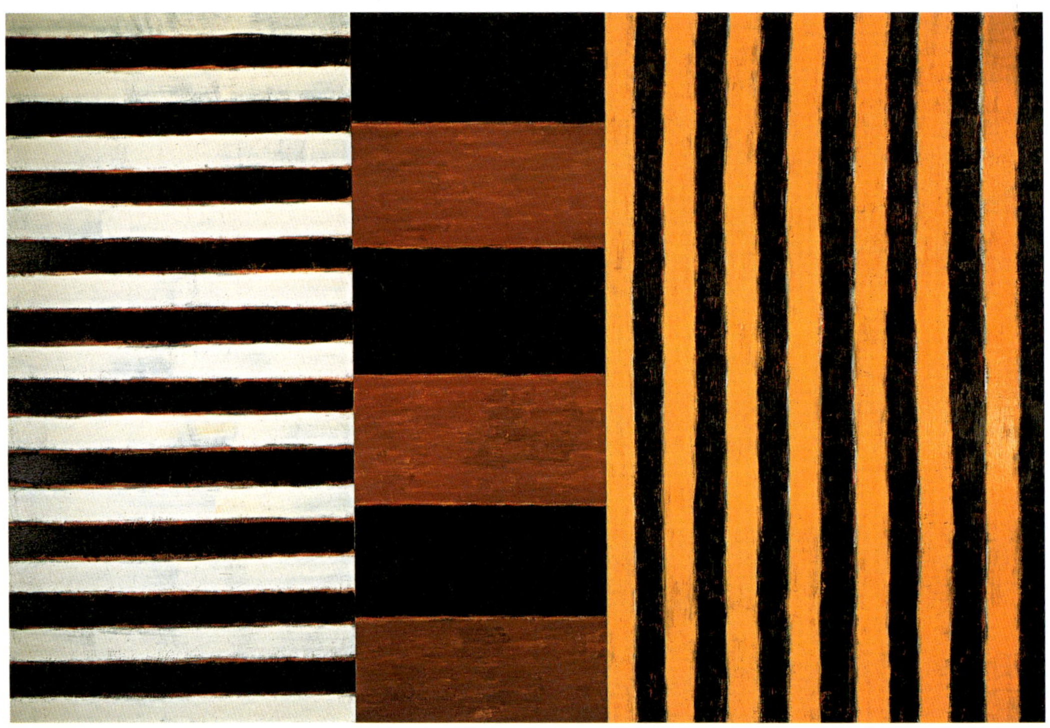

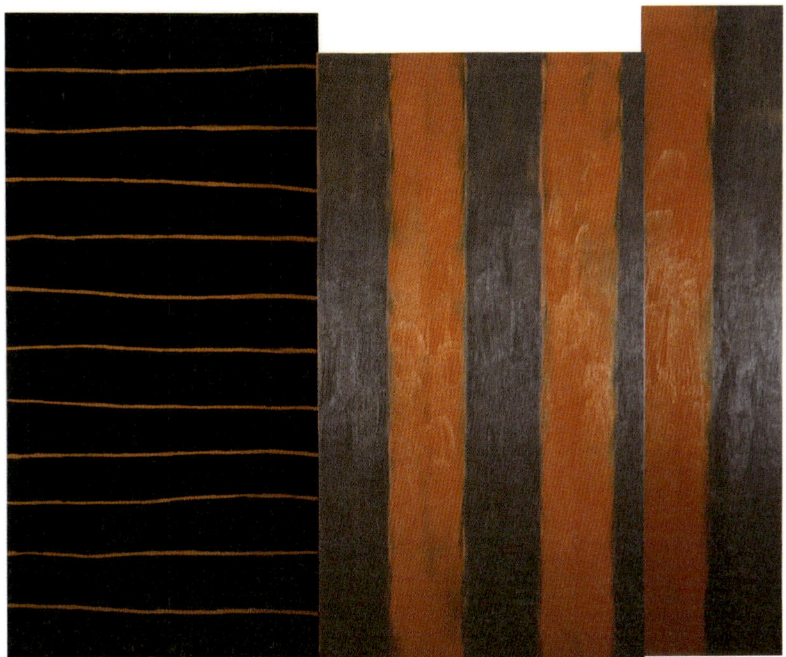

who had never painted stripes before, and in a way I wish I could paint like that every time. You can only paint like that once, in reality. How do you keep the emotion and vitality in the work going? The way I do it is very often metaphorically. I saw the stripes, and I was going up there to get another colour, and as soon as I saw the yellow and black I bought yellow and black, painted the painting, and finished. On the one hand I was using a story about the jungle and about the darkness in the human soul, but the thing that actually resolved the painting was an urban coincidence that was a romance with the back of the post office on Lispenard Street.

This one is called *Come In*. A person came to my studio in New York around this time – she was a museum director – and asked me what the title of the painting was. And I said, "Come in". And she began to interpret the painting architecturally. It's true that the painting does make a reference to architecture, as all my work does. It has something to do with construction work, the way I was building lines at the time, the way you contain and open up space at the same time. So it's an argument that goes across. It's as if the paint is trying to unify something that is physically disrupted: the idea that paint and colour, something so fragile, can pull things together that are not actually together. So she said, "It's called *Come In* – it could be a doorway, it could be a portal", which is true. I told her the story about why the painting is called *Come In*. The story showed me something that I didn't realize until later, and that is that I can't ever be a real American painter in the way that somebody who grew up in America can be. Because that is not my story. My story is in fact that I am a diptych, which is not all that comfortable sometimes.

The story was that [Samuel] Beckett was taking dictation from James Joyce. Joyce was sitting back, reciting. Beckett was writing it down, somebody knocked on the door, Joyce said "Come in", and Beckett wrote it down. Why not? He said it! That was his job. His job wasn't to decide what to write down; he wasn't the author. There is something absolutely beautiful about that – it is so ruthless. I just loved it, and it made me so happy. I think of Beckett as a really bad boy, and that is also interesting to me. The other thing that was interesting was that he was a bastard. So anyway, James Joyce said afterwards, "Why does it have "come in" in the middle of the narrative?" Beckett said, "You said, 'Come in.' I wrote it down so it has to stay in." To me it is very interesting this argument that they had. It defines the reality of how much of a readable narrative Joyce wanted to make. It is a point of crisis, in a sense. Joyce was convinced by Beckett's argument and left it in.

I told this long story to this person looking at the work in terms of materialistic formalism and its relationship to architecture. She seemed slightly bemused by it all, and I was a bit disturbed because I wondered why I told her that. And I thought it was a bit crazy. But that was why I made the title of the painting. But it also had something to do with the idea of allowing something to come into your life that you didn't predict, and that has a lot to do with the intention of my work. I make things in the studio in different places. In a way I am working much more like a sculptor or environmental artist, as opposed to other types of painters who work with the square or the rectangle. I set up bits and pieces which are not entirely within my control. I let something literally come in. I figured that out afterwards.

The one on the right is called *This That*. There is also a painting called *This This*. Really, my concerns are quite consistent and relentless. *This That* has a huge oppressing bulk on the thing below. The area above is painted in a way that makes it lighter and more light-responsive. There are a lot of opposing forces – there is a kind of competition for survival – and I am sure psychologically that reflects something about me, about the life I have led, which I really believe these paintings come from.

I was asked to talk about myself in relation to other artists in New York. I don't like to talk about other artists because I don't feel that I have the right to

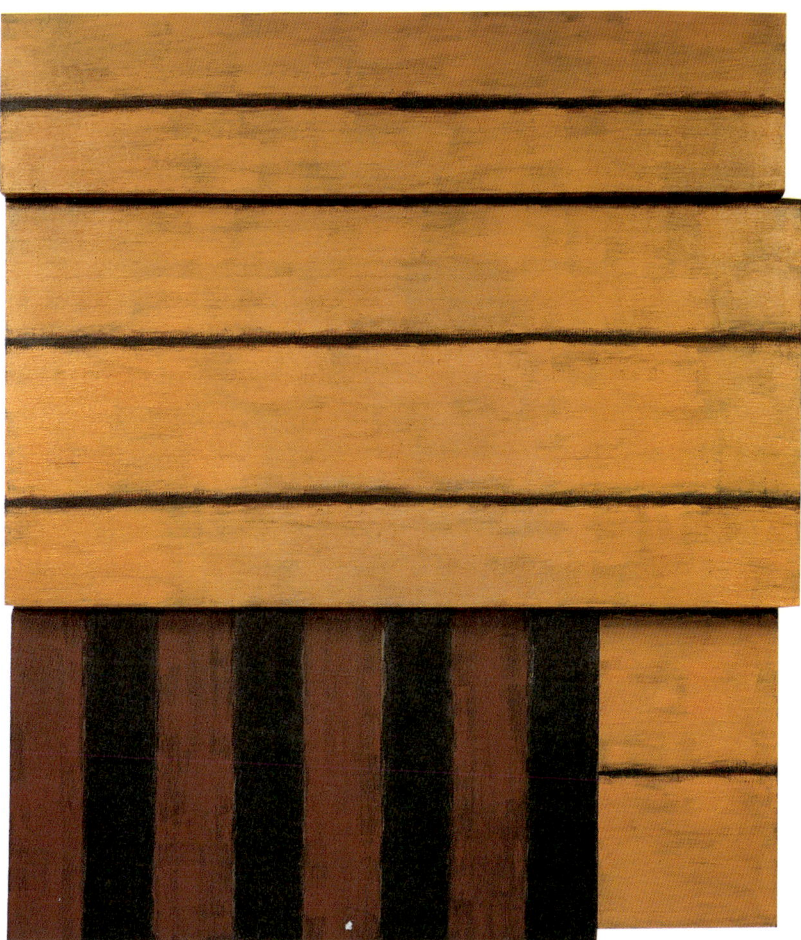

criticize or judge others. I know what I like and am interested in, and it is difficult to contextualize yourself without being somewhat critical. I used to have a friend who was a painter. He used to go round and look at shows, and his habit was to give them a number out of ten. He'd say it was a "seven". This outraged me so much that in the end I just stopped seeing him. Something that might be a "three" six months later might be a "nine", so it's just better not to give it a number and let it do whatever it needs to do within you, and within the culture. In other words you can change your mind about things.

I would have to say that I am not a fully paid-up, card-carrying member of the Lower Manhattan Abstract Painting Club, whilst there have been certain moments in time when I would have liked to have been. Like all human beings, you like to be included. However, my problem with a lot of the people in my generation with whom I have shown from time to time is that they tend to be specialists, following an American example of extreme efficiency and specialization in art. I would say Andy Warhol is an example – and [Roy] Lichtenstein is another – where American artists have been able to become free by travelling light. That causes a certain kind of visual efficiency, to some degree a kind of radicalism, and it definitely has had its upside in the past. It seems to me that when you reach the point where that model has led to a key figure, like Robert Ryman, it has reached its ultimate point. If the medium is going to go forward, I don't think it can go forward in the hands of specialists. If you put all those people together, you might make something. So what I tried to do is to not over-specialize and not be simply an expressionistic, structuralist Neo-Conceptual abstractionist. A lot of different aspects to my painting I try to include. So I would say my position is one of inclusiveness rather than specialization. That makes me quite different.

MOLLOY 1984
Oil on canvas
243.8 x 304.8 cm (96 x 120 in.)
New York, The Metropolitan Museum of Art

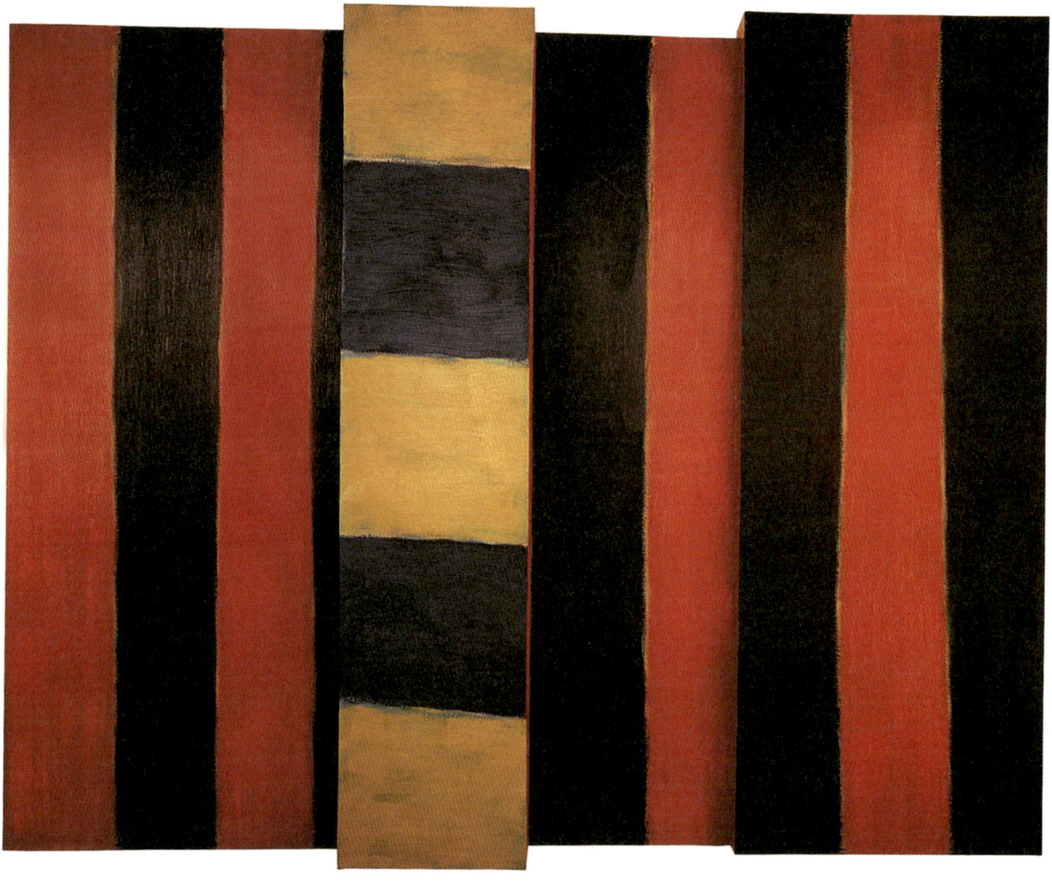

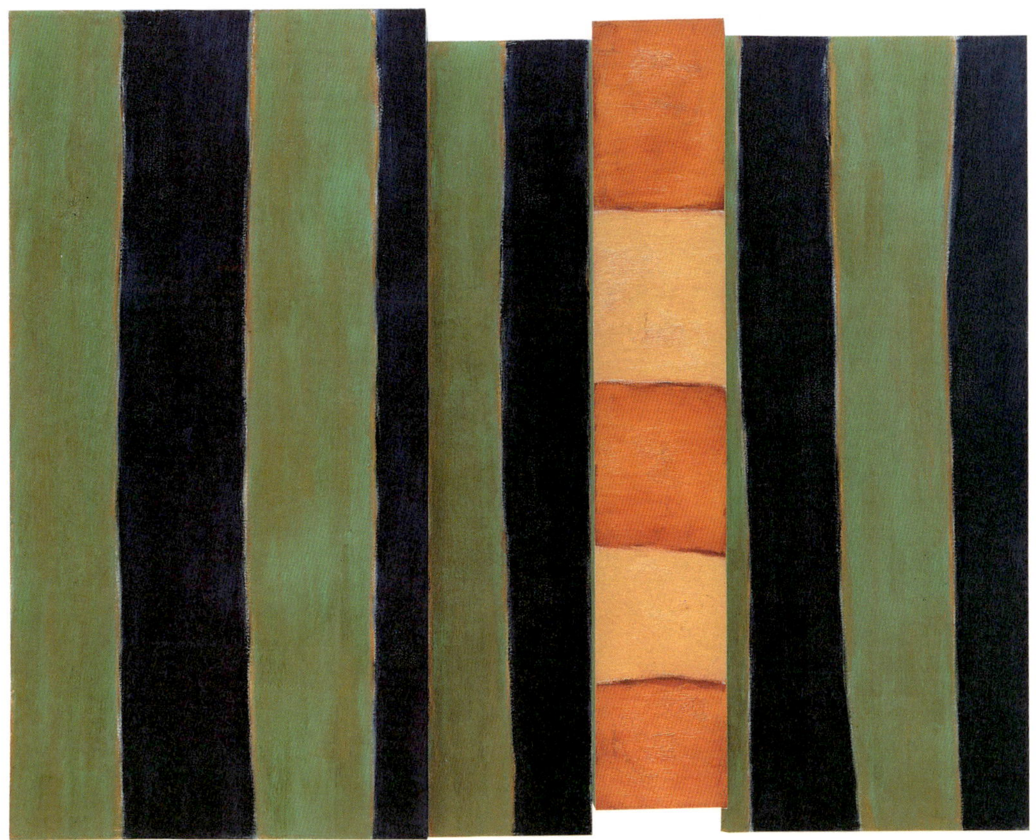

To return to these paintings: it's about putting together the two things that I am interested in. One is a light-filled grid and the other is another type of grid, which is layers of stripes painted in very passionate colours. The emotion in the painting is not represented solely by either. It is manufactured or implied by the combination of the two. It is very much an art of relationship. It's an art that is about 'doing' something rather than 'being' something. Paintings are not, any more, about that idea of the painting representing itself through constituent parts and not about representing anything outside yourself. These paintings clearly try to engage the world in a more direct way.

This one's called *Molloy* and that one's called *The Bather*, and they both relate to the figure. The skinny panels make a very obvious reference to the human body, to a figure in space. In relation to the ethical, minimal stance of my predecessors that were working in the 1970s, these paintings transgress incredibly. They are very impure. I had an article sent to me recently written by a friend of mine who is a Spanish poet. He says that I have said my work goes beyond the illustration of the theoretical questions and that I have spoken about emotional specificity. I think that the way to make abstract painting specifically emotional is to not make an allusion to a particular situation, as figurative artists do. But it is to do something more akin to what Mark Rothko does, which is to make the relationship between form and art so deep that the articulation of those forms in relation to the colours on the surface becomes one of great joy and great pain. That can be true to the point where those sensations can be seen as feelings. They cross the barrier between being something 'felt' and something 'seen'.

I am not an inventor in the way that others, like [Frank] Stella, were. A lady recently came to my studio and is going to write a piece on my work. Her name is Deborah Solomon. She asked me if I had been psychoanalysed. It seems to me that one can do the extreme at either end. As much as I recognize Bruce Nauman's

FOUR DAYS 1990
Oil on canvas
274.3 × 365.8 cm (108 × 144 in.)
Private collection

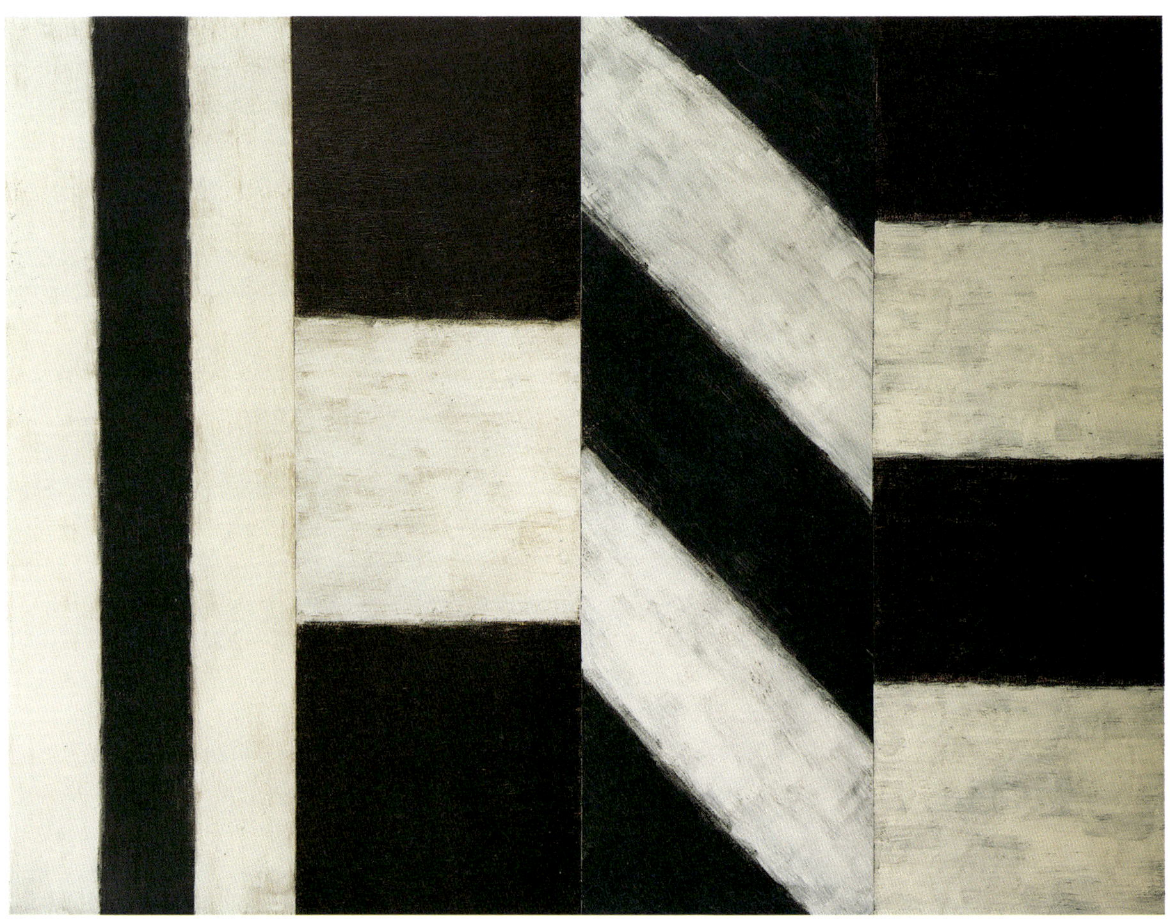

work, I would have to say that my temperament and nature are the opposite. I am someone that works with something for so long that the level of identification becomes enormous. You work at something over and over again. That is at the same time kept open by strategies that I adopt in the studio, by the way that I put things together; and that creates the air in the work, the window in the work.

The art form that I love most, I think, besides painting is film-making. I think that in order to be a film-maker you have to be more equipped to deal with the world than I am. It seems to me that if you work in a medium like painting, which is so stubborn, so inert, so difficult to make happen when you are actually speaking, you need a certain kind of personality. I think of myself as somebody who is too open to be working in the world. I think I would be destroyed if I were working in a medium that had a more direct relationship with the world. I think as a person I am like a tunnel. I think things just drive right through me and go straight through the other side. It also seems to me that, if one has that sort of nature, a medium like painting becomes perfect. There is enough distance from the world to make it possible for me to work without being destroyed, and yet the need to be expressive is so strong that somehow there is a pressure there to make – to speak to whatever degree I have been able to make it speak. When I was listening to Yve-Alain Bois talking about François Morellet, he said that when François made a painting – for those that don't know, François Morellet is a French Neo-Constructivist painter – it only took eleven decisions. When I make a painting, it takes hundreds of decisions. In a sense, they fail a certain test of economy of means. It is not a test I try to pass any longer.

This painting on the left is called *Four Days*. It came out of the conversation that I had with a friend of mine who used to be a film critic. He was talking about a film that he called "Four Days of a Dreamer". I found out afterwards that it was called *Four Nights of a Dreamer*, but it doesn't matter, because what matters to me is that the painting came out of the conversation. So thinking about this painting in terms of the cinema, the way that you can go from sitting in the back of a New York taxi to being in Africa in a split second. That has something to do with the way I make the relationship, the way I put things together. It causes a kind of energy, or a kind of relationship, that I believe to be true to the time in which I am living and true to the energy that I live in, which gets consistently harder. So if I want a break from New York I go to Barcelona, which is described as the city most like New York in Europe, only with a different climate.

These panels were painted in different places in my studio. I am not painting them in a way to harmonize them, so 'taste' is completely avoided; going from one area to another, from Day One to Day Two, I don't have to mediate the

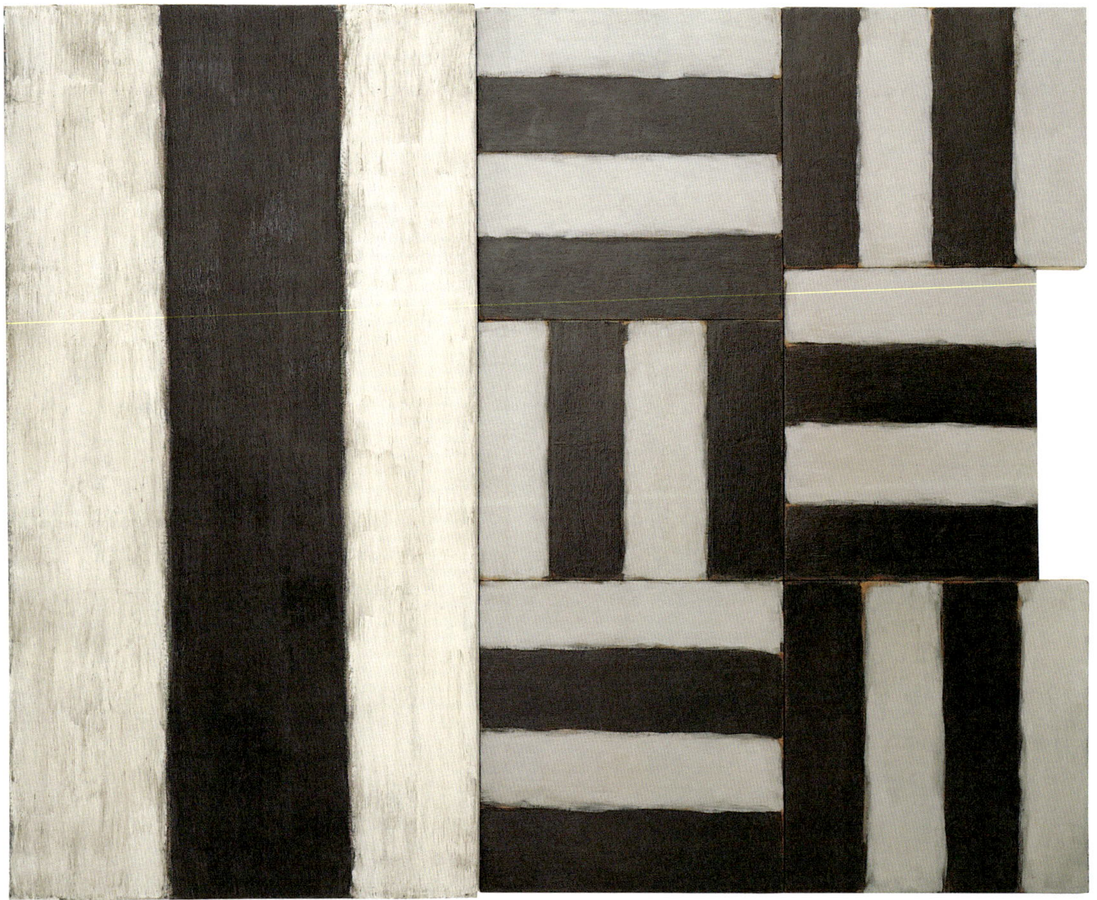

difference. It's like saying you are on one side of the street and describing how you cross to the other side, and that's not what I am doing. I am on one side, then I am on the other side. There is no sense of mediation. The relationship is absolutely blunt. In that sense it is related a lot to sculpture.

The painting above is called *Any Questions*. I called it *Any Questions* because I went to see a concert with Talking Heads, a beautiful concert. At the end David Byrne said, "Any questions?" As if you were going to have any questions about punk rock and roll! What I did with this painting was two different things. I put them together in a way that one couldn't really answer questions about. I thought of the right side as the same stuff as the left side, broken up and put back together again. So when I think about these paintings, I don't think about them in terms of patterns. I know that they are patterns because they are repeated structures, but really I am thinking about different kinds of thought structures. In a way that has something to do with computers. It's not the computer that I am interested in; it's the person that invented the thing that's in the computer. It's the way we think. These are the structures that we surround ourselves with. These are our urban structures, and they are repetitive. One kind of repetition juxtaposed with another kind of repetition – that is how you spend your day in the city – the endless repetition of life, or expression, or beauty, or mystery without avoiding what it fundamentally is. In other words, without making structures that I don't believe are reflective of the age in which I live. I try to make the structures as direct and honest as I can in that way.

The other thing that I might bring up while I am telling you everything is – so that I don't forget to tell you – that when I was growing up I was in south London, which is a desperate proposition. A working-class kid, standing on the street corner waiting for something to happen, feeling empty, I discovered an incredible, ravishing beauty in American R & B. I had a club, which we didn't have for very long because it was closed down by the police. But in any case I think my great love of music was reflected in my paintings, in the constant and relentless beat of

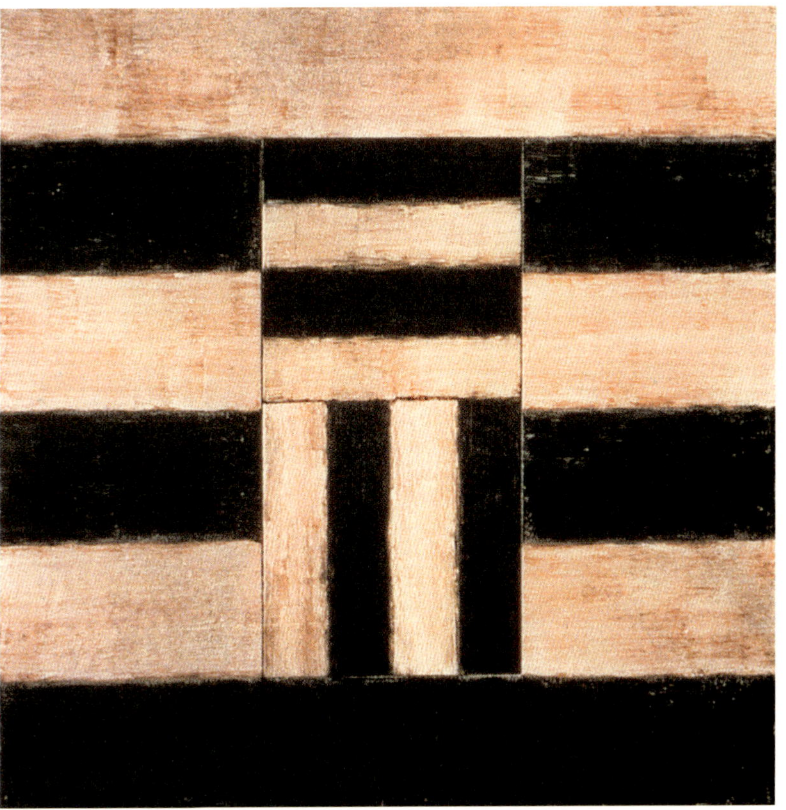

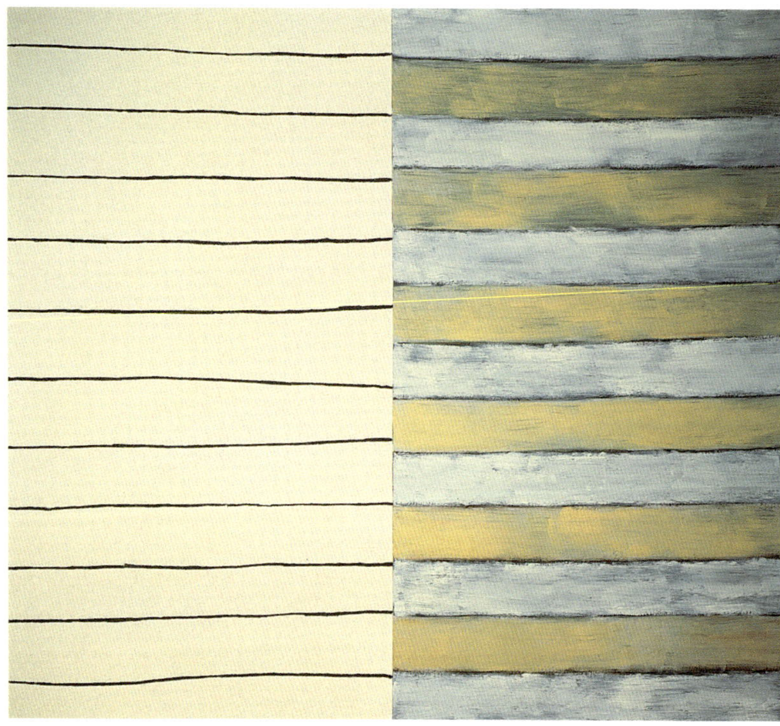

these paintings. It had more to do with that kind of thing than with the juxtaposition of patterns. I don't really think of my work in that formalist sense. It's something that I am doing, everything I am doing, to get away from ... banality.

These paintings were made during a period of great sorrow in my life when my son died. The one on the previous page is called *Empty Heart*. I think it is a very barren painting; there is a kind of ferocity about it that one might see in an African mask. African masks always have a kind of savage beauty. It has a lot to do with this distressed white – there is a pink-white and a yellow-white. A brown-black and a blue-black. Of course, the black and my constant use of black since have a lot to do with those paintings in the 1970s that I made that were all about black, where I was dialoguing with the Minimal-Conceptual paintings. There is also a painting with the centre scraped out, called *Green Gray* (1988).

I think authenticity has something to do with why things are made. If your reason is strong enough, then that is going to result in something that is authentic. So I don't think that authenticity is something that can be corrected afterwards. It is something that has to come from the base, from the concept and from the need. The reason that I raise that is because I was thinking about Gerhard Richter.

His scraping away had everything to do with the war and the need to take away and get rid of the past. I think it is compulsively neurotic, which is why it is very interesting to me. A lot of people that work like that in New York have seen it as a kind of interesting device, have seen it as a kind of pictorial strategy. The reason for doing it is not interesting if you think about it like that. That to me lacks authenticity. That is what I mean by authenticity.

The structure of these paintings somehow is a structure that turns in on itself – it has no point. One is ravaged colouristically. The other is just, in a certain sense, cancelled out. There is no centre. I think, psychologically, the metaphor is quite obvious, as is the title. So my titles are very specific. A lot of people at a certain point in the development of abstraction started to use titles willy-nilly, to make them up as they liked, as they were attached to the painting. What I would like to do with my titles is to make them very specific. That doesn't mean that I want the paintings to be absolutely descriptive, but the titles are not loose in relation to the painting. This painting opposite is called *Angel*, and it's a painting that I decided to make when I was on an aeroplane flying between Pittsburgh and New York. I was looking at the clouds and the colour of the clouds and all that beautiful pollution. The reason that I was calling it *Angel* was because of the idea

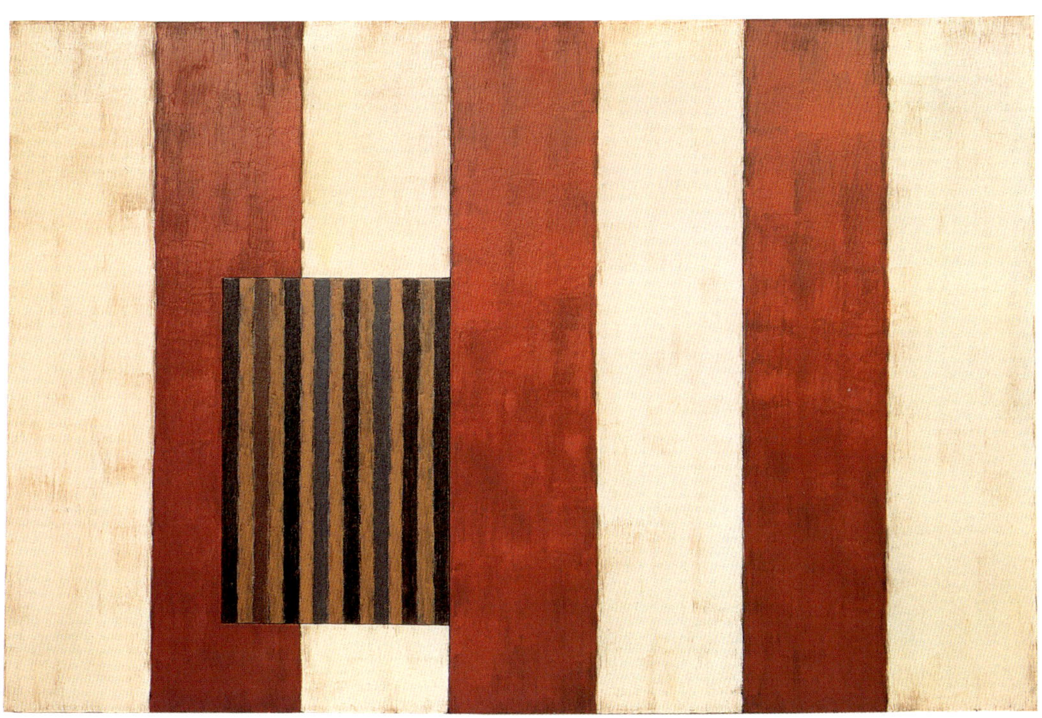

of body and no body. Body and line, painting and drawing. And there is a split right down the middle.

The painting on the previous page is *Pale Fire*. A friend of mine who is an architect looked at the painting and interpreted it for me. I will try, if I can, to tell you what he said. He said it was a very sad painting, because he thought it was about the American flag with a darkness (in the window) in it – like an American flag with a cancerous rectangle set into it, which is more or less what I was trying to do. What I wanted to do was make the field, which wasn't the American flag but the colour field, the optimistic field of stripes that represents security, surety, direction – and it knows where it's going – into a symbol of power. For a long time the painting had a hole in it, and if I had left it, it would have said a lot about the thing I had wanted to say. It was a field, but the field had a hole in it. There was a problem with it. But what I did was put in another canvas; and I did something on the other canvas that I hardly ever do, which was to not complete the pattern with relentless regularity. I was putting something in there that was darker and less secure. It had a lot to do with the way my friend described the painting, and of course the title says it as well. The fire's not out, but it is pale. That doesn't mean that a lot of things aren't possible, and if that can be reflected then that's what I believe an artist should do. I think if you do that then you have made art.

I think one of the main reasons that I make my work out of separate pieces is because of the way that I can paint them without thinking about what they are with. I can paint them in a way so that I am unselfconscious. I am just painting bits. A relationship is made up when they are put together.

The Duomo in Siena is one of my favourite buildings, for obvious reasons. It may have been in fact the first time I got the idea to make chequerboard paintings. But I remember rather strongly a recent experience: I was walking around in Madrid, and there was a huge steel double gate guarding a car park. It was painted with a red and white chequerboard. This gate, situated in a narrow street up against an old wall, full of rust, was so romantically beautiful and savage at the same time; it was very inspiring. The painting opposite is called *Yellow Ascending*. Sometimes I think of these panels as vehicles for ascension. I can also see them as figures, but they generally tend to be painted differently. I think they are not meant to be seen as ladders in the literal sense, just a metaphor for ascension. What is interesting is that the rungs (steps) are going up and they are pushing the ceiling up, but because of the stripes going horizontally there is a sense of the weight coming down; they look stacked. I thought at different points about making sculptures that were very related, but I never got round to it. This is an unrelenting, rather dreary black and grey that has been modified by that strip of orange.

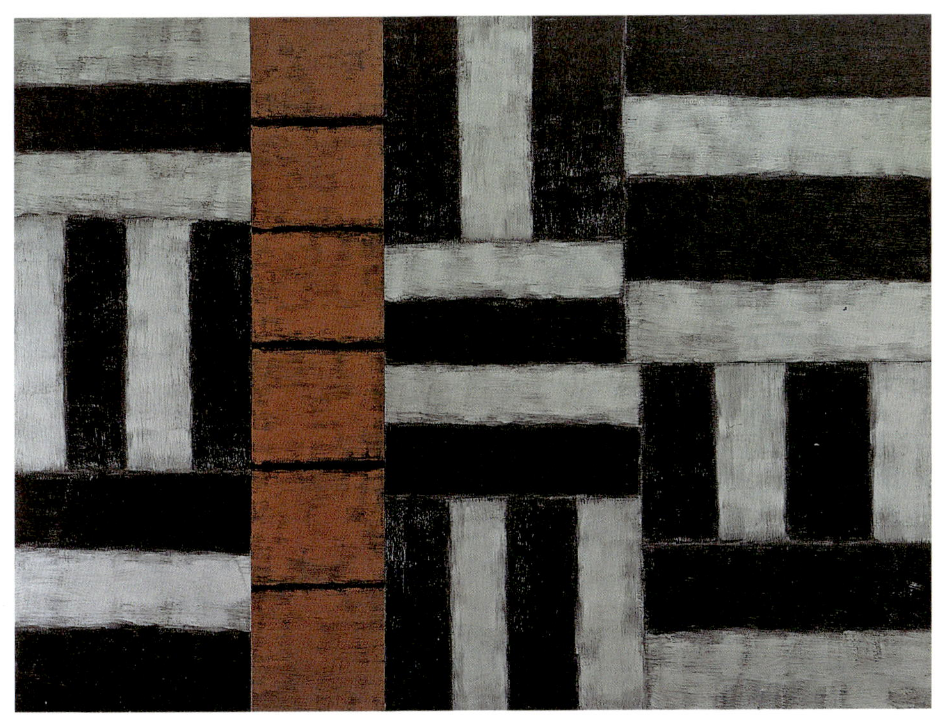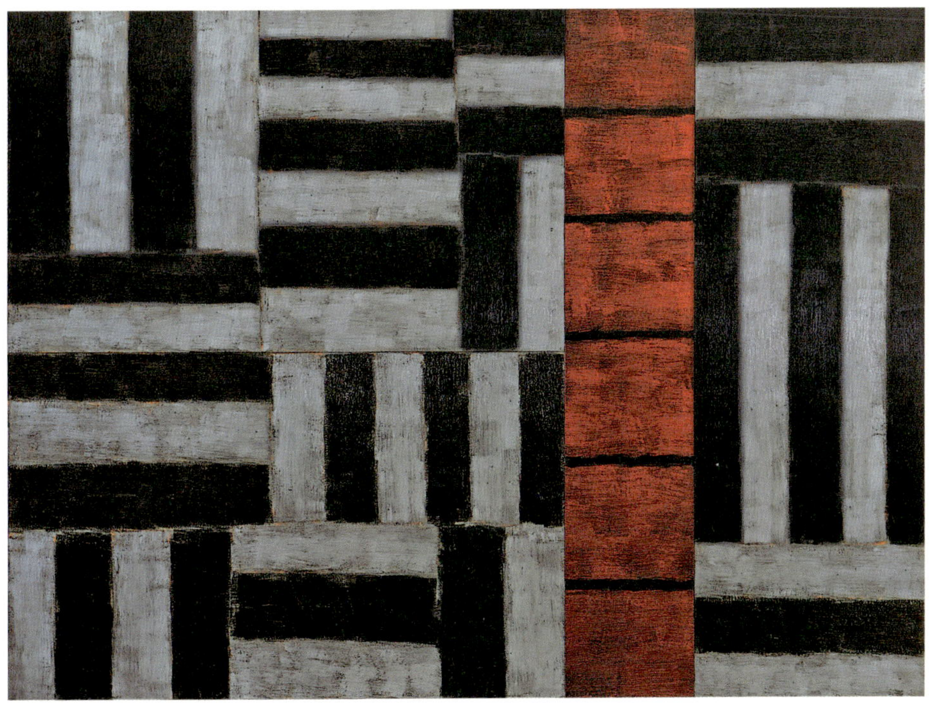

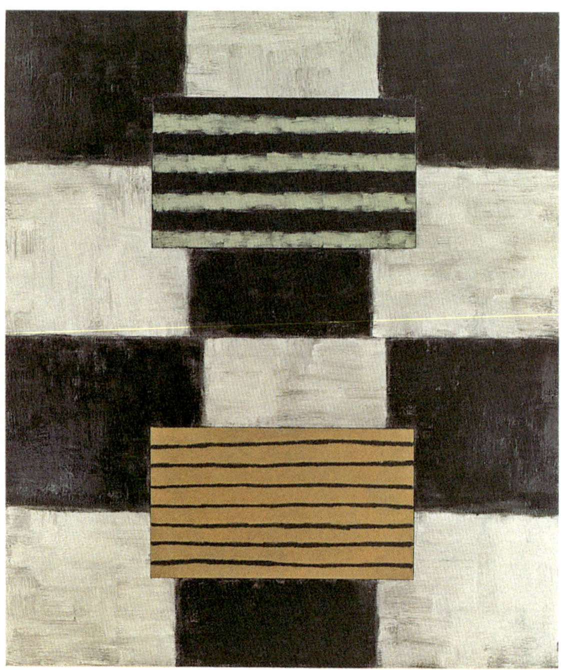 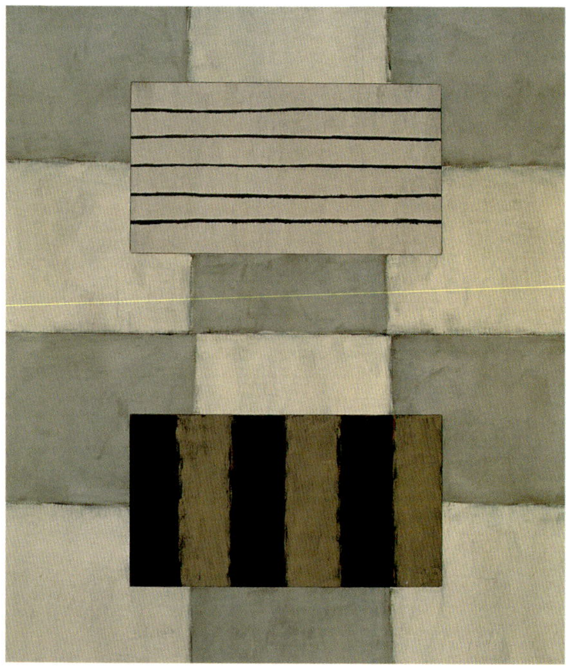

The one at the bottom of the previous page is *Red Ascending*. Again, these two paintings go back to the idea of the diptych. There is the grey and black field. To press it, coming out of the plus-and-minus idea: energy that is going nowhere has a kind of pointlessness about it. It is pulled apart for something else to enter the painting. It seems to me that when my paintings travel, they travel with the relationships taken apart, the pieces separated. When they reach their destination, the relationship is remade. I want to have a sense of that in the painting.

I am doing a series of paintings and giving them the title of women. They have a verticality and a sense of the figure. The one on the left, above, is *Mariana*, and the one on the right is *Lucia*. *Mariana* is dirty and ravaged; *Lucia* is lit up with a pale and delicate light based on subtly different whites.

The two paintings opposite were made at a time when I was reading *Ficciones* (Jorge Luis Borges), which is a story about a place which doesn't really exist – it can't be proven. One of these paintings is called *Ukbar*, and the other is called *Okbar*. In the story people would name the place slightly differently every time, so I added more paintings around this idea. A printer friend of mine came to my studio and saw these paintings and he said, "You know they remind me of places that I don't even know exist." I do believe that empathetic communications between humans perhaps will develop in the future. I thought it was quite wonderful that

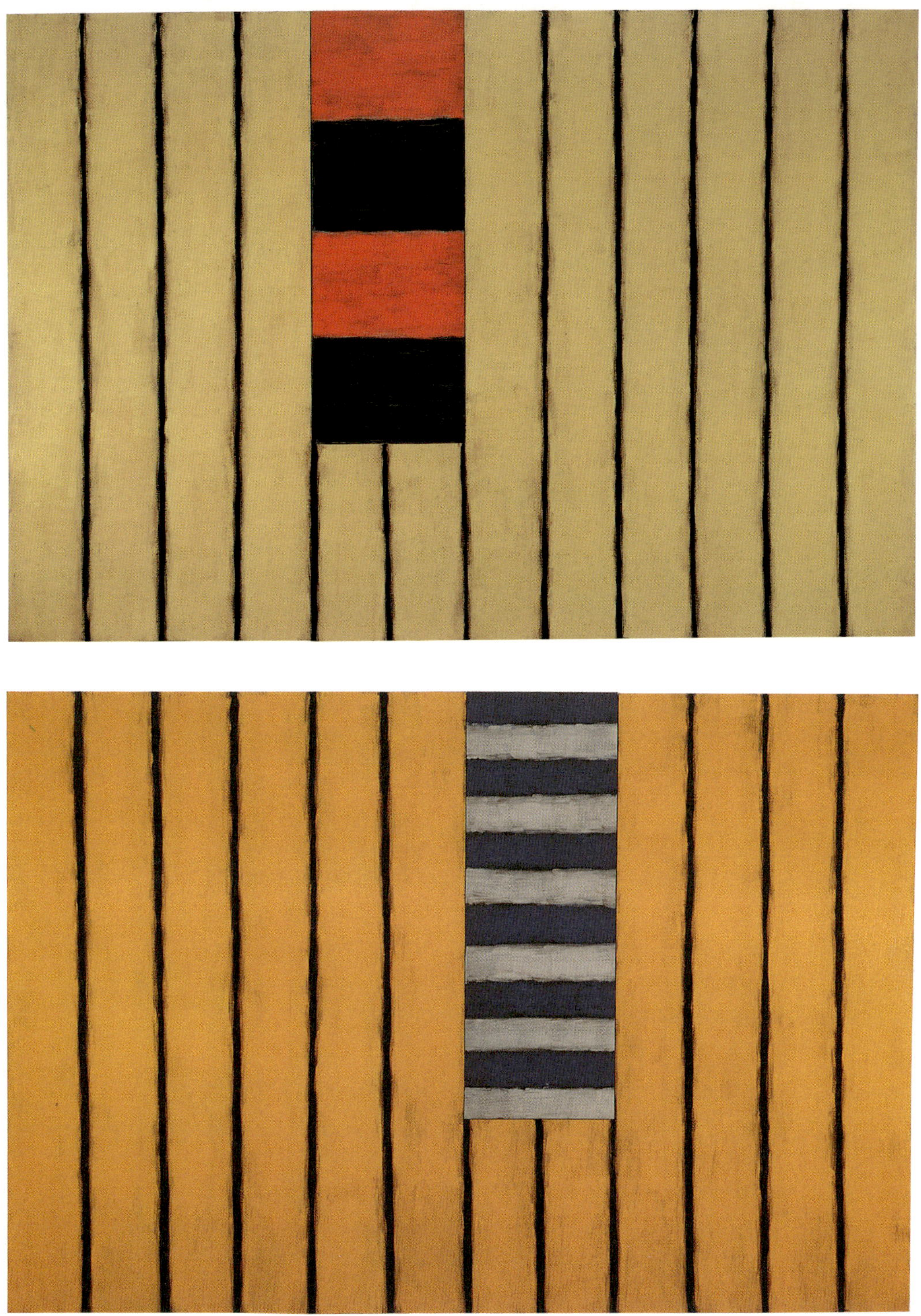

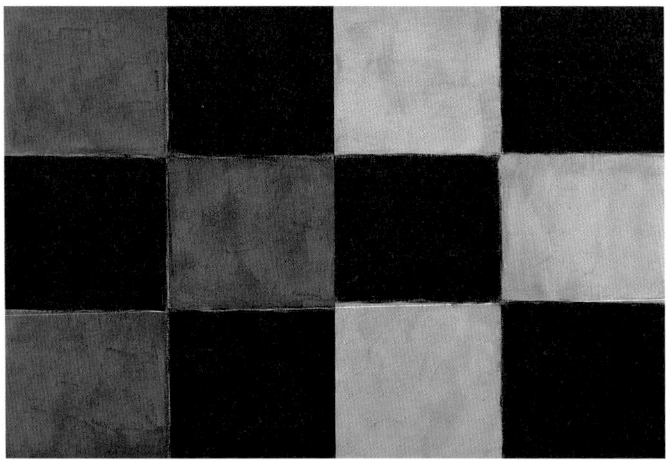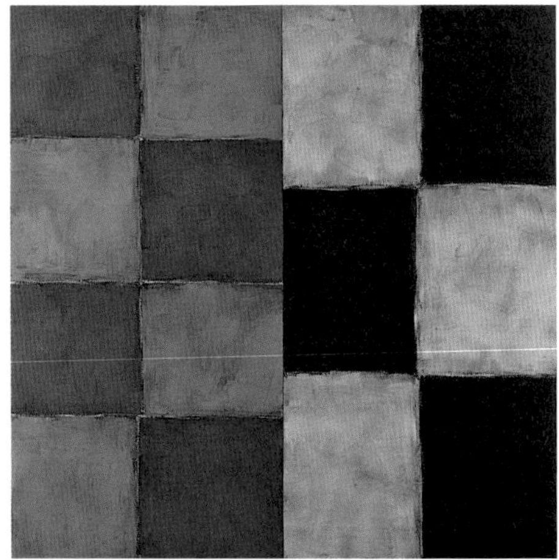

this person walked into my studio and said exactly what the paintings were about, and I hadn't even talked to him about them. So there must be something very strong. Maybe it doesn't work every time, but there has to be something in it. These things (the insets) are dropped in and they are painted separately, of course, as usual. The field is painted with something missing, and the other thing is painted somewhere else with something missing, like an uninvited guest.

The paintings above are all called *Union*. I had a long discourse with myself about using chequerboards – not because I didn't think I could make good paintings with them, but because I think that the continual use of something that is obsessive, compulsive behaviour is very interesting. What I wanted to do with the stripes was to reuse them in a way that they hadn't been used before, not to continue with the formalist game. I was quite happy not to be inventive in a certain way; I was quite happy to use something that everybody else had thrown away. It was equivalent to making sculpture out of garbage. I was making paintings out of something that had been discarded: stripes. I wondered whether it was more interesting to use the same motif, whether that would be a more important point to prove. It would expose something more and would become deeper by using something over and over again. It would have that sense of repetition about it, like people asking me if I had been psychoanalysed. It had that aspect to it that was very attractive. Anyway, after a long struggle with myself I decided to make these *Union* paintings. They are about a softer kind of relationship, and they also imply a sense of wholeness because of the title and because of the impact between the two sides. The communication between the two sides is more reasonable in a certain kind of way. It is quite a different sort of situation from misfits, where the

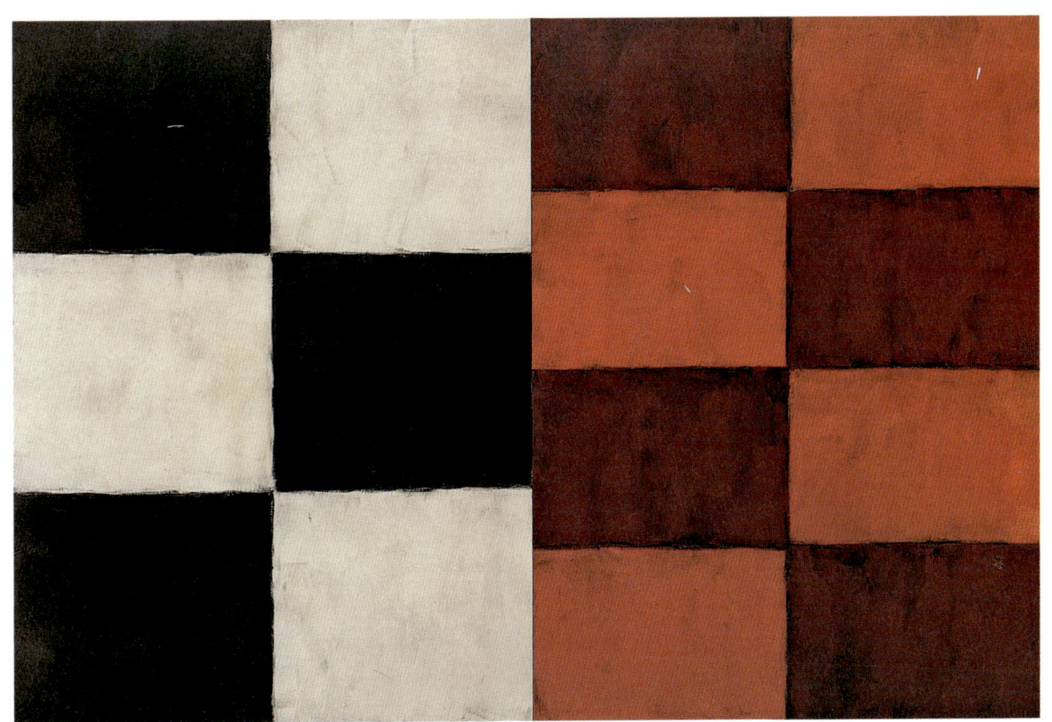

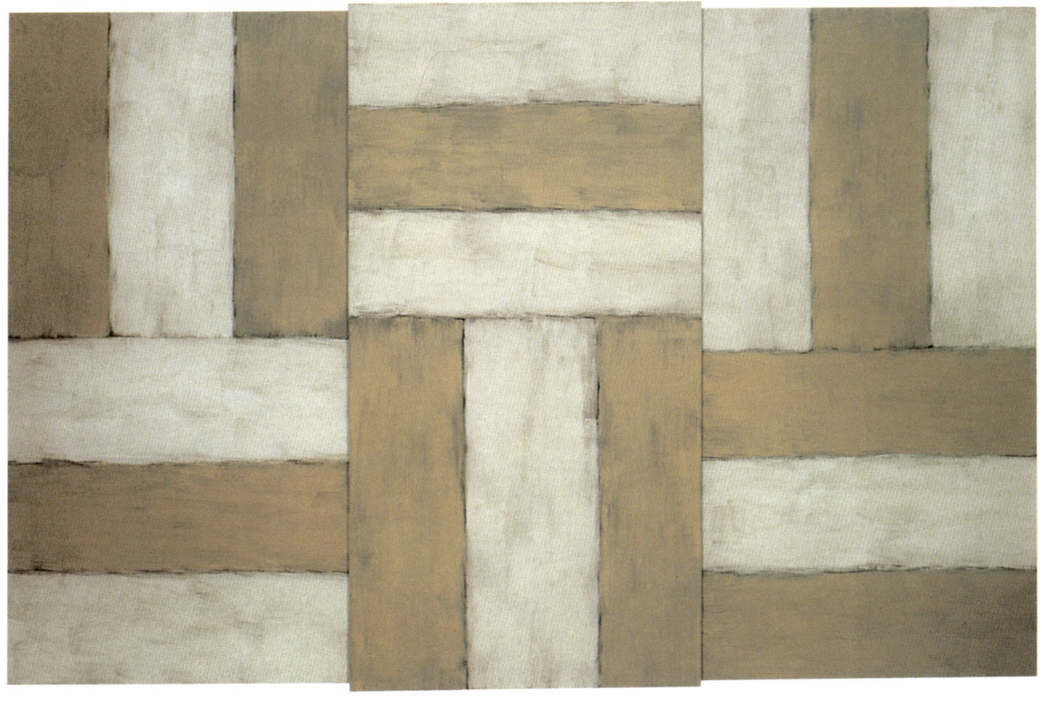

two things are bluntly slapped together and have to live together and make the most of it and survive. These were painted many, many times, by the way. The one on the left is *Union Black*; the one on the right is *Union Green*. *Union Black*: the panel is the same, and it goes back to what I was doing in the 1970s with the nocturnal light. And on the right side of the painting, which is an equally divided – democratically divided – diptych of six squarish rectangles, the two sides are painted separately in the blacks and greys and then they are put together. This is done over and over many times. Painting this probably took me six months. All the edges on this are soft, the only hard edge being that one running vertically down the centre. So the paintings have a more gentle quality, with the abutments not as violent as they were in the striped paintings, where the colour and the size and the nature of the stripes varied tremendously where they abutted each other, causing a kind of rupture. In these paintings, in fact, you get a kind of union: a union that is still making and un-making itself as you look at the painting.

The next two paintings that I want to show you are the *Catherine* paintings (page 65). I have chosen these because they show something important about my work: that it doesn't really progress in a very formal, linear fashion: i.e., according to the rules or game of formalism. The one at the bottom is *Catherine* (1995), which is a painting that relates in form to other paintings such as *Durango* (below),

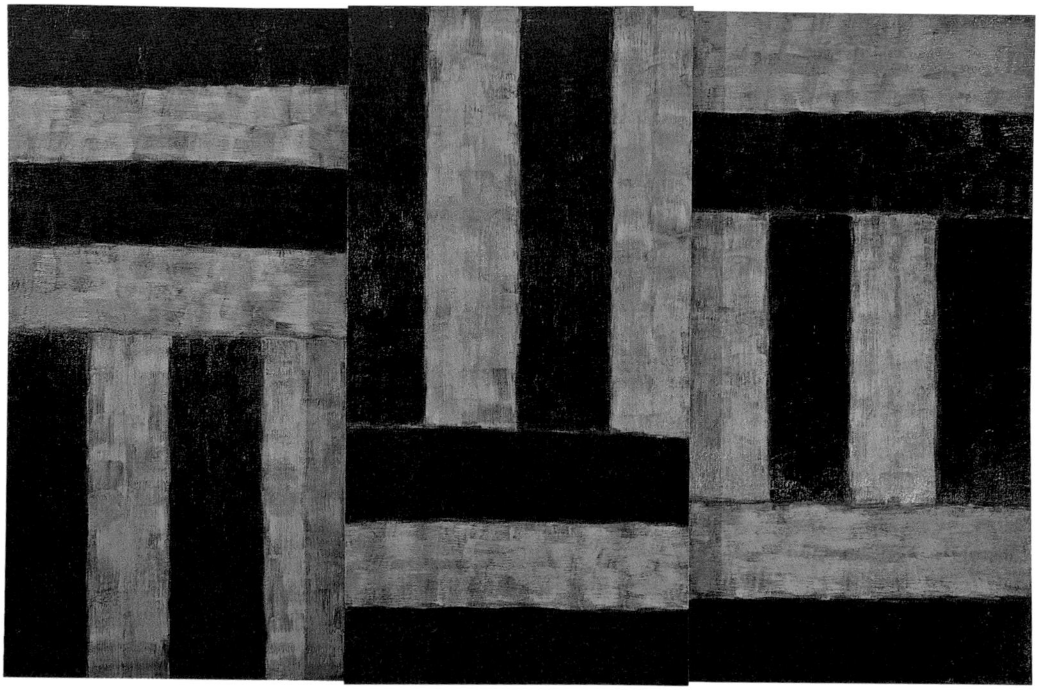

which were painted around 1991; however, the colours are very different. The colours are delicate, fragile and very washed out. And it is monumental; it has about it a risky quality. It is a monumental painting and I think that it is only possible to do that with a form that you know well. The one at the top is *Catherine* (1994) from the year before, of course, and that is a chequerboard painting. It is not that the chequerboard paintings have replaced the stripe paintings, not at all.

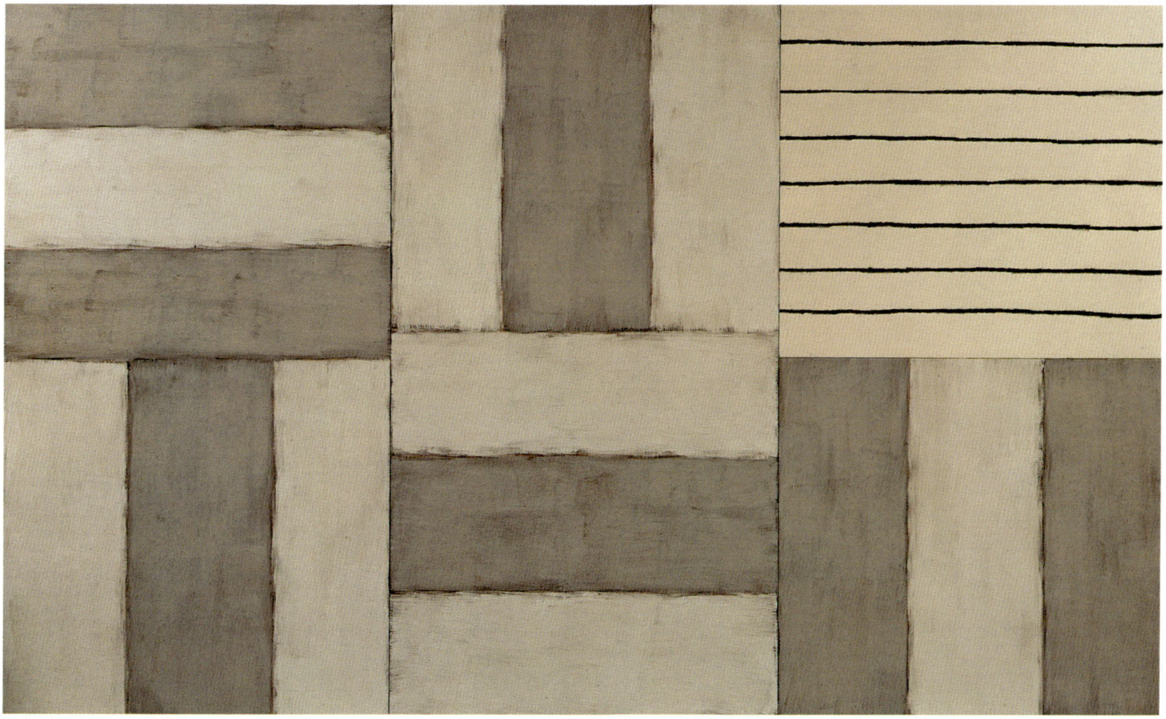

There is always an up-and-down, and sideways, in order to be expressive. In other words, I am not moving forward; I am moving around in a way that is more cyclical and more unpredictable.

The painting above is mine, and the video piece below it is by [Bill] Viola. And Viola's piece is called *Nantes Triptych*. It is a beautiful piece, and I want to talk a little bit about triptychs in my work and in his piece. I thought it would be interesting to talk about his piece in relation to what it is to make a modern triptych. I don't think a modern triptych is based at all on a medium – I don't think it matters whether it is a video piece or a painting. I think it has to do with the psychological structures in the piece. My painting above is called *Angelo*, and is

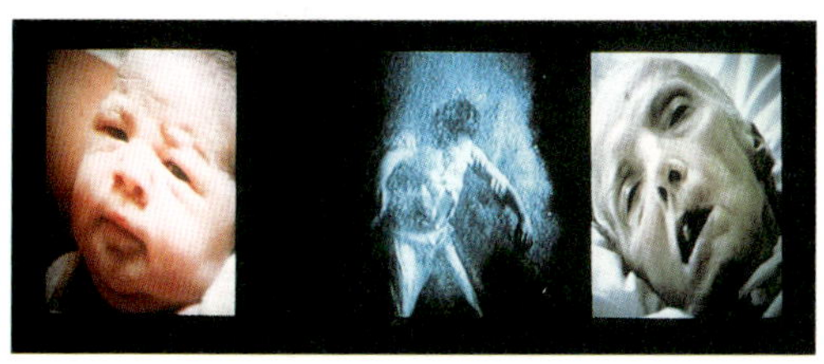

not strictly a triptych; it is a triptych with the right-hand corner separated off. Bill Viola's is a triptych about birth and death and life and death. On the left panel is a woman giving birth. On the middle panel is a figure that is underwater, somehow existing in an in-between state between life and death. And on the right is a video of his mother dying. My piece, *Angelo*, is really about the idea of giving up bodily mass – going into something that is more spiritual, in a sense, less physical. If you compare what I would call a contemporary triptych with a pre-Renaissance triptych, you will see that the middle panel is the dominant panel. It has the central figure in it: the Virgin Mary. They weren't living in a democracy like we are. As the world has become more democratic, this has become reflected in the way the middle panel of the triptych is working – certainly in mine, and it is in Bill Viola's. The middle panel of one of my paintings is used to facilitate communication between the left and the right side, so there is no more hierarchy. It is, I might humorously say, a "lower-archy".

I wanted to talk about a painting that I saw once in Toledo, which is called *The Entombment of the Count of Orgaz*, by El Greco. It is typical in the fact that it is realistic. Usually El Greco's paintings are over-expressionistic. It is not, in fact, strictly a triptych. In this painting a very important civic figure is being buried. The facilitating figure in the painting is the priest, and the priest exists between the world of this and the world of that. His robes are painted with the most exquisite transparency, and that symbolizes the movement between what you can see and what you can't see and what you can only feel. And in the painting I think that is crucial; well, certainly it is to my work. What you can see and what you can

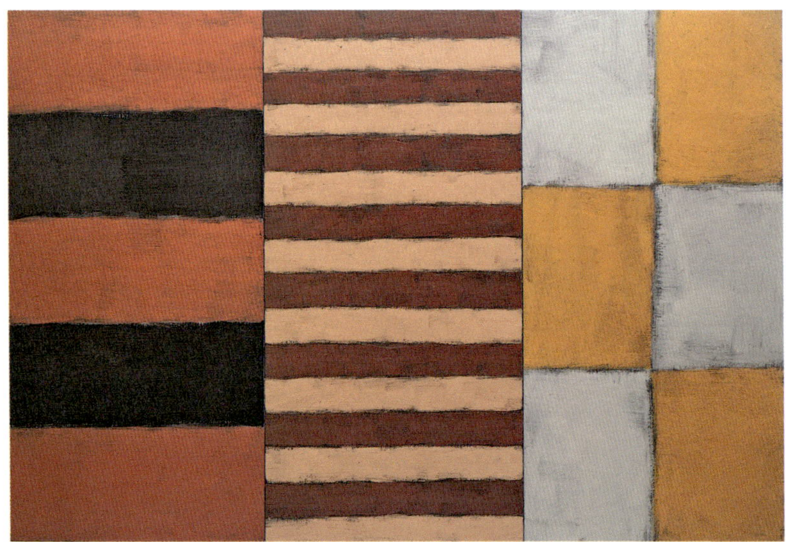

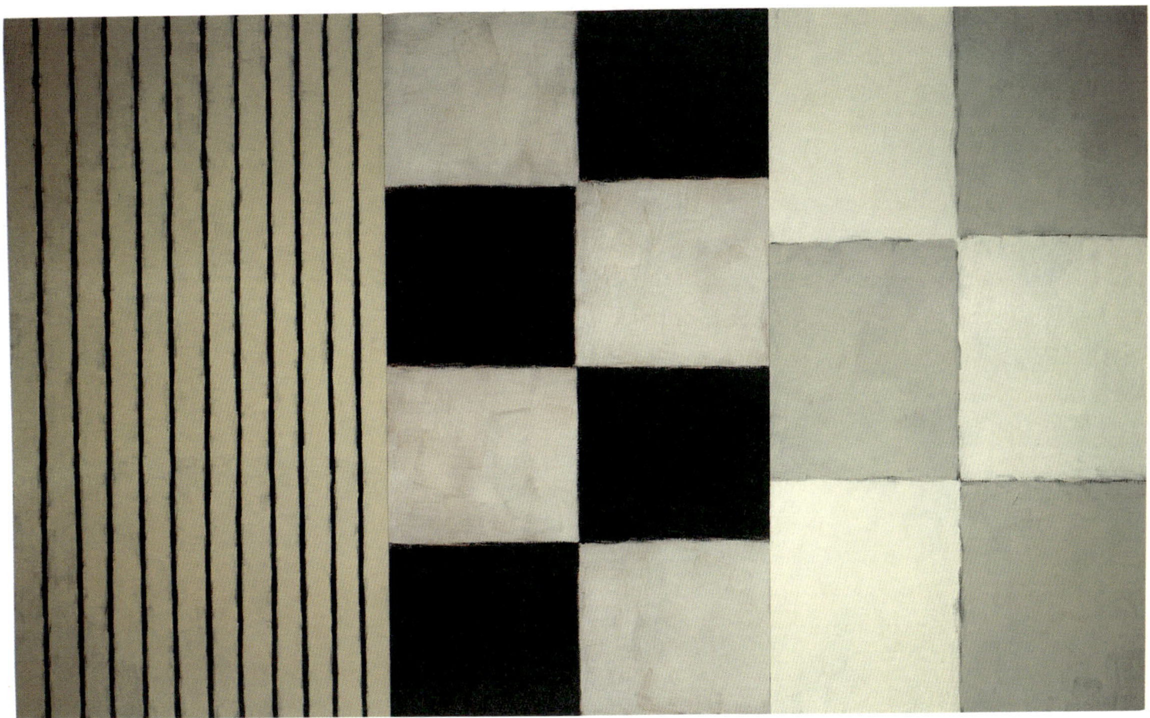

feel, or the way that what you can see conjures up what you can feel: it has everything to do with my big painting *Angelo* (page 67), where it communicates with other paintings I have made and in a way makes a kind of series over time. It starts with *Angel, Angelica, Angelo*. They are all about surfaces that share a drawing idea with a painting idea – a diagrammatic idea, or linear idea, with the idea of flesh and body and the loss of body.

The two triptychs here, which are recent, are called *Demologic Red* and *To Be With*. I mostly give my triptychs, if I can, three-word titles: i.e., one word for every panel. That is because of the democratic nature of the paintings. *Demologic Red* makes an obvious reference; it has this logic of democracy in it. The paintings have drama at each end, with strong colour denoting some kind of emotional signal or response from the viewer. The middle panel of *To Be With*, in black and white, is in a sense more diagrammatic. The two panels on the end are more fleshed out; they add another dimension. In this painting the middle panel is really facilitating the movement from one end to the other, from yellow and grey vertical stripes to the red and blue giant chequerboard on the right end of the painting. Both these paintings are made of three panels absolutely the same size, so that enforces the idea of no panel having hierarchy over the other.

In the mid-1980s I painted a triptych called *One One One*, where the panels
were the same size. It demonstrates the relationship between the panels and the
idea of democracy, so that together, and equally, they make another reality. Here
I am showing you *Painting For One Place*, which is from 1979, and *Spider*, from
1980. The *Painting For One Place* was an environmental piece painted directly on
the wall. I had a corner that went in and a corner that went out and then went
back in again to the wall. It simply follows a wall, but I am choosing where to
begin and end the painting. I cut it off in the beginning of one plane and then
stop it where the wall returned after making a short outward corner.

I made the other painting [*Spider*] in a little apartment in the Turkish quarter
of Berlin. What I did with both of these paintings was to take a certain area, paint
it on the wall and leave it. The painting can only exist in that situation, which is
very different from the other idea that the painting can travel by separating the
parts of the paintings. Those paintings were built for travelling. These paintings
are only built to last as long as the place – in fact, *Painting For One Place* no longer
exists. What was interesting to me about those paintings in relation to the future
was that they led to projections and to paint around the corner. *Spider*, in
particular, was like a painting that had slid into the corner; it hugged the corner,
which is why I called it *Spider*. They were very fertile for me in relation to
subsequent work, making paintings that perhaps weren't environmental but had
implications of the environment in them because of the way they used the space.
In the late 1980s I started to make my paintings flat to get rid of the excessive
physicality. The idea of painting round the corner is still very interesting to me.

Recently I started to make small painted boxes that I started to show. They
come out directly from the wall and also have implications of something invading
the wall, the inward motion of the wall. For example, when I put the insets into
the painting there is a wonderful kind of penetration of the surface by the inset as
it comes back to the painting, and I think that this issue of having a space behind
the painting has always been important to me, as long as I have been making the
painting physically expressive. Even so, by going right back to the 1970s, when
I was making overlays, the idea of something behind the painting – a layer of air
somehow informing the painting – is very important to me and has metaphysical
implications. I was thinking about this idea being taken further, exploded out
from the wall, and I was thinking about having a space possessed by the box. The
way that the boxes are striped is very open. I have only just started to do this, and
I think the way they hang from the wall is very exciting and the way they project
into the space interesting; and in my mind seeing them painted expressively is a
little like saying it is expressionism cubed. They have the physicality of a box but

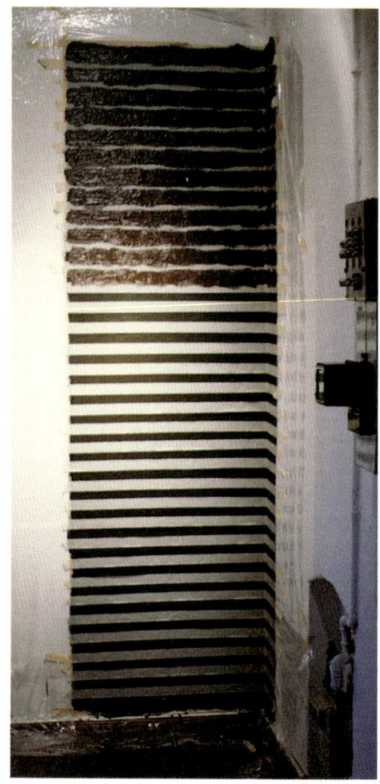

SPIDER 1980
Oil and masking tape on wall
213.4 x 76.2 cm (84 x 30 in.)
Berlin, Museum für (Sub)Kultur
Destroyed

the metaphysicality of something that is quite poetic. These box paintings have a long way to go.

Lastly, I would just like to give you one more quotation. This is by Armin Zweite. He wrote a beautiful essay on my work. He finds my pictures always "balanced on a knife-edge to reconcile the tension between part and whole, conflict and harmony, opaqueness and transparency, coldness and warmth. Plane of space, expanse and restriction. There is a constant interplay of unity and diversity. An endless oscillation between feeling and actual repetition." I think in those two final sentences we very densely establish, very precisely sum up, what I am involved in. That is, the constant search for unity and personality, for expressiveness. How somehow to catch these elements in a single work.

Things have come apart visually. If something looks good, then it is said that maybe it is not good. It is not good because it looks good. It is, apparently, not self-evident.

The famous English journalist Bernard Levin said Stockhausen is not as bad as it sounds. Levin was a famous wit who also, on occasions, could say something profound. And this is one example. One could argue that my painting *Durango* (page 68) is not as bad as it looks. It is indeed ugly. But it is also beautiful, depending on what you are looking for. It's ugly-beautiful, or beautiful in its ugliness. Its brutality gives it power in an art world where art should be visually assaulting. So it can be called beautiful. The attack on painting is part of this. Exhibitions of sticks, photographs and rough TV videos are thought automatically to be 'morally' superior because they are not good to look at; therefore they are better than they look. However, since most of this work is not really scientific, it cannot legitimately claim to be sociological because in this sense, and in a genuinely political sense, it is decorative and egocentric. But it is adored by curators who would like to promote it as sociologically conscious because it deals with issues such as race, poverty, housing *etc*. But since it is not scientific, it is useless in the discipline of sociology. And sociologists would find it impressionistic and self-indulgent.

In order to look for any audience at all this kind of art has to squeeze itself into the world of visual arts, the world which is occupied largely by painting. For this quasi-visual, pseudo-political space to be opened up, something has to be wrong with painting. Hence, the problem of visual excellence versus the issue of quality. It's not as good as it looks, or it's not good because it looks good – or if it looks good, it must be decorative and therefore not good.

This is the most transparently dishonest argument of all, one always put forward by a gang of (mostly European) curators who want to be considered intellectuals but who couldn't go two rounds in the ring with a real philosopher – i.e., a real intellectual, like [Jürgen] Habermas, for example.

A truce between the pseudo-intellectual position of concept-based art and its promoters and the authentic, round, emotional achievement of painting cannot,

I don't believe, be found any longer. I used to believe it could – or at least, I was prepared to give it a go, as I did in my more visually reduced paintings of the late 1970s that were made exclusively in horizontal stripes of grey and black. The problem is that when the visual territory of painting is ceded to the point where it passes the test of being considered intellectually acceptable by the sophists, it is reduced to a grey square. There all the guts, beauty, poetry, personality and, last but not least, colour, are taken out of it. And by colour I mean its courage to be bigger, more generous than mere idea, where the idea and the feeling become an embodiment.

Those who would have us believe, for example, that Marcel Duchamp is the equal of Matisse would also ask us to believe that one is better than it looks and one is worse. The argument that would have to be mounted to convince us, for example, that Matisse is not a visual god is not authentically available. Matisse and a lot of other painters are as good as they look. They look that good because they are that good. And this has nothing whatsoever to do with decoration but has everything to do with the roundness of the visual experience, the compressed embodiment of content.

Stockhausen has a place in history. And so therefore Bernard Levin is right when he says it's not as bad as it sounds. But neither is it Mozart.

Mooseurach, October 2004

It's harder for the serious young painters now. More doors have closed, and they are obliged to pass through a long canyon bereft of opportunities to get through them. Now the painters seem old when they come through. They've had to make something 'theirs' through endurance and through living it. Nothing is given up easily by an art world that's in love with gimmicks and tricks. If the painter comes up with a 'trick' early on, it's possible to achieve success. But then you are, unfortunately, confined by the elegance of the 'trick' which got you there in the first place.

The difficulty of painting is that when it becomes focused and intense and articulate, it simultaneously becomes narrow. [Jasper] Johns made fabulous paintings in the 1950s and '60s of numbers, targets and flags, thus resolving the competing tendencies of serial ordering, Pop art, banal subject-matter, formality and mastery of paint handling. His contribution was huge. And yet the moment he deviated from this perfect fusion his work fell, slowly but inevitably, to where it is today, which is diagrammatic. This is the problem with it and the problem for the young painter painting in a world that has an inexhaustible hunger for elegant solutions that can feed (with a hint of irony) the Art Machine. To work through time in the face of resistance is uncomfortable but infinitely preferable to selling out.

Changing your shape to fit the shape of the space on offer instead of changing the shape of things to fit your shape, your desire and your vision: this is harder and (for sure) not generally requested.

The problem of focus and bigness seems irresolvable in the beginning. It can only be brought together through life – through time, through time lived. This is truly the problem for young painters because nobody, and especially the market, will cut them any slack (thus my reference to the canyon bereft of opportunities). But at the end of the canyon, if you reach it, you find the canyon's end; and then maybe you can make surfaces where your personal spirit can enter and transform the structure. This is why the hand, in our age, cannot be usefully taken out of painting; it cannot because it slowly transforms and closes the distance of what is being painted. That's another problem. [Barnett] Newman ungenerously refers to Cézanne's apples as cannonballs. At least he acknowledges what we would all agree:

they are apples. And second, whether wittily or not, he gives them weight and a sense of fearsome power, since a cannonball is not a brick. This said, Cézanne painted the lowly apple; but then the 'little thrill' that he brings to it, with his unique colour and structure in a staccato dance with transparency, is where he the person enters and transforms what is being painted. In my case I paint the stripe. And we could all agree on that. We would all agree that I didn't invent it, and neither did Newman. And Cézanne did not invent the apple. Subsequently, Agnes Martin did not invent the grid. But we can all agree that the apple, the stripe and the grid are indeed the apple, the stripe and the grid. No one is going to confuse the grid with the apple or the apple with the stripe *etc.* So we know what we mean and we know where we are at the outset.

This was important for me: to find a subject, a subject that was big enough and material enough for the human being and the human hand to enter and slowly transform it, the wall that can be entered. I sometimes think my paintings look as if a family of refugees has been living in them; sometimes that makes me smile when I look at them, gives me a kind of joy.

You have to have a subject that's fundamental, that cannot be found through works that are philosophical. And that subject must be big enough, flexible enough and capable of absorbing nuance to allow you to grow with it as a human being, as an artist.

Mooseurach, July 2005

THE WALL

When I first had the idea to do the wall, I wanted to make it out of material from
Ireland. I had this extremely sentimental idea that I would almost dig my hands
into the ground in Ireland and pull up this wall, and it would come out black and
white. It would refer to the black and white in a lot of Irish façades. It would refer
to the buildings and ancient walls of Ireland, and would be absolutely rigorously
contemporary. But then we were unable to find anybody in Ireland who could do
it, so we had to look outside of Ireland. I love the idea that we found the stones
in China and Portugal, because this corresponds much more closely to my idea
of being universal. Because nationalism for me carries a lot of problems and
continues to cause a lot of problems if one is so invested in one's own little cultural
syntax. I am very fond of the idea of bringing these stones together from different
parts of the world, in a sense forcing them together. Placing them into perfectly
democratic relationships of black and white: the white from Portugal, the black
from China.

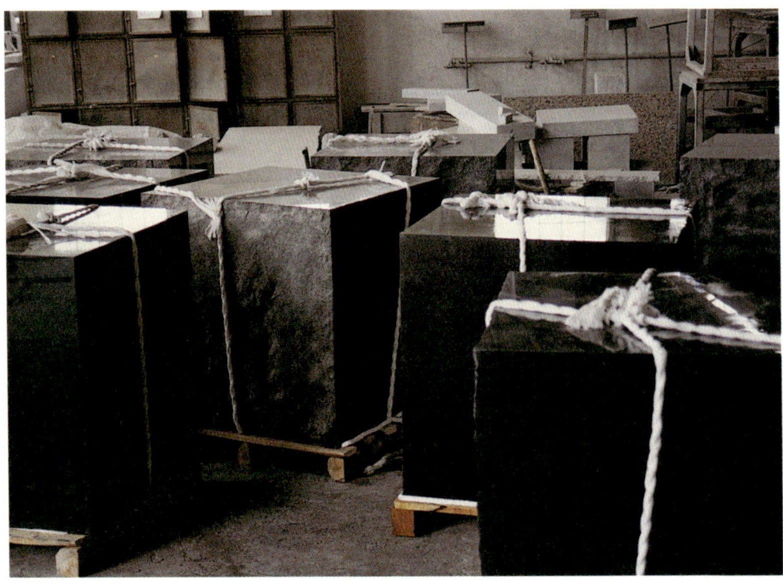

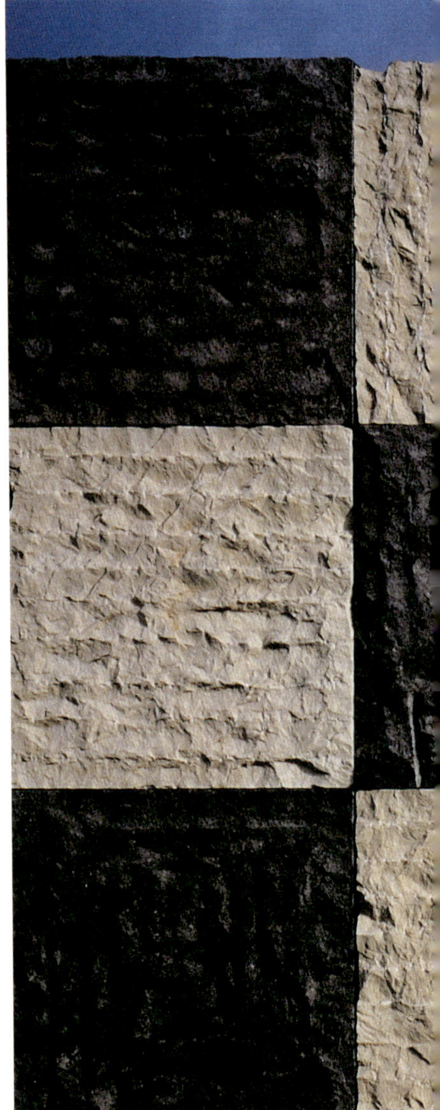

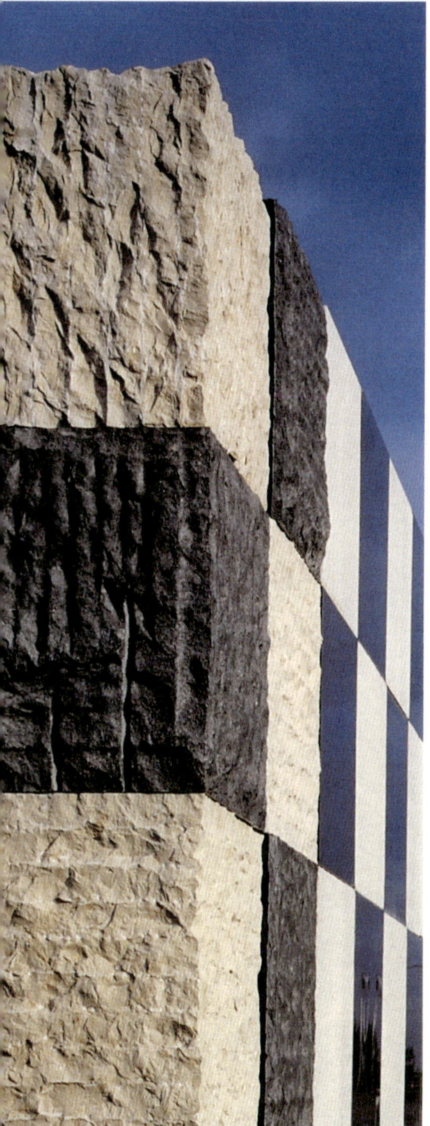

Opposite you see them all wrapped up, ready to come to us. Solid boxes. It's quite beautiful. I made a little inset in the wall because by pure luck we found out we had the stones polished, if we wanted to use that side. I was thinking about an idea of making an inset like some of the paintings. It wasn't my idea. In fact, it was Shane de Blacam's. But he gave me the idea, so now it's mine. The little inset is made very simply. The same material is just turned around very simply, reconsidered, retouched, re-stroked, reworked, and it becomes a signifier of something different. It has an entirely different, distinct quality to the rough part. When you look down at the wall, it becomes almost impressionistic. This window or inset was dropped down into the wall and presents a little problem or a little question. It gives it a point of intimacy. It's like a wall within a wall, which is going back again to the fascination I have with paintings inside paintings or windows inside houses.

I don't know if you have ever been in a room with no window. It wouldn't be very pleasurable. I thought it would be extremely interesting to somehow put a smudge or a stain on the relentlessness of the slate. I must tell you, the wall is made of stacked stones. There is the same number of black stones as white. It is exactly fifty–fifty. It's the rhythm the two have set up emotionally and visually.

Taken from a lecture given at the formal opening
of the *Wall of Light* sculpture at the
University of Limerick, October 2003

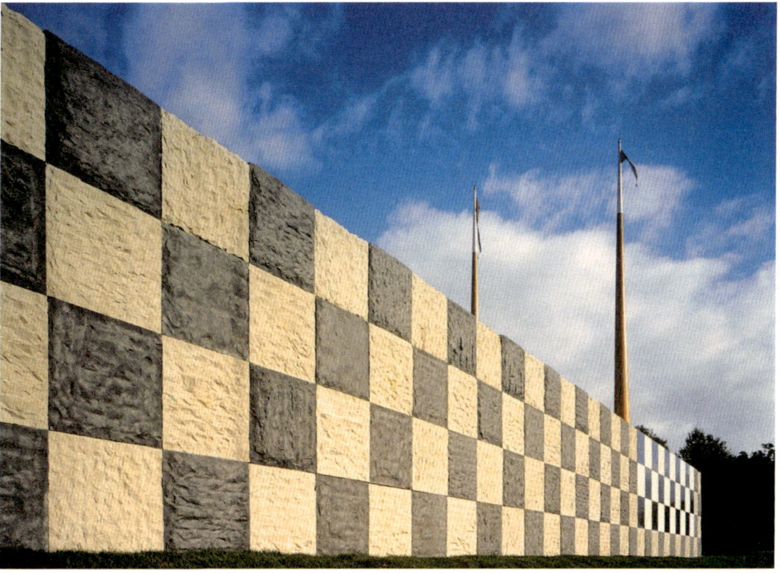

What I found fascinating recently, because I am organizing shows of earlier work, is that when I left London for New York, I also broke the grid, or, to put it another way, my grid, which wrapped the painting, became uncrossed. In retrospect it seems psychologically loaded. I left Europe and the order of Europe, and I went to New York, where there were no stabilizing verticals in my work. They simply disappeared, and I started to make the grey and black horizontal paintings where the lines just run from side to side. People tend to think of abstraction as abstract. But nothing is abstract: it's still a self-portrait. A portrait of one's condition. I took out the vertical, which was my column and my architecture, and what I was left with was the horizon. And so I could begin my journey along it.

Zurich, March 2006

I use oil paint because it has a disobedient and mysterious nature. I use it because it is an active, volatile material that, no matter how much one knows about it, one can never know completely. Oil paint and all its companion media that can be put in any order – put in any combination to make it dry fast, slow, shiny, matte, opaque, transparent – give painting an expressive range of possibilities (always slightly out of control) that cannot be matched by any other painting medium. It engages issues of alchemy and mystery that resist the deadening ambition of the modern world to control everything, absolutely.

New York, April 1995

Art is not something that can ever be mechanized or repeated. Or, in other words, its inner secret can never be resolved or formulized or passed on as a repeatable process, one assured of success. Art always has to be reborn. And this is especially true of painting, which depends on extreme human effort and expression. Painting in particular is 'original' in a sense that no other visual art form is capable of competing with. A painting is the embodiment of human action and feeling and thought. If you're working with video or photography, for example, you can certainly show images of fascinating human drama and action, but they are not the embodiment of that action. They are only an image of it. The embodiment of that action is the action itself, not the film of the action. It is therefore not original, not in the way that painting is. Painting is the thing itself, irreducible and irreplaceable. It is a moment in a body, a thought and feeling embodied – and thus, original.

Mooseurach, Aug 2002

The artist who can provoke empathy is the one who simply completes your thought, or makes visible our desire (yours and mine). I'm not trying to say anything different from what you want to say; I want to say the same thing. I want to make visible what we feel, not just what I feel but what we feel. I want my paintings to be obvious, so that when you see them you feel that I have painted something that you were thinking yourself, as if I have stolen the thought from you. This is what I mean by empathy.

New York, November 1986

My edition of Robert Rosenblum's *Modern Painting and the Northern Romantic Tradition* has on the front cover Caspar David Friedrich's *Monk by the Sea* (1809) and on the back cover Mark Rothko's *Green and Blue* (1956). This tells us much about the nature of Rothko's work and his exalted place in the world of art. The Friedrich painting shows a lone ecclesiastical figure in front of the awesome majesty of the sea. It is thus brilliantly elemental and symbolically religious in a single stroke. Rothko in effect closes the book. His position could not be clearer: he extends into the twentieth century the great Romantic impulse and, at the time of his important text's publication in 1975, he has the last word. So with *Mark Rothko*, [an exhibition] at the National Gallery of Art in Washington, D.C., [3 May–16 August 1998] we were recently given a stunning retrospective of an artist who is relatively contemporary and yet admitted unreservedly into the pantheon of great painters.

However, Friedrich's narrative symbolism and Rothko's naked sense of sublime could not be more different. With Rothko the figure has gone, though there does remain a figure-ground relationship. This formal dyad, along with the drama that it produced, ultimately drove Rothko's work and made his message human and relevant. The figure and the ground, the sky and the sea, as well as all the experiences the artist has lived and all the stories he would like to tell, are distilled into rectangles that have the solemnity of the stones of Stonehenge and the weightless turbulence of Turner's air-and-seascapes. In relation to Romantic painting, Rothko, with his exquisite compression of style and intent, has it all.

Moral force can generate a kind of simplicity of form and also, at times, a stringent painterly approach – as in the case of Mondrian. Rothko, on the one hand, is severe and geometric, but on the other, he is inhabited by a sensual despair. It is not a despair that tormented him, like the anguish Van Gogh expresses through his swirling linear forms, but one that is held in a melancholic sexual embrace. Nothing in a Rothko is hard, nothing is secure, and nothing is definite. He works sadly and constantly against the dying of his own light, which he cannot prevent, even with his radiant reds, oranges, yellows and blues. In his use of black and grey towards the end I see not so much subjugation of sensual imagination as an acceptance of his own closure and conclusion. Life accompanied art, and art reflected the passage of life – the two as inseparable as a body and its shadow. Once the artist consented to the loss of light in his black and grey paintings, he continued to work, and he continued to produce masterpieces. This darker period lasted for almost a decade. Rothko flowed with the inevitability of water towards his end.

In this exhibition the dark late paintings began in earnest with a beautiful grave work titled *Blue and Gray* (1962). A sombre, squarish rectangle whose hue vacillates between creamy yellow and grey hovers above a flattened horizontal rectangle of dark purple-blue. Both these forms are laid down on very dark grey, making a virtual night scene relieved only by the lightness of the upper rectangle. This shape moves forward out of the painting and offers dynamism, though its solemn nature tends to imply a further darkening in the artist's life and work.

To begin at the beginning of this story, we have to go back to the figurative paintings that Rothko made in the 1930s. The show started with a self-portrait painted in 1936, when Rothko was thirty-three years old. This image is a half-figure vertical portrait – painted predominantly in red, dark red, black, white and translucent burnt yellow – of a young man, clearly intent on becoming a great artist, staring stiffly out at us. In terms of portraiture the painting is not very impressive, except in one respect: its relationship to Rothko's mature work.

In 1936 people weren't making huge abstract paintings concerned with sublime tragedy. They tended instead to paint portraits and landscapes, a convention to which this Rothko canvas conforms. But if we compare it with other paintings like *Untitled (Purple, White and Red)* (1953, page 82) or *Green and Tangerine on Red* (1956; page 84), we easily see that all three works are by the same painter. The sonorous temperament of the colours is the same, and the compulsion to layer paint thinly (dark over light, light over dark) is unchanged. Remarkably, these paintings, which span a period of nearly thirty years, are in essential respects the same. Rothko's jacket, in the self-portrait, is painted as a group of vertical blocks in magenta and brown-black with blurred edges. This could also be said of many other works by Rothko, including the great dark paintings given by the artist to the Tate Gallery. In that jacket one can almost see the room of paintings in London, with their vibrating junctures of maroon and black, and the impossible-to-locate space that results from the visual hum. What started out as instinct in 1936 became, twenty years later, a fully understood and realized achievement that takes place alongside those of other great masters of transcendental art such as Cimabue, Masaccio and Rembrandt.

Those earlier artists emphatically represented religious themes, since that was the social and political currency of their day. By the time Rothko came along, the church no longer dominated most lives. Rothko's art is abstract, but in terms of sentiment he is paraphrasing for his own time the great spiritual ambition running through one major branch of Western art.

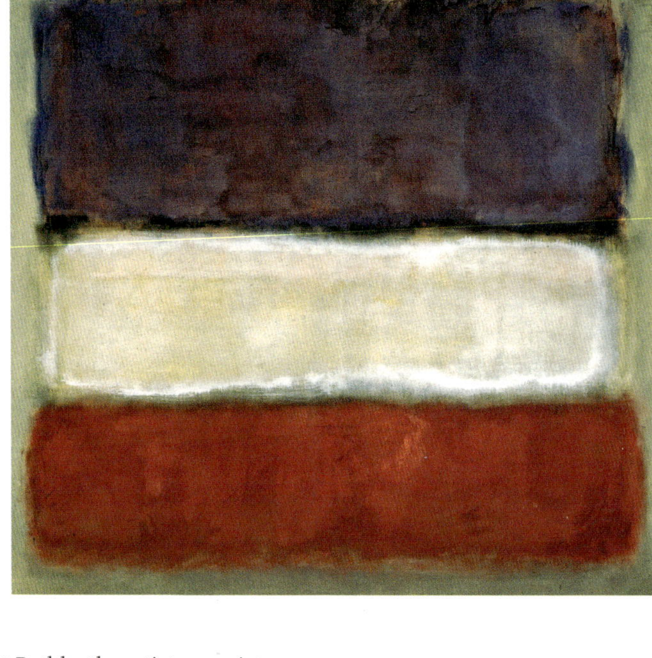

Any major survey of his work tends to prove that Rothko the artist came into the world virtually ready-made – not as a greatly gifted painter but as possessor of high-minded attitude. His sensibility was formed by the experience of life, and the only question was how to make it manifest. Rothko's early work is for the most part interesting but not outstanding, as the stylized doll-like figures from the 1930s confirm. One can argue that all artists struggle along until they find their voice. But Rothko is the most extreme example of this that I know. His paintings needed to be organized symmetrically, with his blocks stacked one on top of the other. Once he had found this single compositional device he became Mark Rothko the great Abstract Expressionist. His compositional organization gave him a degree of security, and he was able to pour emotion and profundity into his work with an intensity not seen before, certainly not in abstraction.

Mondrian offers an interesting comparison, since he was also an artist with spiritual aspirations, trying to find a way for abstraction to somehow be 'religious' in a new, unfettered way. He, however, was from early on a great painter. The powerful quality of his trees and landscapes is undeniable; they hold up very well to his later classic paintings of black-and-white grids. Rothko was different. He was never interested in just producing paintings. He was always driven to make elevated works that were devastating in their spiritual force. This, of course, considerably reduced his formal options and his ability to experiment.

Robert Stanley, who was a New York painter and a close friend of mine, once told me he thought Rothko got his idea of painting blurred edges, in colours influenced by brown, from staring down at the wooden bar of the Cedar Tavern in Manhattan, where the Abstract Expressionists drank in the 1950s. I drank there in the '80s, though by then the location had changed and the place was not nearly so much fun as I imagine it was when you could get drunk with Willem de Kooning, Jackson Pollock and Joan Mitchell. I have no doubt that Rothko, in his morose cloud, did gaze down at reflections in the brown shiny bar, but I don't believe they gave him his compositional idea. Rather, I think the sight confirmed what he already knew: that the edges of the world and everything in it are blurred by mystery and sadness.

Rothko was born Marcus Rothkowitz in 1903 in Dvinsk, Russia. He spoke Hebrew and Russian until he was ten, and attended the Hebrew school at synagogue. In 1913 he arrived in America with his two sisters, Anna and Sonia, all three wearing labels explaining that they could not speak English. This is how they travelled by train to Portland, Oregon, to reunite with their parents. There Marcus entered immigrant school, where no English was taught. To survive his childhood trials Marcus had to take what he knew with him. A little boy sitting on the train, chugging across the vastness of America, he brought the old world of Hebrew and Russian mysticism with him. It would be his only protection. The romantic, in embryo, had at the age of ten encountered the grandeur and harshness of the new world, as a social mute. A sense of his own self-made space would become his focus and his sanctuary. And this preoccupation, given the nurturing power of time, became a grand obsession, lasting the whole of his life. As an adult in Manhattan he spent many hours, day after day, remaking his fervidly private emotional space – one that was ultimately destined to be exposed in public. But during the second half of his childhood he lived in the damp mists of Portland, where the horizon line regularly blurred. By the time he went to Yale in 1921, Rothko the young adult was made: a perfect fusion of the ancient and the new.

Then he took this extreme sensibility to the intense geometry of Manhattan, and his ultimate path of veiled, vulnerable formality seems in hindsight inevitable. He was already an artist looking for a way through.

In the late 1920s Rothko met Milton Avery, who made charming, simplified paintings heavily influenced by Henri Matisse. It was Rothko's exposure to Matisse's painting *The Red Studio* (1911) when it came to New York in 1949, that opened a huge door to his own future. *The Red Studio*, as radical as Picasso's *Les Demoiselles d'Avignon* (1907), was painted with a flat red colour that completely covered – and thus simplified and unified – the entire surface of the painting. This work profoundly affected Rothko and made it possible for him thereafter to put down colour without bothering to model it for the sake of description.

Rothko even went so far as to paint a homage to Matisse. But, as the exhibition demonstrated, he did not have Matisse's pictorial curiosity or his range of technical possibilities. Thus the difference between the two great artists (one from the first half of the twentieth century and one from the second) does much to illuminate Rothko, and to help us understand the nature and importance of his gift. Matisse was essentially a bourgeois French gentleman who spent his entire life in comfortable surroundings. His extraordinary work is an exercise in one-ness and sheer invention. Rothko, it might be argued, had none of Matisse's imaginative facility. But Rothko was an American who used to be Russian and was always Jewish. Ultimately, he went to live in the most challenging and difficult art environment in the world. His life from the beginning was always more embattled. His work lacks variety by comparison with that of Matisse, but it has a moral and emotional force permeated with sensual pathos that is unique in the history of painting. In this respect, his œuvre marks the arrival of abstraction as a genuinely expressive art form.

Barnett Newman, Rothko's contemporary, was forever talking about the dissolution of his zips into the field. Thus he claimed they disrupt the figure-ground relationship and so achieve a kind of pure metaphysical state: openness. Rothko, though, was not trying to escape the traditional figure-ground relationship: he was trying to explode its potential. His paintings can and should be read as a plane upon which figures are painted. He presents a new and radical way of exploiting the figure-ground relationship, without having to tell stories. The colour in Rothko's work was 'found' by working the surface so that the picture's chromatic character and luminosity are inseparable from its texture. This distinguishes Rothko from his contemporaries, especially Newman, who was consistently railing against the 'European-ness' of Mondrian because the Dutch artist included 'touch' in his work. While Newman was laying down flat colours in giant formats with simple geometric divisions, Rothko was activating the surface almost as Veronese or Titian would have done. This gives Rothko's art an extraordinary power.

One aspect of Rothko's genius is that he is able to collapse great stretches of time. Drawing shapes characterized by frontality and heroic simplicity, a practice that

Mark Rothko (1903–1970)
Green and Tangerine on Red, 1956
Oil on canvas
237.5 × 175.9 cm (93⅜ × 69¼ in.)
Washington, D.C., Phillips Collection

connects him to the avant-garde concerns of his day, he simultaneously through 'touch' reaches back across centuries of art history. It is this grand dialogue with the past, and the breadth of his understanding of time, that will ultimately separate him from his peers.

"I adhere to the material reality of the world and the substance of things", Rothko averred in 1945, showing us how un-abstract and connected his paintings are, at least in intention. The remark also sheds light on the specificity with which elements in the painting are rendered and the sensuality of the way the colour is laid down. Rothko's paintings are universal, but they are never simply the manifestation of an idea. They bleed emotion, in terms that come directly from life experience. No one figure in a Rothko work can be separated from its partner or partners, since they have all been painted deliberately into place: they embody emotion through the layering of material and time. Their meaning for us lies not only in their cultural, art-historical compression of chronology but also in their suggestion that personal time can be layered. In front of a Rothko time stands still, and we are free to make are own 'abstract' poetic relationship with it.

In 1947 Rothko said, "I think of my pictures as dramas; the shapes in the pictures are the performers. They have been created from the need for a group of actors who are able to move dramatically without embarrassment and execute gestures without shame." Of all his famous statements this one is the most original, and it clearly asserts that his work, though abstract, was also very human and figurative. If we take this avowal literally, as I do, it shows that Rothko's paintings are in essence as dramatically representational as Rembrandt's.

The belief that Rothko's paintings also aspired in some sense to the emotional condition of music can be justified by what he said about his favourite work, *The Red Studio*. He described it as being like music, and that clearly was the highest of all accolades, since he was speaking of his hero Matisse. Rothko's canvases, with their multiple veils of colour, are also musical but it a different way. They do not emphasize linear rhythm, but rather seem to suspend sound in colour – radiating visually as if two or three deep sonorous chords had been struck at once and held indefinitely.

Rothko once famously asserted that he worked towards clarity and the elimination of all obstacles between the painter and the idea. This pronouncement, which appears on the cover of Jeffrey Weiss's excellent catalogue for the exhibition, says much about the artist's conscious intention. But with Rothko that is only half the story and, in my opinion, less than half the reason for his enduring appeal. His conscious, disciplined drive towards conceptual and visual clarity results directly from his intellectual rigour and moral outlook. Yet his abiding ability to evoke mystery comes from a more instinctive, more deeply emotional source. It comes, I believe, from his own life history – and his tragic attachment to the idea of our shared past.

At this point the image of the small boy on the train, speaking no English, travelling across the great expanse of America, again comes vividly and poignantly to mind. Besides the bags that he carried he must have brought to the new world another form of luggage: the memories of the old world, of the mysticism of Hebrew studies in the synagogue in pre-revolutionary Russia. The layering of one experience over another, the old colliding with the new, is always central to the psychological and cultural complexity of Rothko's paintings. It is the richness of meaning that has, despite all his work's austerity, kept it so vital.

Rothko said many times that he painted large in order to be intimate. This was not unique to him at that time. [Franz] Kline, [Clyfford] Still and [Jackson] Pollock were also painting big. It was part of the message of Abstract Expressionism that the picture should be open and vulnerable and capable of being emotionally entered by the viewer. This raises a very interesting issue about the orientation of Rothko's paintings. Nearly all of them from his mature period are vertical and therefore relate historically to the standing portrait tradition. They also evoke doors and portals. In this they are very different from the works of Rothko's two great contemporaries Pollock and Newman, who painted mostly horizontally – Pollock making from his dance of paint a direct link to the vast American landscape, and Newman (much more urban and urbane in spirit) stretching the paintings horizontally and pointing the way towards Minimalism and the environmental art that appeared in New York in the 1960s.

With Rothko the relationship to the history of painting is treasured and used to powerful effect. In works from his great period, when the colours were still burning bright (1949–62), we are confronted by a huge 'door' with a series of stacked figures on it. The images are big, but not so big as to make us disinclined to mentally engage them. They are monumental, certainly, but they are not spectacles like the giant works, based on themes of heaven and earth, painted by [Francisco de] Zurbarán in seventeenth-century Spain. Rothko developed a new scale for vertical picture-making in the twentieth century. His paintings offer a generous arena for the viewer to 'step into' and for the colours to breathe in, while the ever-present 'horizon lines' that separate the floating blocks give the whole work a sense of amplitude. One vertical painting shown in the exhibition is about 20 per cent larger than most. *No. 14* (1960), at 114 by 105 inches, tends to suggest the massive and the heroic. To my mind it falls just within Rothko's idea of the big painting that is not authoritative but intimate and approachable. The image consists of one nearly square rectangle painted in uneven, sensitively modulated red, hovering above a very horizontal blue rectangle. The figures play out their drama of continual mating and separation on a field of the darkest brown-red.

The presence of *No. 14* pointed up how Rothko's small-scale alterations work perfectly from painting to painting, echoing the various changing relations between the rectangles within the clear edges of his canvases. These subtle, constantly shifting differences in proportion and position take a vital role in keeping Rothko's painting experimental. They are impossible to codify, and they never submit to mere idea or programme. There is never a reliance on the mental and emotional laziness of formula. The rhythms that these intuitive changes set up are hypnotic, mysterious and free of any didactic agenda.

Rothko said that the surfaces in his painting either expanded or contracted, and that between these two poles we can find everything he wants to say. His idea was not to describe but to make a theatrical arena – a space so authentic emotionally and so clear conceptually that it was capable of holding essential human passion. His own high ambition for art was so compelling that he was forced to blur his edges, simplify his forms and complicate his colours so that his paintings would have enough mystery to hang naked in public.

Abstract Expressionism was a quintessentially American movement, and it marks the triumphant period in American art. There is no question that the style has its roots in the luminous nineteenth-century paintings of the immense New World landscape. But this American movement was built on European memory. When Europe was pulling itself apart during the Second World War, nearly all artistic opportunities were transferred to the USA. Here European immigrants confronted the majesty of America's terrain and the up-for-grabs nature of its customs and culture.

Manhattan is not the art centre that it once was, when Rothko, De Kooning and Pollock were painting, nor the epicentre that it became in the 1960s, during the reign of Pop art. Rothko and his peers made the city important, and Pop art cashed in. After Pop, after that crescendo of fast images and banality, New York little by little began to face challenges to its position as the unassailable capital of the international art world.

Pollock, the other great Abstract Expressionist, painted elementally, incarnating the pure American hero who even conjured up, in modern form, the mystic power of Native American sand painters. But it was Rothko who gave us the more complex gift. Today we do not seem to believe in the transcendental or sublime, as did many of the artists and writers working in New York in the '50s. The world, it is said, has changed – and become more cynical. I suspect this is an eternal argument.

What has changed, to Rothko's advantage, however, is the relative positions of the USA and Europe in terms of cultural power at the end of the twentieth century. Rothko's fusion of American luminosity and openness with European moral density finds its contextual equivalent throughout the Western world these days. His work has a capacity, given this opportunity, to reveal yet another of its many aspects.

Towards the end of the exhibition there was a room of dark, magnificent late paintings, where the glow of Rothko's light breathes its final breath. *No. 8* (1964) is a vertical canvas of slate grey upon which floats a solitary vertical figure of grey-black. The effect is gravely beautiful and abjectly lonely. Now the figural rectangles no longer sway in each other's company but stand alone, hovering towards the edge of the painting and the edge of Rothko's world.

The great luminous paintings in yellows, reds and blues are expansive not only in terms of palette but most specifically in the way that they radiate out into space, implying an abundance of feeling. They communicate a fully lit and orchestrated generosity. These are paintings that can be hung in huge halls or placed in more modest spaces. Wherever they are placed, the works inhabit and light the space without trying to control it. Theirs is simply the act of giving.

Mark Rothko (1903–1970)
No. 8, 1964
Mixed media on canvas
267.3 x 203.8 cm (105¼ x 80¼ in.)
Washington, D.C., The National Gallery of Art

As we enter the period of the darker paintings, this feeling changes. The canvases become more prescribing and controlling in relation to the space that they occupy. The stark ashen images mirror Rothko's soul, which at the time was troubled and defensive. We are limited, controlled by the artist – forced to stand close to feel the paintings' warmth. Rothko no longer permits us to move where and how we want, bathing in his illuminated space.

Five years later, in his final move, Rothko did something crucial. Having already reduced colour to grey and black, he now gave up the narrow breathing band that followed the perimeter of his paintings and kept his actors on their stage. His tremulous relationship with the edge had once held Rothko in his own world and had given his figures space to breath and act. But now the mysterious tension was broken, and the border became thinner and hard-edged. In *Untitled [Black on Gray]* (1969) the balance between sensuousness and austerity is broken in favour of austerity, and drama, which carries possibility, is replaced by the desolation of a single horizon line that extends off each side of the painting. Rothko was unable any longer to maintain the rapport between tragedy and hope. In effect, he slipped off his own artistic stage.

Friedrich Nietzsche's great book *The Birth of Tragedy* had a profound effect on Rothko. Nietzsche's idea that the artist has the power to transform tragedy into beauty is very close to Rothko's central truth and the primary reason for exceptional grace in his work. For how could Nietzsche's idea be physically demonstrated, unless the artist was prepared to push tragedy and beauty to their extremes?

Rothko's life ended in suicide in 1970. In 1889 Nietzsche had stood kissing a horse in the street, eleven years before he was to die insane. But by the time these artists met their sad ends, their gifts have been made and given.

In my view a great abstract painting offers one the possibility to travel without having to endure the tedium of a journey. Rothko created many great paintings. Now the question can be put: does art like his make a difference to the world, as he would have wished? Or, to phrase it another way, would the world be less without it? The answer to both questions is a very simple yes.

This article was published in *Art in America*, July 1999
A shorter version appeared in the *Times Literary Supplement*, 6 November 1998

Mystery in art is very important to me. I feel that a lot of that is being squeezed out of art in today's mechanized, digitized world. A number of the twentieth-century artists I most admire – artists like Barnett Newman, Giorgio Morandi and Ernst Kirchner – created mythologies in order to keep mystery at the core of their work and to fight off a sense that they were becoming disconnected from the natural world.

By mythology, I don't mean art that refers to Greek and Roman gods. For me the mythic involves the idea of legend and mystery and something you can't trace all the way back; you can't just unravel it or decode it. It may be something that is at least partly comprehensible to a broader audience or something more specific and auto-biographical – what I am calling personal mythology – which can be hidden from all but a select few. In a democracy, where everybody becomes or is able to become their own world, people sometimes capriciously establish their own idea of myth and – in a rather extended relationship with Marcel Duchamp – say that certain things are special just because they say so. That can close off meaning, however, and in this essay I present some of my concerns and thoughts about it. The essay is a kind of argument with myself about the function and the importance of modern myth.

Recently I gave a lecture on this topic, and I began with Barnett Newman's *Zim Zum*. He made two versions of this large steel sculpture, which creates a corridor for the viewer to walk through. *Zim Zum* in Hebrew can mean a number of different things, but one of them is 'sacred space', and that is the way I interpret Newman's titling of the work. Newman is trying here as on many other occasions to create his own mythology – to suggest that he is a great religious artist, or quasi-religious artist, one who compares himself rather charmingly to Michelangelo. Thus he presents *Zim Zum* not as a mere arrangement of minimal shapes, but as the cradle of a special and mystical place.

Newman tried to make a space that was spiritually charged, and that is what I try to do in my work too. I basically believe the world is filled with spiritual energy and am very involved with things that attract it. Of course, it cannot be proven that *Zim Zum* is a 'special' place, but Newman asked us to suspend our disbelief and co-operate with his reference, with his act of creation and designation.

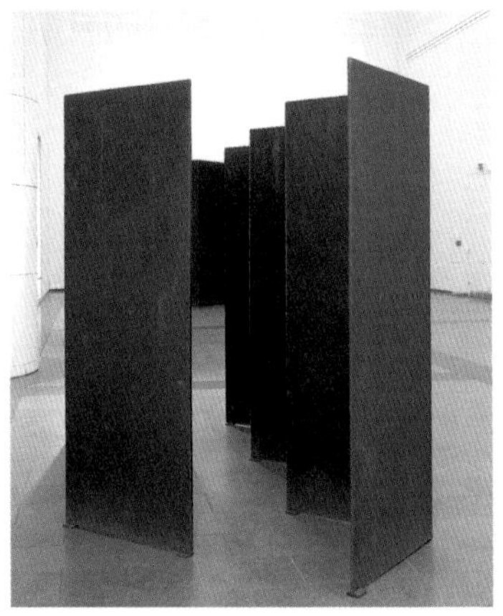

Barnett Newman (1905–1970)
Zim Zum, 1969
Cor-ten steel
244 × 184 × 457 cm (96 × 72½ × 180 in.)
San Francisco, Museum of Modern Art

The zigzagging steel planes might be compared with the design of an African mask, the kind that inspired Pablo Picasso and other Modernists in the early twentieth century who turned to the 'primitive' for inspiration. But the mask usually does not attempt to tell stories like Newman did. Take for example a Songye mask I saw in the Metropolitan Museum of Art in New York, which is made of wood and straw. Its point is to gain the maximum in expression with almost no consideration for the appearance of things. It goes back and forth with tremendous force between the rhythmic stylized linearity of the drawing, which expresses and does not express the appearance of a head – though it does express the life and continuing rhythm of death – and the straw. It embodies in its constant fluctuation between the straw material and the deeply stylized rhythm of the drawing the belief of the people it is made for and by. It is made to summon the gods, and the people who used it and viewed it knew this about its play of realism and non-realism. I'm not really a collector, but I used to have a Dogon mask I kept at my house in New York, which had a repeated vertical rhythm; it's supposed to be a bird, and it looks nothing like a bird. Its maker understood that you don't make a representation of a spirit; you make something that a spirit would be attracted to inhabit. That was the idea of the African masks. Instead of conjuring up the spirits, they assume the spirits are already there, the way the flower and the bee work. I 'used' this mask for a long time myself. It made the point that this is not mere space or geometry. In the same way when one hears jazz today, the original structure of a song played by John Coltrane is constantly lost and found and brought repeatedly to the edge of emotional crisis. That's what is happening with the mask too. It is made to attract the gods, to get the gods to somehow inhabit it.

Barnett Newman was extremely interested in attaching himself to great themes. He painted, for example, *Onement* (part of a series begun in 1948), as if this would be the one moment, the beginning, the origin. He wanted to get to something that was fundamental and pure, to sweep aside that confusing, polluting, compromising and dialectical European shadow and make a pure American art, a new beginning, and that's what his paintings constantly try to present. Newman also painted *The Stations of the Cross* (1958–64; Washington, D.C., National Gallery of Art), the tragic story of Jesus being tried, taken out to Calvary and executed. He painted this in black and white stripes as if they could express this story. He has attached himself to this story. He wanted to create his own mythology and to do it with stripes. But in many ways he created an art that is for experts and for devotees. In order for a myth to take root, to have power, it must have more than one devotee. There is a schism between what an artist like Newman says and what is self-evident, going obliquely back to Duchamp. In other words I have difficulty with Newman's assertion that his paintings are stations of the Cross, because they are not self-evident, and so I am not convinced. I find the title stronger than the evidence. For example, I could stand on a stage, drink a glass of water and then declare that I have just made an artwork through my performance. We have a crisis of what artists say and what they can support. I have it myself; I live with it on a daily basis.

Works become mythic in other ways. Brancusi's *Endless Column* (1938; Târgu-Jiu, Romania), for example, is not endless, but we are asked to believe in a sense that it doesn't end, that its spirit or idea is bigger than its physical form. Alberto Giacometti's *Tall Figure* (1949; New York, Museum of Modern Art) is a figure ravaged, which stands mute and dignified; it too has in it a sense of myth, something that one can only feel, not see. Giorgio Morandi painted jars and jugs in endless silent conversations on a modest scale, and they also fit into the category of images that become mythic because they are not explainable, images that, like Giacometti's figure, stand silent and reverential. A Morandi painting becomes a vessel for meaning, a vessel for feeling. In Native American culture they have people who are called 'contrary' – they are the ones who do everything backwards. Giorgio Morandi was also a contrary. He painted too small with not enough colours and wouldn't do exhibitions; he found exhibitions to be an intrusion on his private time. Can you imagine that?

There are, of course, many myths of the land, including myths of the Native Americans. Recently I have been teaching and working in Germany, and I feel the power of the German landscape. The land in Germany gave rise to the movement that we call Romanticism, which flowered in England in a similarly opulent green landscape. In nearly all countries the land, nature, is referred to as mother. That in itself is mythic, the mythic mother, the one we walk over and through and unfortunately build upon. But in Germany it is the fatherland, something that strikes me as rather distinct.

I have been working in the countryside, and the first painting I made in my farm studio there was green, a healing and regenerative colour. The German Expressionists, like Ernst Kirchner, at the beginning of the twentieth century felt an incredible need to reconnect with the solace of nature. The First World War was on its way, riding towards them like a dark horse, and the artists were reacting to this. Kirchner's *The Four Bathers* (1910) comes to us with the life force of nature. His figures are flat, and there is a beautiful, humble sense of material in the German Expressionist paintings; they used very simple canvas and dry paint because they wanted to be with nature, not to make something separate. There are countless paintings of people in the lakes and by the lakes in Bavaria, which have a magical, mystical, mythic importance for the people, and the link between the people and

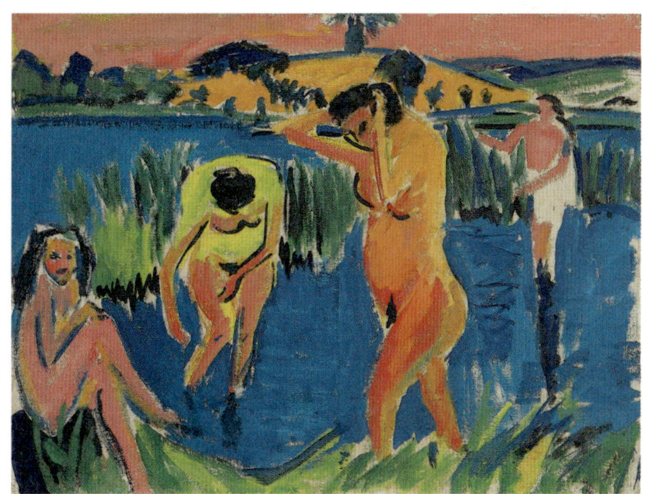

Ernst Kirchner (1880–1938)
The Four Bathers, 1909/10
Oil on canvas
75.5 × 101 cm (30 × 40 in.)
Wuppertal, Germany, Von der Heydt-Museum

their landscape is profound. Even now you can find people doing the same things the people are doing in that painting, communing with other human beings and with nature. Kirchner's blue is vital, a blue you would only see in your dreams. The painting is horizontal, ambitious, open and hopeful. Above all, the water flows through the composition, giving it energy, mystical power and movement. The painting is a section of the bigger idyllic world. It is an extremely optimistic, emotionally expansive painting where we as human beings immerse ourselves in the forgiving water of nature.

You know, a lot of people think these German Expressionist paintings are all the same, but the personalities who painted them were different. Otto Mueller's compositions tended to be vertical, less open, more contained than Kirchner's. His colour is extremely delicate and melancholic, the colour of memory, and you might compare it with Morandi or Agnes Martin later on. He is not illustrating optimism, but only a hope, a faint dream. Karl Schmidt-Rottluff painted uncompromising pictures that release the force of nature through direct, primary colour. And Emil Nolde was attracted to notions of purity. Unfortunately, he sought the approval of the Nazis, or couldn't understand why they didn't like his work – a testament to our power of self-delusion. So he went to the South Seas and identified strongly with the people there, making drawings and portraits of them. He wanted to unravel, to escape from this edifice we have built, this cultured trap that we have made for ourselves, and get to something where we are once gain in union with the mythic and regenerative power of nature.

One of the best examples I can think of about making a truly personal mythology that closes off meaning instead of opening access to it is the story of the tattoo on the left arm of my student Hedwig, a very good painter who came to study with me in Munich because she couldn't get in anywhere else. She was in a rock band, and when she arrived she was covered in tattoos. I thought seriously of not accepting her, but it has turned out great. On her arm is a picture of a bird, and the bird represents her flight from Berlin to Munich. It is not decoration, but it is also not decipherable by anybody and everybody, the way the instructions in a telephone box are. It's another example of our attempt, our need to create personal mythology. It goes along with the freedoms of democracy, where everybody becomes either king or queen of their own castle. So, if you were to see her walking along the street and you were to look at her arms and her legs and some of these symbols, you wouldn't understand what they were, but if a Masai was walking through an African village marked up, the other Masai who understand the language would know what those marks meant. And that is a big difference, for now we don't agree on anything any more. Everything is in crisis in a sense, everything is up for debate, and it is possible that these body marks may be more permanent than any human relationship this young artist will ever have. This, I believe, is a powerful strike against the way things are going, this interest on the part of young people to mark themselves up, put things on themselves and make a commitment, the kind of commitment that you can't make on the internet, where you press a button and it's gone.

This kind of gesture, a way of doing something to yourself that you cannot undo, is body art, and there are a couple of artists around who exhibit their bodies. But people only understand the story behind Hedwig's tattoos if she explains them. So that means that these tattoos communicate to about ten people.

I guess I have created my own personal mythology too. For example, I made a painting called *Precious* (page 30), which, like Hedwig's tattoo, involves travel, but I want my work to be more accessible. I had been talking about my leaving Ireland with my parents and how the boat got lost. I was thinking about this, and I made a painting with a little insert inside. I was very small when we came over from Ireland just after the war; it was dangerous, because there were many loose mines in the water, and the boat got lost, and I remembered it and then I made the painting. That word 'precious' is based on something my mother said, that I was a "precious cargo". So I made a painting within a painting; it's encased, protected by a bigger painting, a 6-foot painting. So there's personal mythology right there.

In a sense my work is a question of trying to retrieve the irretrievable. My work has a lot of yearning in it. There is a structure, and the structure is being undone or subverted by a sense of emotion and of loss.

I'm kind of moving in a different direction to the way the art-world majority is moving right now, I believe. I'm including mysticism, mystery, spirituality in my work. I believe the problems artists had at the beginning of the twentieth century, which caused such a reaction, which caused such an upsurge in the pursuit of the 'primitive' and the mythic, again happened after the end of the terrors of the Second World War because of the crisis they faced, because of what they saw come to pass. The world became mechanized, and this irresistible juggernaut rolled over everything and has given us the world that we live in now. In my own response, I like to speak through the language of rhythm. Rhythm is direct, and you can feel it. If I stand in the wrong place in the wrong time in the relation to the history of art, I like that just fine.

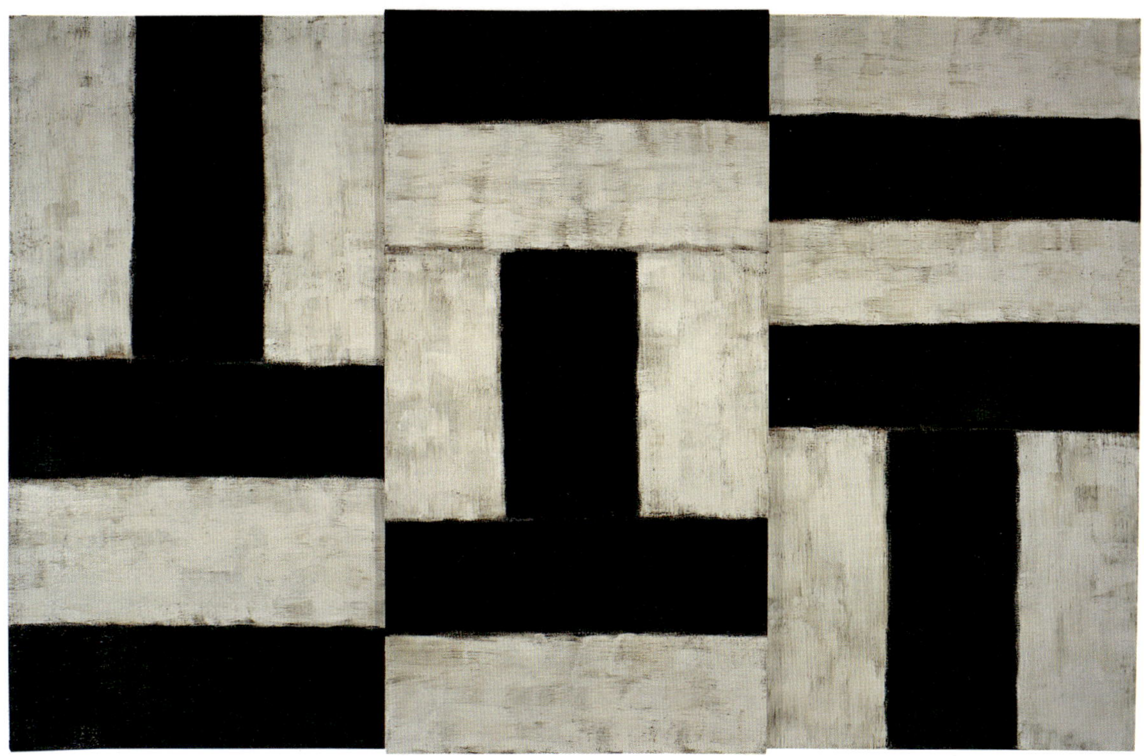

The painting *Hammering*, for example, embodies a primitive form of rhythm. The colours I use are black and white, and *Hammering* is aggressively painted. In these paintings in the 1980s and on into the early '90s I was trying to re-find, retake, reconnect myself with something very particular to painting, the ability to do something that is, in fact, fundamental and impossible to improve on, technologically speaking. In other words, it is me with a brush and a bucket of paint in front of a canvas, and it always will be. The light in the painting obviously is a battle between light and dark; a battle is being hammered out on a huge format, but the white in the painting is not as white as the black in the painting is black. And that represents, I imagine, a flawed or damaged sense or limited sense of hope. It is not a battle between light and dark, but a battle between nearly light and very dark.

Sometimes when hard times come, I just do what I can do. After the death of my mother recently, I made a small painting called *Ivy*, the name everyone called her, which reminded me a little of Brancusi's *Kiss*. It was exhibited this spring in the cowshed of a *Kunstpalast* in Germany with a series called *Holly*, in fourteen parts. When my son Paul died, in 1984, I made a painting for him that was related to a kind of altarpiece format I had used for my *Maestà*, which is a homage to Duccio's painting

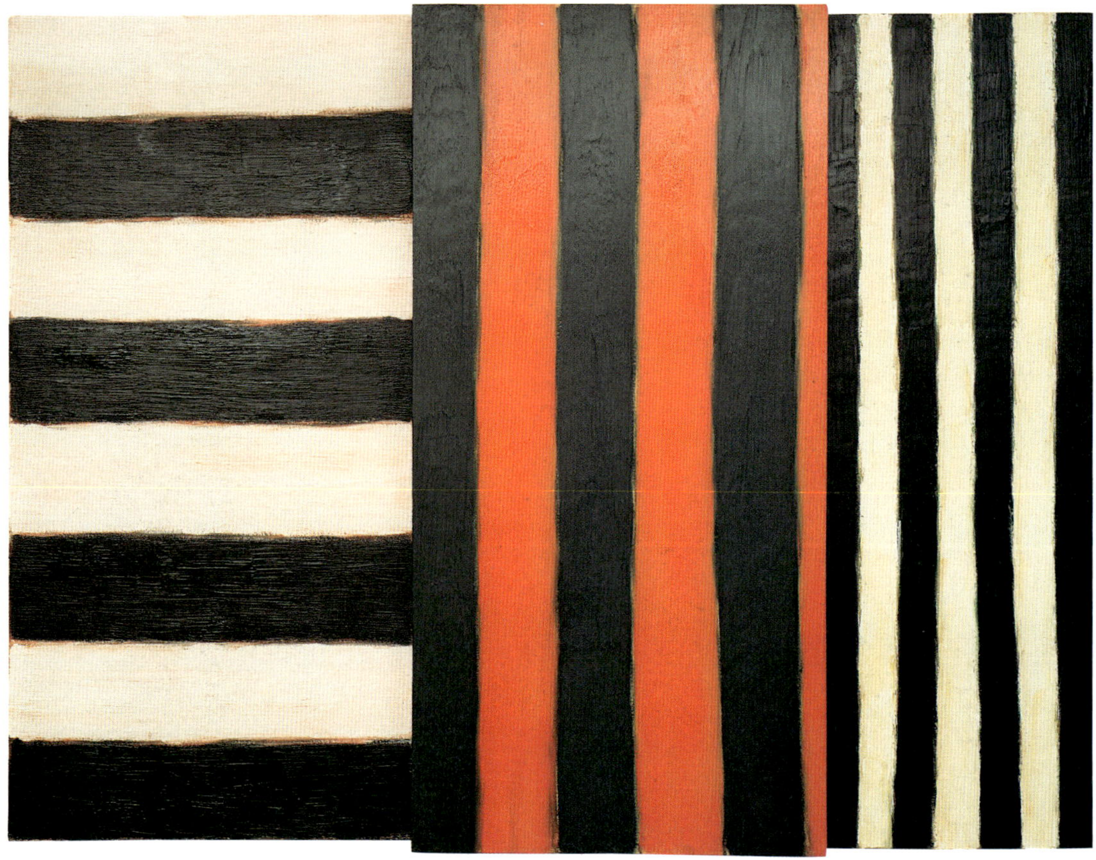

in Siena, Italy [Duccio di Buoninsegna, active 1278–1318], to the art of the sacred. The idea with both of my paintings is that the middle panel has body and weight and it projects out into space in a sense like a figure, like an aggressive figure, or a figure that could be moving out of the painting. *Paul* has a central panel that is body-size, the width of a body, in black and white vertical bands, and it's set into a kind of landscape pink and grey on one side. And *Maestà* takes the colours of Duccio's great *Maestà* of the thirteenth century. Sienese painters were very fond of blue and red, blue taken from the Virgin Mary's robes. And then what I tried to do with the outside of that one was to make it into something very elemental in a sense. It is devoid of colour, because I believe that colour is connected to living life, the natural world, and black-and-white is connected more to the world of idea, concept or thought. That's how I tried to use it in that painting. *Maestà* came first, then *Paul*, also in the triptych format.

These autobiographical narratives can be points of reference that help explain how paintings came to be. Artists do derive images, colours and ideas from a

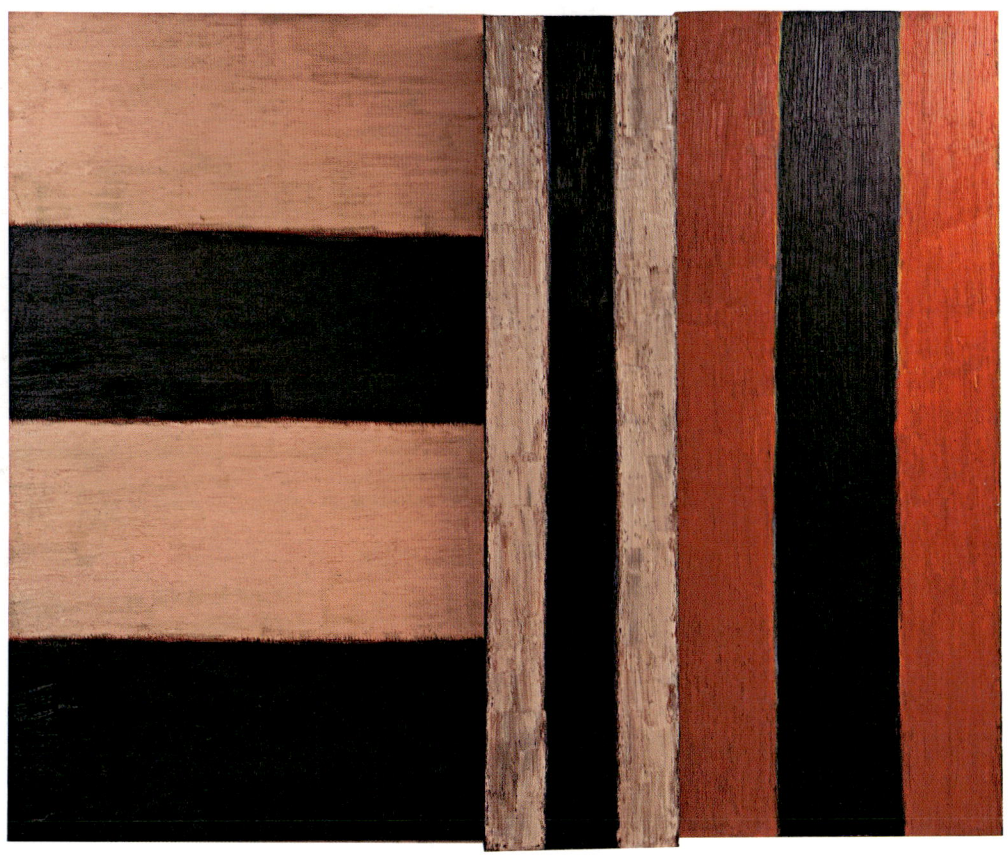

personal narrative, a memory bank, that can build or be called a 'myth'. But in truth the major goal of my art is that play between rhythm, the inner rhythm of things, and ideas. (I wrote my master's thesis on the rhythm transformed in Matisse's *Dance*.) Art is not a really a question of conclusions or closed opinion. It is something that keeps us alive, and it becomes more vital as the world continues on its merry slide. I want mine to be more accessible than Hedwig's tattoo. That's nice if you know the story, but I'd like my work also to speak through the universal language of rhythm. Rhythm communicates in a primal way, directly and through feeling. You look at all my paintings, and you see different rhythms: it goes fast, then it goes slow in different sections of a painting, and then the colour changes – from idea to body, and then back to idea or back to spirit.

This essay is adapted from the lecture 'Mythology and Abstraction', given at the University of Madrid in July 2003. It first appeared in *American Art*, the magazine of the Smithsonian Institution, XVIII, no. 3

THE PROBLEM WITH COLLECTORS

Well, of course, the really big problem with collectors is that when you sell them something they think they own it. Before that they're all as sweet as pie, but once they get what
they want they turn into castle walls. And if they don't want to be breached or reached,
they won't be. If I could figure out a way of selling things twice, that would solve the
problem – or even better, to sell things and keep them.

New York, November 2005

NOTES FOR AN UPCOMING EXHIBITION IN GERMANY

In the constricted world of Manhattan, where real estate equals money, which equals
gallery space, which aspires to equal the power to pay for and overcome the price of real
estate, it's not unlike the SoHo of thirty years ago: more or less impossible to be experimental with gallery spaces. It is a question in Manhattan of art equalling money and
therefore power. Art equals power. And galleries are measured in terms of power and lack
of power – power, of course, being better than lack of power. But in the end, power and art
should not be in bed together (though in Manhattan this seems virtually impossible to
avoid). And it all comes down to real estate.

With an exhibition like this we need the physical space to put things together that
don't necessarily have an obvious, saleable connection in order to allow nuanced corre-
spondences to appear over time, during the tenure of the exhibition. This kind of
exhibition can happen in Europe, where one can still find buildings that sit in the margins
of commercialism.

Mooseurach, April 2005

Concept art or the art of pure idea is, at its purest, freaky. Freakish, since it has no age. If something is redrawn, remade and can be considered original, it separates itself from human-experienced time and it has no pathos. That's the idea: like Dorian Gray or Dracula, to be forever young. To be forever young and perfect is to be disconnected from the human experience. Even the work of Joseph Beuys ages and accumulates pathos as it ages. Painted surfaces reflect time, are damaged by it or are aged by it; but they are also empowered by the accumulation of this experience.

Mooseurach, October 2005

I travelled up to Newcastle in September 1968 from London, to start my fine art course at Newcastle University. My mother was born in Durham, as was my grandfather, who was a coalminer. My grandmother was a woman of sour disposition, since she came from a great family in Scotland and had married for love instead of position. Now my grandfather was a sweet man who had his left arm on backwards from a mining accident, and they had no great house, no servants, no car and one outside toilet, which one could reach with the help of a torch during the night. And that's where I stayed: 54 Hallgarth Road, Durham City, which was opposite the university where Ian Stephenson went to study art, when it was more solidly attached to Newcastle University.

Of course, I didn't know all this when I arrived. I had heard of Richard Hamilton, and was happy he wasn't there. But, I didn't know much about Ian Stephenson until I arrived. But when I found out what he was doing, I was excited.

He seemed to be sweetness personified. Tender, yet absent. He wore a white jean jacket, usually, and matching jeans. He was ten years older than me. This is important, because he was older than us students, but not much. So he, in other words, was cool. Ian was the famous artist, who was an artist first and a professor second. And he was the one who was somehow of his own world and was allowed to be, because he had the paintings to back it up.

He was especially famous, and still is, because his paintings were used in [Michelangelo] Antonioni's highly successful film *Blow-Up* [1966]. At that time London was the centre of 'cool'. David Hemmings played the sexy photographer who accidentally shoots a corpse in a park, and Vanessa Redgrave played the sexy woman who tells him. There were other films made around that time, such as *Performance*, which starred Mick Jagger as, more or less, Mick Jagger. All this contributed to the image and attraction of London as a centre to rival New York. So, by extension, this aura of hipness was transferred on to Ian Stephenson, who strode gently through the corridors of Newcastle University Fine Art Department as a person who seemed to be unaffected by any of it, and interested only in his dots.

The inclusion of his paintings in the Antonioni film made him fashionable, but there was also a profound reason for it. The film is haunted by Ian's paintings, because it is a story of uncertainty. The point and atmosphere of the film is that visual evidence creates as many mysteries and problems as it provides answers. The paintings are transformed into the medium of film and they represent enigma, though the artist who makes them plays the opposite of the superficial fashion photographer who stumbles across a possible murder. The systematic *sfumato* of Ian's paintings is transferred on to the photographs that are thought to maybe show a shadow lying under a tree in a park. The techniques of photography and film and painting become intertwined in a plot of hard-to-decipher surfaces. The uncertainty and the authentic mystery of Ian's paintings become the psychological background for a very important film. Film-makers have made films of artists before. But here was a film of the first rank whose theme was underpinned by a painter's content, though not by the painter as subject.

Ian started to come to see me after I started making my paintings. I didn't have to ask him. He was a hunter who knew what he was interested in, and what he wasn't interested in. He never told me what to do. But he used the term "beautiful" as a kind of indicator of wrong direction, right direction. Not unlike the way kids play hot and cold when they hide things. Hot being right, cold being wrong, and warm being not bad. Ian would say, "That's beautiful" if he liked it a lot. And, if he liked it less than a lot he'd say, "It's beautiful but not as beautiful as the other one". And if he didn't like what I was doing, he'd stop coming for a while, until I'd got over it, whatever my infirmity was. He was once talking to me about the work of a 'Dada' art student in the sculpture department, and he told me he thought that his apartment was too beautiful in relation to the kind of work he was doing. Thus he seemed to measure good, suspect and negative by the use of the word "beautiful". His own work was famously beautiful. The mystery of beauty, and what beauty was when it was beautiful and what it was when it wasn't beautiful, seemed to colour his world.

He gave me a lot of his time, but it didn't seem to have much to do with his parents and him coming from Durham or my mother and grandfather coming from Durham. I would say it was exclusively connected to the paintings and what we were mutually interested in.

He had gone to Newcastle University himself, and his contact with the analytical and circumspect mind of Richard Hamilton had probably given him a kind of counterweight to the emotionality of his nature. Kurt Schwitters had worked in Ambleside, and we had the Merzbarn reconstructed in the Hatton Gallery. So I saw it every day. So did Ian Stephenson. Thus the influence of another tradition as a way of asking questions about the validity of abstraction was ever-present as a curtain of scepticism. I personally wasn't interested in the scepticism, but I was interested in overcoming it. As, I suspect, was Ian Stephenson. William Feaver was there too in the Art History Department, and was the incandescent rising star of the British critical scene. He wrote very well on Ian Stephenson, and subsequently on me. It's important to have someone around who can put the whole thing into words and, just as importantly, get those words published. It gave us our Newcastle word window on to the world. That time, which was of Tim Head, the memory of his friend Brian Ferry, the departed but somehow present Stephen Buckley and Mark Lancaster, with the shadow of Victor Pasmore, made Newcastle classy. It gave it weight. A counterweight to the much more heavily endowed London. We didn't have the Tate, but we had a history of distinction and, close by, the long, spectacular beaches of Northumberland, that nobody wanted to visit. Thus their majestic loneliness was permanently uncompromised.

Ian had his swan-song exhibition at the Laing Art Gallery in Newcastle in 1970, and inevitably I was asked to write on it for the student review. The usual critic was a good friend of mine – she was a sweet girl, but had no idea how to handle the work of Ian Stephenson. This is largely the case today, though now there are perhaps ten people who understand it instead of three: those being possibly William Feaver, Kate Stephenson and maybe me. A Romantic conceptualist working towards such extreme states of visual denseness is destined to leave the majority of the public bewildered. However, the paintings are undeniably beautiful, and they should slowly move from the margin to the centre of the page of painting in Britain, and take their authentic place among the images that we see constantly.

Ian said his goodbyes to Newcastle Fine Art Department in 1970, to become head of postgraduate painting at Chelsea. There our paths crossed yet again, when I became a lecturer at Chelsea Art School at the tender age of twenty-seven, in 1973. I used to see Ian from time to time. He liked to ask me to drive him around in my

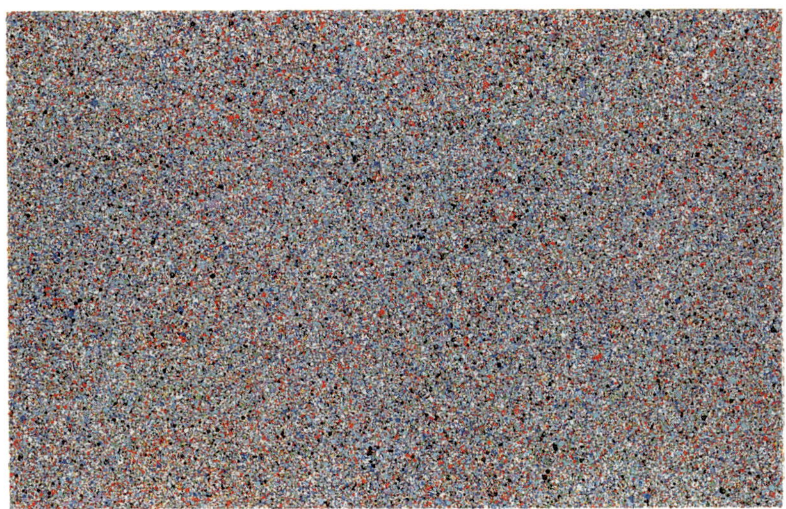

Ian Stephenson (1934–2000)
Flaxman: Understudy, 1972
Oil and enamel on canvas
167.8 × 267 cm (66 × 105 in.)
Private collection

van, if he needed to go somewhere. And I liked it when he asked me. I always admired him, and I always, like a protegé, wanted to make him happy.

One day we were interviewing the applicants from all over Britain for the places available in the postgraduate school at Chelsea. And competition was tremendous. A fairly aggressive, cool-looking young guy, who had certainly been told he was very, very good, arrived from Sunderland, with his enormous paintings on top of his car. He strode into his interview inhabited in equal measure by the forces of confidence and fear, which resulted in a mistake that he maybe regrets to this day.

His paintings were slick, taped up and sprayed, and visually declarative and powerful. A kind of abstracted Pop art, one might say. I made the cavalier remark that they, like a beautiful Italian suit, were "snazzy". This was an unfortunate choice of word under the stressful circumstances, since he had driven all the way from the 'proletariat' North to the 'corrupted' South, and was no doubt tired and 'young-bloke' defensive. He subsequently launched a tirade of abuse at me, since he objected to my remark. This was sad, since I was more than inclined to vote him in.

Ian, however, stood up, walked towards him, and told him to wrap up his work and get out, and never talk to a lecturer like that again. The cool young guy from Sunderland left robotically, far too stunned to either protest or say thank you or ask where the nearest petrol station was. He simply exited, never to return. I sat, amazed, having witnessed the absolute transformation of Ian Stephenson gentle and sweet into Ian Stephenson tiger. I realized that day that Ian's relationship with me was protective. I have never quite understood that and, since hardly anybody was ever protective of me before, it touched me deeply. It also demonstrated that

there was something fiercely ethical in his nature. That disrespect was unaccept-
able and furthermore represented a force to be knocked down. So behind all the
poetic discretion of those modestly patient surfaces there was a man who knew
how to fight, once he'd identified a clear ethical issue. The character of his paintings, of his method, is driven by a constant obsessive fidelity. He rains down his
colour with the even-handedness of nature and the endurance of a farmer.

"The details are the paintings", he said. One can say this about all human
endeavour and all human relationships, not just the natural world. For in its details
one can understand and see demonstrated the truth of everything. What lies
behind, and causes form, shape and appearance. What the thing is really, in its
symphony of elements. Eventually he discarded the forms, the buried shapes, and
showed what he was destined to show all along: exclusively detail. The paintings
arrived at their inevitable destination and became detail as monumental blocks.

Air, earth, water. Britain is a land of coast, where the elements of air, earth and
water struggle against each other every day, and have done since Britain was made.
This has given the country its character. In Europe, out of Europe. Desirable but
difficult to invade. The Spanish Armada was chased all around the coast of Britain
and Ireland, by sailors who understood that navigation (the ability to blow with the
wind) was more important than big guns. It was that chase that caused the great
Armada to self-destruct incrementally, detail by detail. And, it is this space that
exists between the border of things that has made the British character. It has given
the British character its patience, its tolerance, its sense of independence and its
Romanticism. Ian is the exemplar and the heir, made visible, of all this. The eternal
emotional space between the land and the sea and the sea and the sky is responsible for Romanticism. It is the space between things that represents eternity and
gives us the luxury to fall into it and feel profoundly. It is no accident that *Wuthering
Heights* takes place on the rain-soaked moors of Yorkshire or that Wordsworth, the
great Romantic poet, wrote in the Lake District, where water, air and earth are visually mixed up for most of the year. Ian Stephenson is a Romantic. But he is a
systematic Romantic, an artist who understood conceptual art, as it related to
painting, very early on; and this was manifested with great beauty by the relationship between process, and its own strange ritualistic dance, and visual result.

"I insist on the details in a picture." The paintings are made by details. But
they are also made by gravity. The force that holds all our world together is what
carries the drops of paint vertically down on to the horizontal canvas, from Ian's
hand and brush. The paint falls to the canvas in imitation of nature as rain would
fall evenly, and without favour, on to a deserted sandy beach off the north coast of
Britain. Everything arrives as it should in an even, measured dance that covers what

arrives first. So time is represented by layering, and what ends up on top is what arrives last. It is a picture, a perfectly true mirror, of process. Just as the rain is what it is, and not other. A strip of land being as wet, exactly, as the amount of rain that falls on to it. A painting by Ian Stephenson is a mirror of adding and covering, until what is covered cannot exist as a clear visual reality. Then the painting is full up. Then the painting is detail-laden, to the point where it can take no more. Then it is free of him, and ready for us: as a clear, conceptual conundrum. Because the systematic painter has, by simple addition, made the Romantic inscrutable. Ian has made a painting that begins to empty itself out of specific narrative and meaning, whilst simultaneously being made of inestimable detail. But detail in this work contradicts describable content, just as the Romantic urge is not to articulate emotion but to provoke it.

He talked of the macro and micro – in other words, of opposites – and by compressing two traditions he arrived at originality. Georges Seurat declared that he had found an entirely new way of painting. He had made painting 'artificial' again. He had taken it out of nature and put it back into the artificial world of the studio. And, by putting paint down systematically, in small dots, he had got rid of gesture and the hands' direction. He would stand painting in front of the painting for hours without having to step back to look at it. His work was above mere appearance and, in fact, had become conceptual. One could argue that he was the first conceptual artist, because the theory determined precisely the result. Although this doesn't explain the poetic charge of his smaller paintings.

I had an exhibition once in a museum in Gravelines on the north coast of France, which is where Seurat came from. Now it is famous for having a nuclear power station, which gives the place a slightly creepy quality and makes me wonder about the influence of Seurat's scientific particles. There you could see the famous lighthouse that appeared in his paintings. However, when I looked across the inlet to the jetty on which the lighthouse was planted, the air was vibrating with dots. They say it's a phenomenon of the place that there are dots everywhere, and that it is impossible to see the air as empty. And that the explanation lies in the way the light is reflected off the water. So, everything comes from something. Or nothing comes from nothing. Goethe says that nothing can come out of darkness.

My father was a barber, and outside his barber's shop he had a barber's pole, striped in red and white. I used to visit him, a lot, when I was a child, and now I'm painting stripes. That seems weird.

Ian Stephenson painted watercolours with his father when he was a boy. And he painted standing on the sandy particles of the beach on the north-east coast of England, where the horizon line is a blurred strip for half the year, and every colour is fluctuating between definitions. The light of the north-east is clear and bright, and it is closer to Scandinavia than Cornwall, and the weather is thundery and unstable. If you stare into the yellow-green-grey mist that is the colour of Ian's paintings, you can feel the ships cutting the waves in the distance. You can feel what the mist will not allow you to see. So the mist holds, obscures, shelters and endangers, and is the teacher of the Romantic spirit.

Jackson Pollock, the great American Abstract Expressionist painter, developed a style of using a rhythmically circular motion of dripping paint on to canvas that was lying on the floor while he was walking around on top of it. He was therefore literally in the painting. He, like Seurat, dispensed with touch, but he replaced it with drip. This created distance and movement. Pollock achieved a very great body of work made of swirling rhythm, and in *No. 32* (page 18), which is in the Kunstsammlung Nordrhein-Westfalen in Düsseldorf, he closed the gap ferociously between process and result. It is a giant horizontal rectangle, where black paint is dripped rhythmically and evenly on to raw cream-coloured canvas. In this work Pollock achieves the ambitious power of a painting with the brevity of a drawing. This accounts for its impact and its conceptual elegance.

Ian Stephenson was a man from the north-east of England, but he was a man who understood the past and the present. In addition, he was sophisticated internationally, and he knew all about American art of the twentieth century.

When the influence of Jackson Pollock rubs up against a Romantic spirit like that of Ian, who is steeped in the history of fairly recent French painting, the result is easy to see in retrospect. However, the accommodation of this influence (I mean action painting) pushed through the net of his own European tradition yields a fascinating result. Ian Stephenson pushes together two opposites, where they meet on his own clouded horizon. There he combines the sky and the sea. The systematic structuring impulse of Europe dissolves into all-over painting. So that freedom from description is achieved, without denying the supremacy of detail.

In preparation for his retrospective at the Laing Art Gallery, Ian painted in the huge rooms of Newcastle University's Fine Art Department during the summer of 1970. The bright northern light was filtered through old windows, the result being old bright light. The stretchers were beautifully made as huge horizontal rectangles. The linen was the best, all the way from Belgium, and it was stretched to perfection, with the attaching staples put into the wooden frame at exactly regular intervals. And since the dots of paint on the front side were going to be a paradigm of evenness, the back, in attitude, was the same as the front. The paintings were made with utter commitment from the moment they were conceived as paintings to be. Every action was a deepening component in what led inevitably to the clouded rectangle that was an unnameable colour made of thousands of particles of nameable colours. Detail heading towards oblivion.

Ian walked around steadily flicking and dropping the paint from above on to the huge rectangle, horizontally below. Not unlike the seed-sower in Millet's great painting, *The Gleaners* of 1848.

One day the paintings were gone, and there was a negative rectangle on the floor where they had lain receiving their dots. Around the rectangle on the old wooden floor was the necklace of dots that had missed the canvas and now faded out into the space of the room. The students all loved Ian, because they recognized him as a true artist, and what they all wanted to be. I was thinking later that we should have kissed what was left of him on the floor, but, being British art students and disobediently opposed to idolatry, we didn't.

Written to accompany Ian Stephenson's exhibition
at the New Art Centre, Salisbury, May 2005

LILIANE TOMASKO
THE THIRD SHORE

Liliane Tomasko was born in Zurich in 1967. But this is not where the cause of her story begins. And by "the cause" I mean to say, the reason she is a painter and why she is the kind of painter she is. The painter of the lost and the left. And the painter of memories.

Her parents were both born in Hungary. And like many others, they fled their ravaged country in 1956. They ended up as separate refugees in the refugee camp in the south of Switzerland, by Bellinzona. There they met and fell in love and married. Valeria and Arpad Tomasko had three daughters in Zurich: Gabriella (the eldest), Liliane and then Susan. Even now Liliane has relatives living in Budapest and in the countryside around Lake Balaton, in Hungary. Thus her identity and her point of view are those of a Swiss woman with the soulful memory of a Hungarian woman. Since her early twenties she has lived in Paris, London (where she studied art), Barcelona, Munich and New York. So, in European terms, she has been everywhere. And like many from Switzerland, she thinks and speaks in several languages. Her view of the world is not nationalistic. It is a special quality of Switzerland that its people have for centuries developed the capacity to think outside their own borders, in the idiom of bigger, more powerful states. She has this ability. And with it comes a weakened sense of national identity, but a greater vista of options in which to think and speak.

London has marked her painting. There is no question of that. The earlier bed paintings that were made soon after she graduated from the Royal Academy are not 'school of London' paintings, though they bear its dull light. The masterly and physical paint handling carries with it the scent of bohemian London, the disobedient relationship to tradition, that so marks the painting situation there. These paintings are stubborn and difficult in their tough, traditional awkwardness. And the blue, grey,

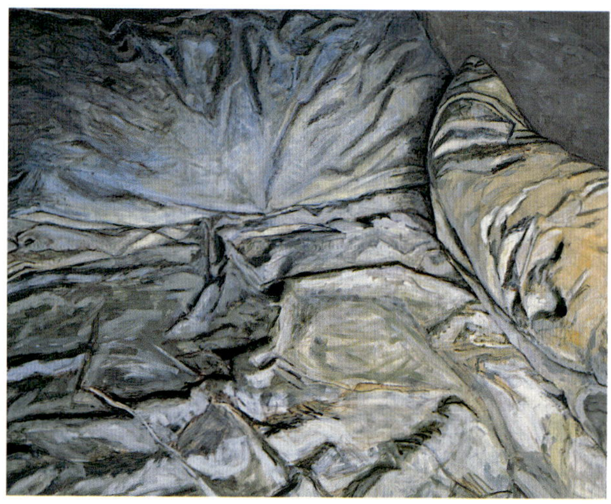

Liliane Tomasko (born 1967)
Bed III, 2001
Oil on canvas
122 × 152.5 cm (48 × 60 in.)
Private collection

dull brown of the grey northern urban light is everywhere in these works. *Bed I* to *Bed IV* (2000–01) are all reminiscent of difficult interior landscapes. *Bed III* is muscular, and it seems to writhe with classic painterly restlessness. This is not a bed in repose. This is a bed that is struggling against its own condition. The condition of being used and left.

As a metaphor for dreams and abandonment, the bed is profound. This is the loving battlefield of sex. The soft platform where dreams are made, that undo the difficulty of the day and where we make preparations for the next day, and the days after. And this is, above all, the place that lies abandoned in the day, except when we are sick or so sick with love that we cannot go to work. Gradually cooling when we leave, the bed lies cold, just there: ready for the night.

It is a place left.

When the character of the mother in Ron Howard's film *The Missing* (2003) – a story of kidnap – understands that her daughter is missing, she pathetically visits her bed. She is not there. But she was there. And so she has left her outline on the sheets. Recorded, sadly, as low-level relief sculpture. Human and brutally inhuman, in its memory and absence. The mother stares at the bed, willing her child to come back. But she cannot. So we are left with outlines. These are abstract, like absence itself. And in this case, dull pain.

In 1956, when Valeria and Arpad left their separate houses and their separate families, they also left their beds, their rooms, their photographs and the walls against which they had leant their belongings and their own bodies, and against which they would lean no more. And thus on the bed there is only the obscure and tantalizing outline. And ultimately this gives us nothing. Nothing but the evidence of absence.

Now the painter steps in to refill this brutal absence with life. Here the possibility for renewal, earned at art school, earned in the studio, earned through work and through understanding of the medium, steps in. She carries the life of dreams into the actual. And puts back, transformed through painting, what has been lost. These bed paintings show what is not there. But equally they show what is there. Or what can be there. What can be put there. Yes, we disappear. Yes, we must leave. But we can retrieve. Through the activated surface of these works these beds come to life. The absence of human life as evidence is compensated for by the hand and its power to evoke colour, light and a sense of domestic landscape. Here the sense of dream returns. Not simply as it was made: a place to lie. But a place to look. To dream while looking. These are landscapes. Their cold light is northern. Yet their active hand is passionate. And the undulating forms are transformed from cotton sheets into another material that is the property of dreams. A landscape that can only exist in a painting. The place where a dream or a vision can be passed intact from one human being to another. Made in paint.

MATERIALITY IN PAINT

In Diego Velázquez's (1599–1660) painting *Pope Innocent X* (1649–50) the pope is locked in his chair in opulence. And opulence equals power. The contradiction here is that the pope is the custodian of the gate. He has the ultimate knowledge. He is God's ear. Yet in Velázquez's painting the satin red of the pope's robe reeks of power and sensuality.

In Titian's (*c.* 1485–1576) sumptuously austere painting *The Man with a Blue Sleeve* (1511) what seems to be a self-portrait is distinguished by the strange title. What marks out the sitter is the blue sleeve; otherwise he is simply a man. The title of this work and the composition, which is utterly dominated by the shimmering blue silk of the right sleeve, display perfectly the importance of material in Titian's work. The largest area by far in the foreground of the painting is the sensually painted blue silk sleeve, which is in a dramatic competition with the intense gaze of the young man. A forcefully balanced double view is achieved between the psychology of the stare and the psychology of the blue that renders the silken arm.

El Greco (1541–1614) painted a masterpiece that now resides in Toledo, Spain. *The Entombment of the Count of Orgaz* (1586), besides being a wonderful composition, is also a narrative told in material. The key to this narrative is the material worn by the priest who presides over the service. Here El Greco achieves a classic mastery of light and transparency. The white robes of the priest are painted as a metaphorical bridge between two worlds. The pale faded white of the priest's gown quietly dominates this great work, since it creates a surface that can be seen through.

In a daring compositional device the priest has his back turned towards us. This serves to isolate him as a personality, whilst making the delicate transparency of his robe more forceful, since it occupies almost his entire body.

El Greco's *The Opening of the Fifth Seal of the Apocalypse* (1608) is a picture of human beings caught up in the swirling materiality of the world and its drama. The composition is, in fact, dominated by the piece of red fabric in the foreground of the painting. It is painted with personality. And is more particular, more specific, than the humans in the drama. Thus the dramatic materiality of the world is more in focus than the people caught up in it. They are generalized and pale by comparison. The material of the clouds, the landscape and, above all, the contorted

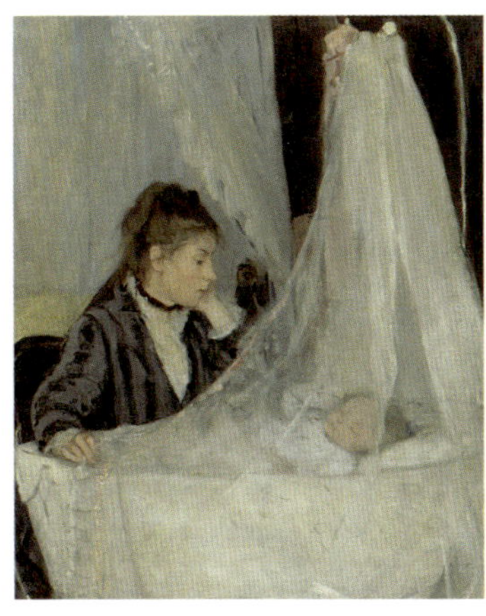

robes of the players carry the abstracted drama of the story. The near-white nudes seem virtually defenceless against the force of its fabric.

In Berthe Morisot's (1841–1895) *The Cradle* (1873) the story of the painting is told almost exclusively through material. Here the interior is all darkness, except for the lyrical transparency of the white material that covers the window (thus transforming and domesticating its light) and the canopy that shades and protects the cradle. Here the baby who is the treasure of the painting lies in a composition of gentle white and light grey transparency. All hard edges are painted out.

There are countless examples of the emotional power of paint as material and material as paint in painting that would serve equally well here, simply to make the point that the materiality of the world's surfaces has transformed the meaning and the story of art. Since it has become the signature of the surface of the artist.

When Goya paints a picture of a drowning dog (in one of his black paintings), he shows matter overwhelming life, and thus absorbing life into its molecular force. The dog is drowning and so it is still a nineteenth-century painting, because the battle between the particular depiction of struggling life and the heaving cosmic power that can engulf it has not yet been emphatically decided in favour of the cosmos. Once the dog is drowned, and once it disappears from the picture surface, narrative tension drowns with it. And we would be left with a late twentieth-century painting.

There is a painting by Liliane Tomasko that carries the title *25.09.2000*. This painting is contemporary. It is not sentimental, nor is it religious. And neither does it tell a story. It is, though, concerned with a form of depiction. The subject is a

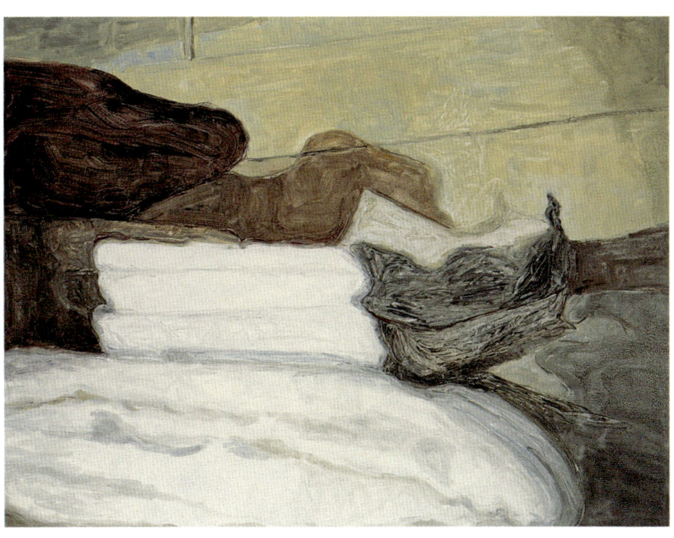

stack. A stack of towels. A stack of material or a stack of sheets. It is important that it is a stack. Because it is a stack made by her. In other words, it is a domestic sculpture. There is no such thing, I believe, as an accidental stack. It may be argued that it is not art. And certainly since it was not made to be art, directly, it cannot claim to be so. Yet, on some level, it was made to sit right, to be a composition. And on an even deeper level, since she is a painter, it might be argued that it was made to be painted. Not the way a model is arranged to be painted, because the model cannot be left for two weeks without attention. But gradually Liliane Tomasko, the painter, will wander back to her 'still life' or her sculpture, in order to paint it. And since she was a sculptor, who left it for painting, we can find, once again, her ability to retrieve that which was abandoned.

And so a simple stack, or a not-so-simple stack, becomes with time a complex and lyrical painting. Here the towels/sheets in the foreground are bearing the entire weight of the centre of the painting, and yet they seem to levitate with a ghostly light. The scratched out and awkwardly placed folded material, in grey, to the right, is an uncomfortable complement to its lit-up cousin. The sour yellow backdrop is both theatrical and deadpan. The painting gently sways between deep shadows in brown that have weight to their reliance, for support, on areas that are both solid and solid light. A sense of surrealism pervades this work. The almost inexplicable too. This was once a simple domestic convenience. Now it is made as a dissolving, scratched-out dreamscape.

THE DRESS

Women have the capacity to transform themselves. Especially so with the dress. It is a skin. But a skin of fiction. And when the fiction of appearance is played out, the dress is dropped to the floor and left. The snake sheds its skin to begin again. Who is not fascinated by the beauty and strangeness of abandoned snakeskin, which carries with it radically distinct connotations to stolen snakeskin, where the animal is killed and robbed of all it possesses, for its beauty? But a snakeskin left is miraculous.

The dresses painted by Tomasko occupy the paintings more or less in vertical orientation. As if they could be animate but will not be, because they are empty. Empty of her. And thus empty of life.

She paints not a self-portrait, but a portrait of what wraps the self. Of what envelops the self or decorates it, makes it sensual, erotic and fictional. So it is a portrait of the skin. When the snake has shed its skin, it leaves, and does not look back, since it does not value a double view of itself. Only we do that. To step out of her skin, and to make that her quasi-self-portrait, is once again to return to the portrait of her leaving. But not the action of her leaving. The evidence that she has left. Then it is ready to be painted once again, because it is abandoned. Now she can rescue it with paint.

In *Pink Dress* (2002) and *Grey Dress* (2002) she paints both dresses with an extreme degree of delicacy. Both seem to be almost animated in their readiness to begin the dance of life without their owner. In *Pink Dress* the delicacy of the

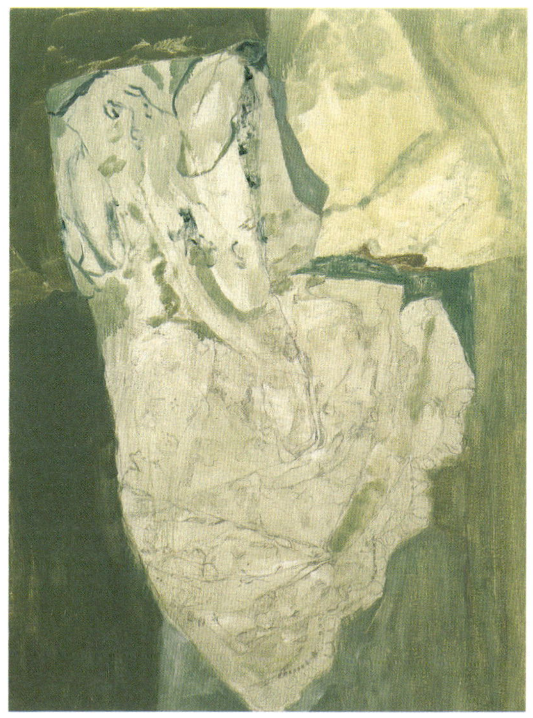

Liliane Tomasko
Grey Dress, 2002
Oil on canvas
101.6 x 76.2 cm (40 x 30 in.)
Private collection

painting is so extreme that the fragile pencil drawing that underpins the work appears to come up through the paint. Exactly the same could be said of *Grey Dress*. It hangs on the painted surface manifested with a materiality constituted of transparency. The composition is dominated tonally by the bottom left corner, which is occupied only by shadow. Thus shadow is more solid than material. The paint is thin, and the dress hangs in the centre of the painting as poetic fragility. They are sensually active, and the paint is used with great virtuosity. Yet this is in a dance with their gentle melancholia.

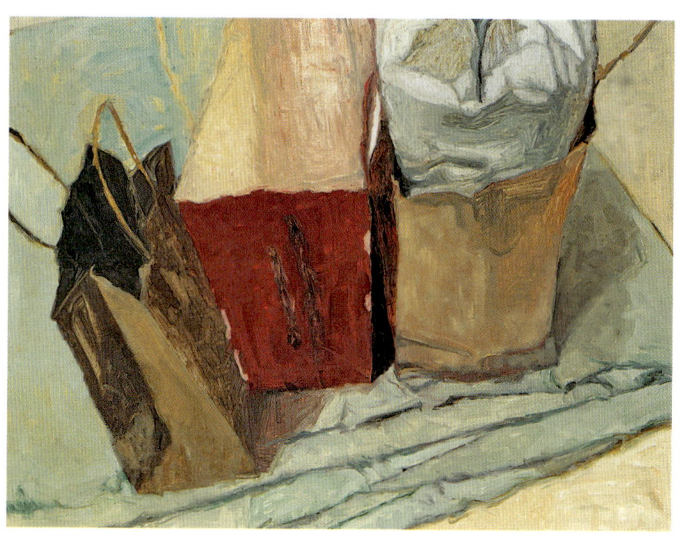

Liliane Tomasko
Paper Bags, 2000
Oil on canvas
76.2 × 101.6 cm (30 × 40 in.)
Private collection

BAGS AND TRANSPORTATION

In the bag paintings the colour tends to be exuberant. Red, green and pale yellow inhabit these paper vessels. They are filled up, and they are emptied and left standing side by side (often in threes) in an armless embrace. They can be picked up. They can be put down. And when they are put down, they lean against each other, as a little family. Almost comic in their slightly crooked stance. In *Paper Bags* (2000) the angle of view is down, and the bags cut the edge of the picture plane, as if they are snapped with a camera. The brushstroke is active, and the scratching returns to pull out the separateness of a folded sheet pushed down into the paper bag that sits on the floor ready to be taken off again.

Unlike Morandi, there is no pretension of permanence here. These bags are not made of ceramic, the most permanent of all art materials, as in the case of Morandi's timeless arrangements of jars; these are bags made of paper. And even new they don't stand up straight. These bags are disposable. Yet here they stand for 'all time' in a painting of highly abstracted colour. Empty and full.

Photography, which is central to the beginnings of these paintings, has been used by painters for over a century now. Tomasko takes little Polaroids to start up ideas for paintings. And why not? It's quick, it's convenient and, in addition, it's cheap. Slightly out-of-focus Polaroids have the advantage of abstracting and simplifying, since as a photographic tool they are only approximate. Polaroids don't have the ability to record everything. This, of course, is the whole point. She needs them to be rough and cheap, so that only the broadest and biggest items in the composition are recorded.

There is another crucial advantage for the painter who uses photography. And this is the most important of all. The camera frames out. Thus forms and objects seem to be falling out of the paintings, because they have been cut off. This could be done with drawing directly. But it is more likely not to be. And it is no accident that Bonnard, who was the great master of the broken edge and the object cut out of the picture, also used photography.

Bonnard's photographs might be called snapshots, since they were also taken with an affordable amateur device: the little Kodak. The 'first look' innocence of Bonnard's compositions is not set up laboriously in the professional photographer's studio. And it's the falling-in and falling-out quality of the framing that gives them their radical innocence. Colour in these photos is absent. As it should be, since Bonnard was the great colourist and could fill it in himself.

In Liliane Tomasko's Polaroid photos colour is distorted. This helps the painter even more, since the strange colour only assists her own project, which is to transform the objects into light and surface and take them to the edge of recognizability. However, if the colour in the Polaroid is not useful, it is discarded. Thus she is free to invent on top of what she has already invented in the arrangement of objects (which has been described previously as a sculpture), and the further invention made in the photo. Eventually everything is returned to painting, where her dream is finally realized as a personal surface.

Her closest ally in history is, in fact, Edouard Vuillard, the friend of Bonnard. In Vuillard's radical small-scale paintings the fabric of domesticity engulfs nearly completely all those who live in it. As an aside, it is almost incomprehensible to see an artist realize his vision so uniquely and then discard it so carelessly twenty years later. He is not the only one. But in his case the contrast between the ravishing intensity of the small interiors of the 1890s and the dull society paintings of the 1920s is numbing.

It is, however, the patterned surfaces painted in energetic brushstrokes that interest Tomasko. She wants to transform the banal. Anyone who has carried a mattress from one room to another will understand that this is material inert: a shape that becomes a lump, a dead weight when lifted. However, her mattresses are lit from inside. Painting with thin

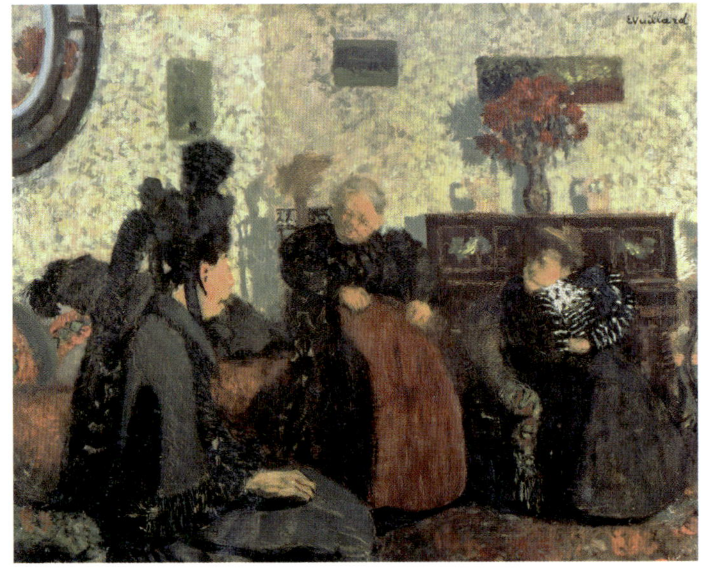

Edouard Vuillard (1868–1940)
The Widow's Visit, 1899
Oil on paper
50.2 x 62.9 cm (19¾ x 24¾ in.)
Toronto, Canada, Art Gallery of Ontario

paint, using the transparency of the painted material, she allows the under-painted colour literally to shine through. Thus the mattress (all dead weight) becomes the broad banded shape that crosses the picture plane, as monumental light.

In *White Border* (2003) the corner of the mattress provides enough perspective to keep the painting in the realm of the representational, though only just. It is taken to the very edge of abstraction but then put back again into the world of things. The pattern, painted in out-of-focus blue, insists that this is a painting of something that already exists. And, reminiscent of Vuillard, it sets up a pulsating rhythm that runs counter to the bigness and almost minimal brevity of the composition. The soft edges cause the bands to float. So the work becomes once again visionary. The mattress on which we dream becomes the dream to be looked at.

Liliane Tomasko paints flexibly. By that I mean she has numerous possibilities in the way she makes marks, and in the construction of her surfaces. They run from opaque to transparent. From scratched out and fought over to laid down like painted breath. And these are the emotional registers and realities of her surfaces.

She wanders between the shores of realism and abstraction to bring it all back to her own invented shore. A reality that is only radiantly possible as image in paint.

This essay appeared in the catalogue to accompany an exhibition of the paintings
of Liliane Tomasko at the Sala Pelaires in Palma De Mallorca, Spain, 2004

It doesn't matter how horrible the world gets;
there's always room for rebellion. And that's
life. Art is part of this. It always offers the
opposite and the free-thinking, open-ended
other possibility. This gets played out in artworks and in the response to them. And this
depends absolutely on a free society. Thus, if
you think about it logically and historically,
art replaces religion. Since art doesn't rigidly
define behaviour, it helps us to evolve.

When it comes to human beings
I am very religious
When it comes to the Church
I am not very religious.

Barcelona, March 2004

When they made the 'Millennium Dome' in London, they divided it into zones of interest (e.g. science, music, history, commerce), and they went out and tried to get sponsorship to support these specialized zones. All of them received money and investments with the exception of one, and that one was called the Spirituality Zone.

I thought that was symptomatic of our time, a time when facile entertainment and slick entrepreneur-ship can gather all sorts of cash around them while spirituality lies in the corner as a vaguely unpleasant, complicated and unnecessary problem. I wasn't entirely broken-hearted when the Dome project went bust.

It's interesting, and complex, how it is almost impossible to give any kind of quantitative value to the importance of the spiritual. Though history proves again and again that when you take it away everything falls down.

Barcelona, March 2002

It takes three seconds to draw a line through somebody's country, and it takes three thousand years to get over it. And my question would be: why is it always a British general who wants to be the artist, the one with the pencil? As in India–Pakistan, Ireland–Northern Ireland, Iraq–Kuwait? Let's say the United States found oil in Quebec and that after constructing some fairly infeasible justifications, say about the way the Canadian government is ignoring the rights of the Native Americans, it decided to turn Quebec into a separate sovereign state. Then what? Maybe the Canadians would just lie down and say, "Yes America, you are right. Thanks for the lesson. And we understand it's not just about the oil. Though it helps to oil the argument. And you need that for your tanks anyway. It's all the snow we get up here that blinds us to our mistakes."

Let's burn the world with Bush. Let's burn it all down, especially the part we don't live in. In Iraq it was the oil. The British and the Americans want to control the oil, and a mountain of lies is built on top of that simple economic imperative. That's why a British general took out his pencil and became the architect of disaster.

Barcelona, 2003

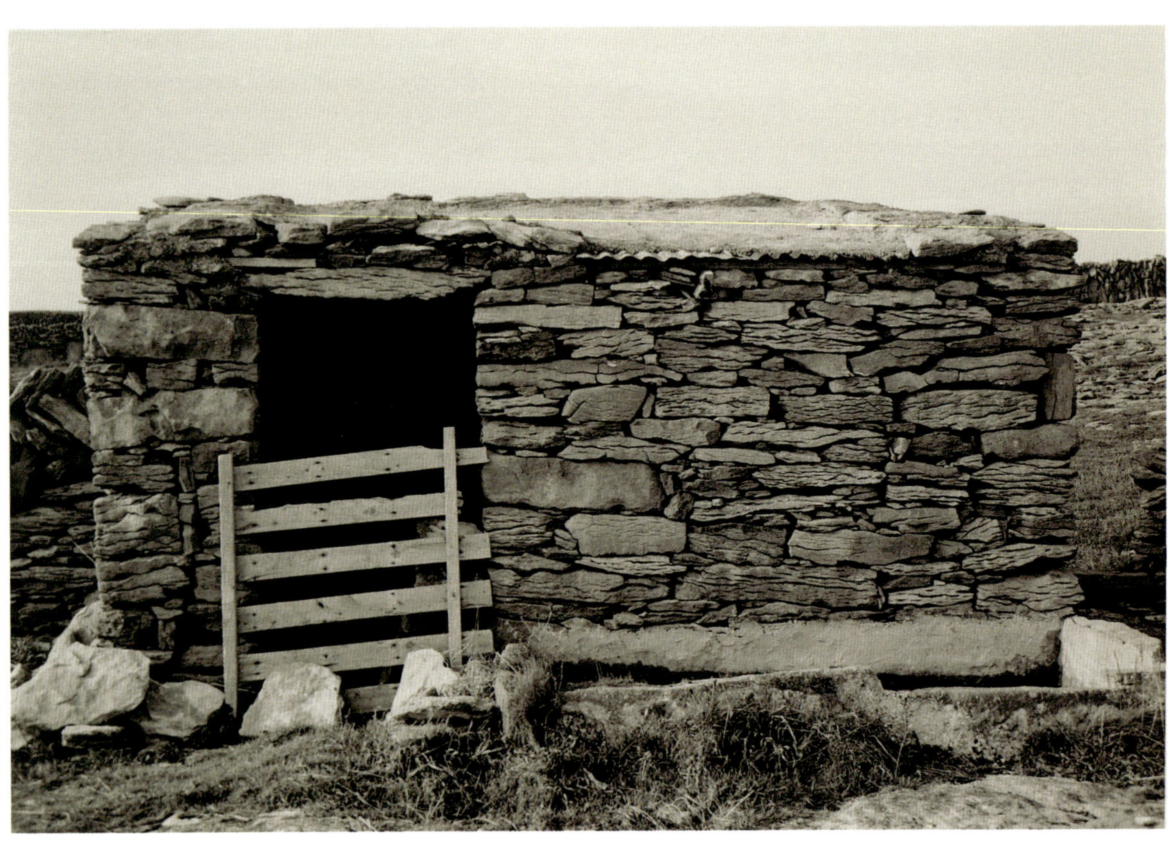

ARRAN HUT 1994
Gelatin silver print, edition of six
32.4 x 47.6 cm (12¾ x 18¾ in.)

In the nineteenth century American painters went down to South America with sketchbooks and made paintings on their return. I use the camera as a way of taking or, in a sense, making 'travelling pictures'.

I take photos of surfaces. When I see how the surfaces of the façades tell the story of the passage of human culture and the power of time, I can't help but react. I have to grasp it as it looks. And the easiest way to do that is to take a picture. Most of the subjects I shoot are in the margins of the world, for in the streets made of humble buildings I have to react. At the same time, my level of comfort and identification with these surroundings is intimate: I started out in identical circumstances.

The fundamental difference, though, between my working methods and those of the painters of the nineteenth century who made travel sketches is that I don't use the images of what I've photographed, only the emotions.

A CORNER OF BARCELONA 1997
C-print, edition of eight
72.4 x 101.6 cm (28½ x 40 in.)

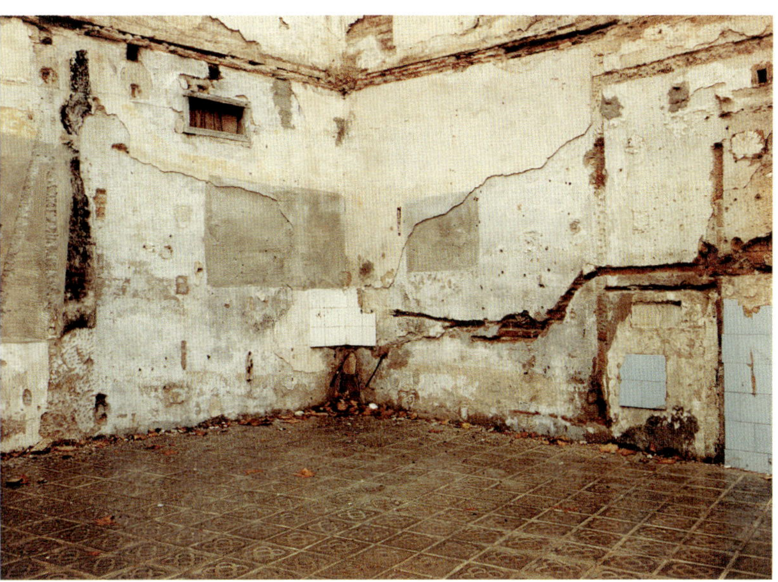

The great limitation of photography is that it cannot (so far) overcome its imagery. With painting it's the opposite. When I make a painting the emotion is embedded in the surface, and the mystery of its making has to be bigger than the image. It has to transform it into feeling every time the engine of the painting is restarted by the spectator.

I had an old friend living in New York who had painted paintings of pornographic subject-matters, but they were never called pornographic paintings. However, photos of pornography are invariably called pornography, thus closing down the space between the medium and the image. That's a strength and a limitation.

I'm always excited when I get back to New York with my travelling photos. When the proofs come back, it's as if the sensation of a Mexican town has literally entered my studio in Manhattan. And it's that feeling and that sensation that find their way into the surfaces and the light of my paintings. But now the paintings have to be 'bigger' than architecture, bigger than mere image.

Barcelona, September 2002

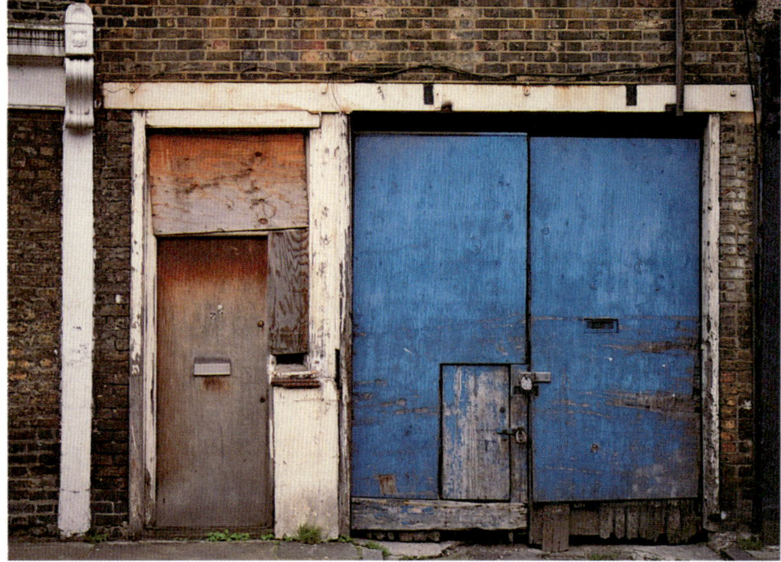

DEPTFORD BLUE DOOR 1999
C-print, edition of six
85 x 114 cm (33.5 x 45 in.)

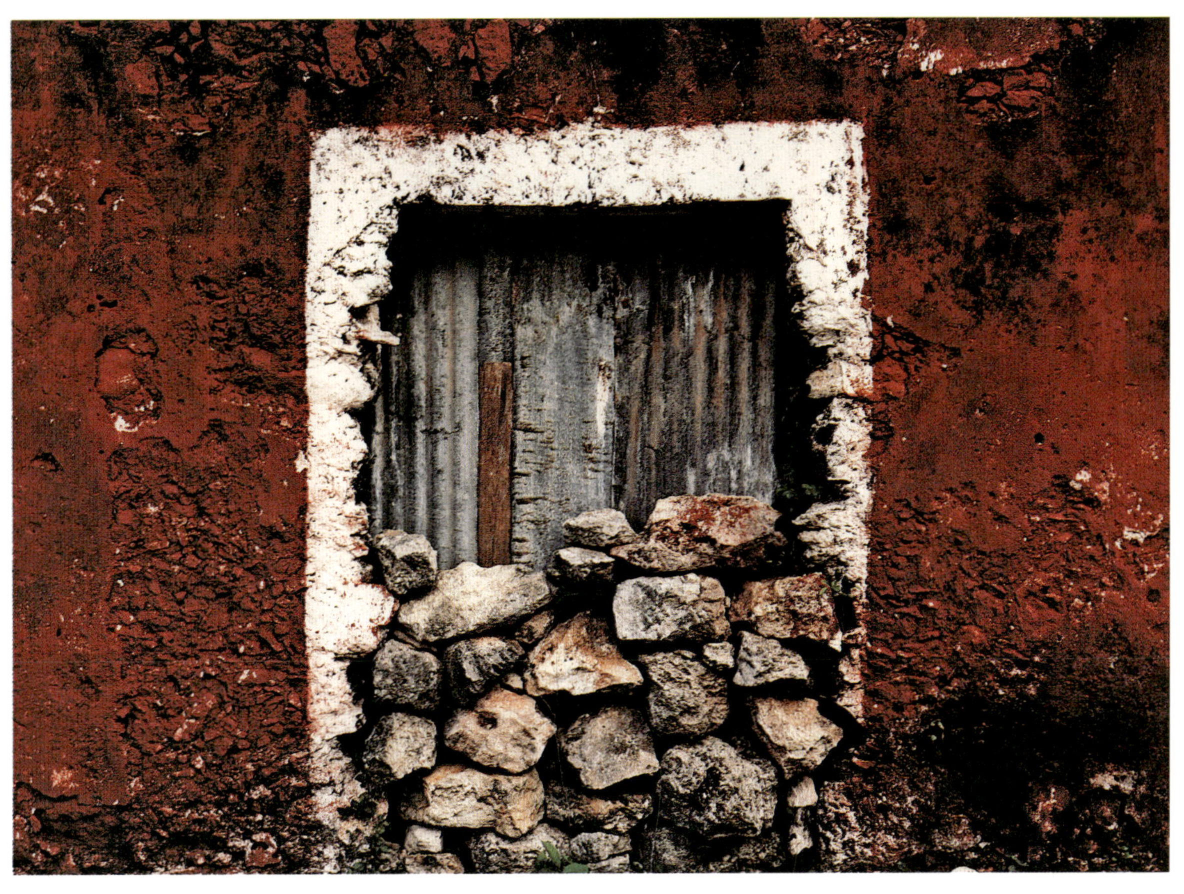

MEXICO RED WHITE 2001
C-print
91.4 x 121.9 cm (36 x 48 in.), edition of six
121.9 x 153.7 cm (48 x 60½ in.), edition of three

The power of a painting has to come from the inside out, not the outside in. It's not just an image; it's an image with a body, and that body has to contain its spirit. A painting, really, is made by its reason for being there. What's behind it decides everything. It's not just a question of attractiveness or correctness; it can't be fixed afterwards or by additions. How it starts will define how it ends. So it's the weight of the intention that defines everything.

Philip Guston said he went up the mountain of abstraction but then remembered he left something behind. That's his nature: as good as he was, he was a failed abstractionist. So he had to go back down because he was utterly bound up with the pictorial appearance of things. He wasn't obsessively abstract. To go up the mountain is one thing; to be happy up there is another thing. To be free, not longing for what you left behind, is a fundamental question of temperament, outlook and nature.

Colour is a key problem and opportunity for a painter; it has to be expressive. Philip's colour is not interesting. It's not nuanced or expressive, and it doesn't contain content and mystery. It's almost like painting by numbers, expressively. Green-orange-pink-black-white, or white-black-pink-red – but with almost no variation. This was his key problem, I believe. He wasn't free. These abstract paintings are not full of joy; they're inhabited by caution. Philip wasn't able to nuance his abstract paintings through colour. That's why it had to stop. I own one myself and I like them, but De Kooning by comparison was on fire because the colour was endlessly creative, open and nuanced. It was only when Guston stopped trying to be high-minded and fell into his authentic personal rage that he became important. Then he could escape his difficult relationship with the sublime abstractions of De Kooning.

Mooseurach, summer 2003

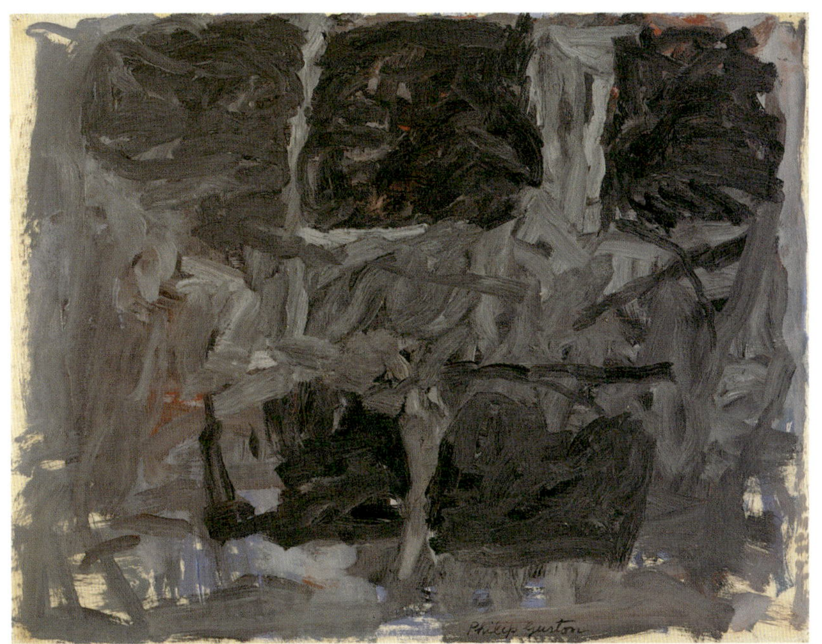

Philip Guston (1913–1980)
Dark Day, 1962
Oil on canvas
76.8 × 101 cm (30¼ × 39¾ in.)
Collection of Sean Scully

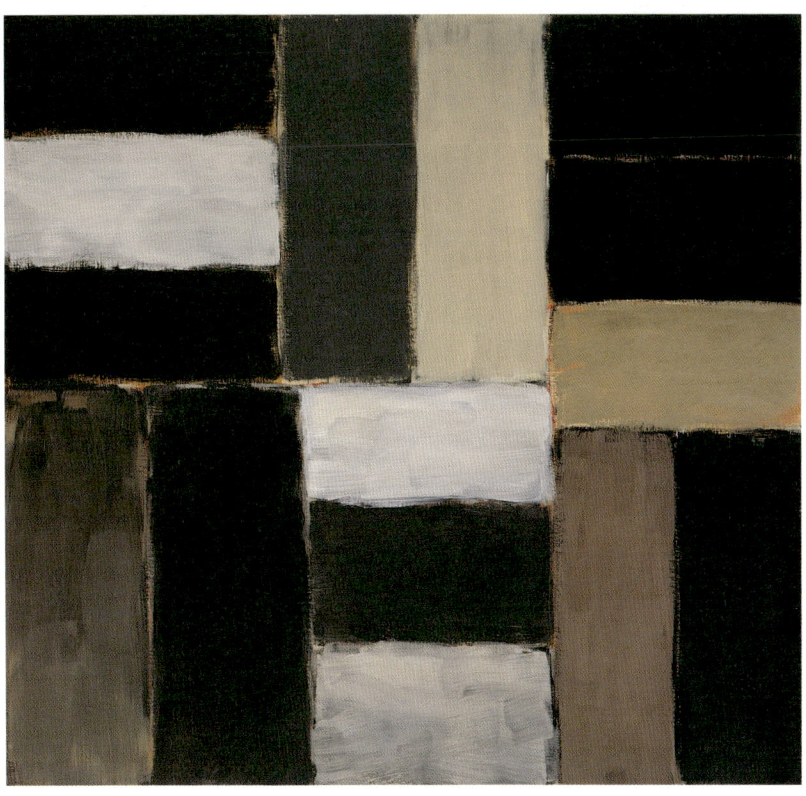

DARK DAY (FOR P.G.) 2001
Oil on canvas
190 × 203.2 cm (75 × 80 in.)
Private collection

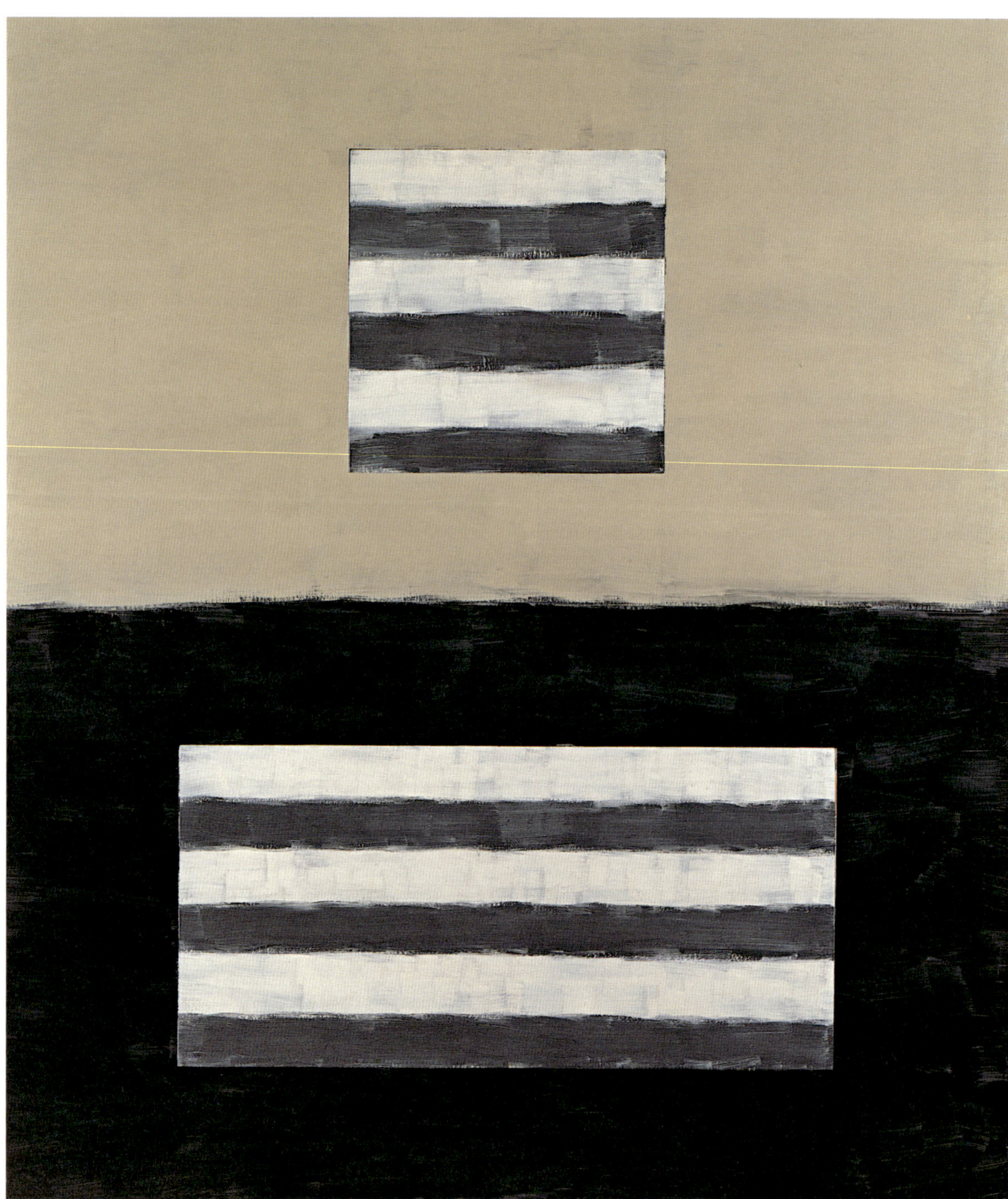

I was always looking at the horizon line – at the way the end of the sea touches the beginning of the sky, the way the sky presses down on to the sea, the way that line (that relationship) is painted. One day I was standing off Ireland, on the edge of Aran Island, looking out. Next stop, America. Standing on the Old World looking out at (and thinking of my new life in) the New World, as many people have done before ... looking out at and hoping for an arrival in America. I think of land, sea, sky. And they always make a massive connection. I try to paint this, this sense of the elemental coming-together of land and sea, sky and land, of blocks coming together side by side and stacked in horizon lines endlessly beginning and ending – the way the blocks of the world hug each other and brush up against each other, their weight, their air, their colour, and the soft uncertain space between them. I'm putting these into paintings: *Landline Sand*, *Landline Sea*, *Landline Blue*.

Mooseurach, July 2001

LANDLINE BLUE 1999
Oil on linen
243.8 × 213.4 cm (96 × 84 in.)
Dublin, Irish Museum of Modern Art

E V A

A man in Munich came to my gallery one Saturday night at almost, but not quite, six o'clock. He said that his daughter of fourteen years had seen my big exhibition at Haus der Kunst. And she had loved my photograph called *Land Sea Sky*. It is a picture taken in Norfolk, England, of the sea endlessly kissing the shore, as it does all over the earth. This father on the edge of disaster told my dealer that his daughter was dying of cancer and that she only had maybe a day or two to live and that the thing she wanted more than any other thing was to say goodbye to my photo. So the father bought the photo, put it in his car and took it to her and mounted it at the end of her bed so that she could see it all the time.

My own guess is that she understood that she was going into the space between the sea and the land, that she would become part of that eternal movement.

When she died, the father sent me a photo of her smiling bravely in the garden of a sanatorium. She was standing frail and embattled in a simple hospital dress. But she was not beaten. She still loved her life, as hard as it was, even if it was just for that one sunny afternoon. And she also had to protect her parents.

This whole incident, besides making me sad, made me proud to be an artist. And I was thinking that children live in a world of images, and that as we get older those images gather weight and layered depth and can turn into paintings. Her name was Eva.

Munich, October 2004

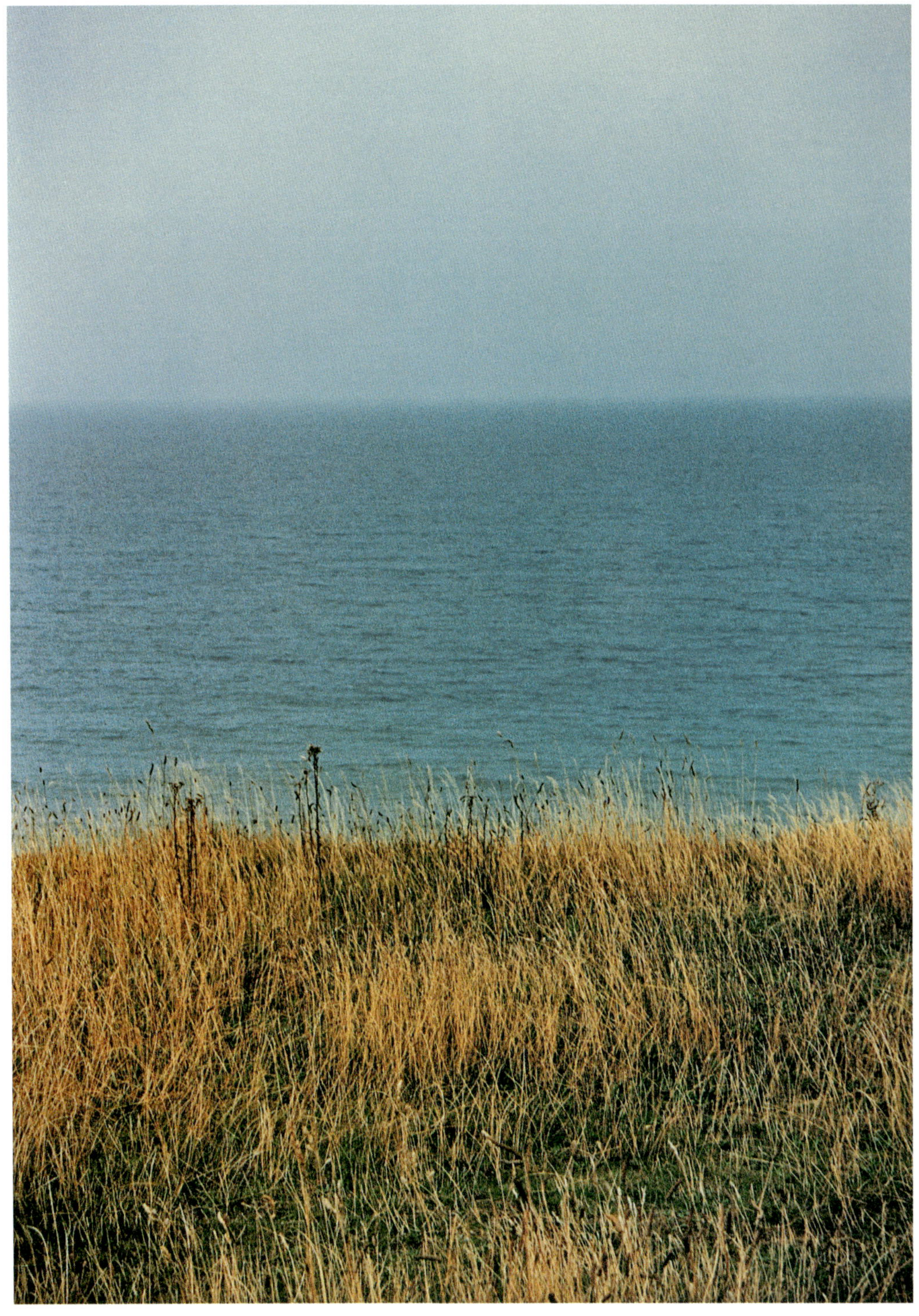

When I was twelve years old, I lived in a south London hamlet called Sydenham. My younger brother Tony and I used to call it Sunny Sydenham to hours of delighted laughter, which mystifies me now. I can only imagine we were training ourselves to achieve superior mental distance over the folks who live in suburban London. This mission has been accomplished, and we both left in our separate ways. It was a pretty distressing place to grow up. My little road: Tannsfeld Road, Sunny Sydenham, south London, a small house of the terraced, claustrophobic variety, with pebbledash walls and bay windows planted in the centre of a slow hill that dead-ended at the high street at one end and curved plainly past a flat park of big boring green lawn, the regularly cut variety, at the other end.

Next to the park, with a degree of character and maintained to the Victorian ideal of rustic romantic charm within the city limits, stood the house of the subject of this story: my choice.

A woman opened up for me the mysteries of the world occupied by small animals that fly around over our heads and crawl around, feet-level, in the spaces we forget to occupy in the cities we build: small wildlife.

She was old, but with a face like a big soft English rose. And she was tall, which gave her a certain aristocratic bearing. Even though at that time I was pretty busy painting and breaking into people's houses, I somehow made a few minutes in my busy schedule for her; and so did she in her curious and amused way for me. We met across a great divide of time and knowledge (plenty on her side and none on mine) over the issue of animals – their wonderful nervous world, the relationship between their little lives and their little deaths.

She knew about this. And even though she and I were wildly different in more or less every conceivable way, the deal was that she would show me her secrets. And when she left to move to an old folks' home, or to something even more abstract, I would become her. And even so, if the animals in all other parts of London were without a guardian angel, the animals of Sunny Sydenham would not be. They would be protected, protected as much as it is possible to protect anything from the unhappiest aspects of being what it is.

She showed me everything she knew, and I went to her every day. Each day a new secret unfolded and another small animal was coaxed back to life or sheltered unterrified as it passed into death. Hedgehogs, squirrels and sparrows were all handed over to her in blankets, scarves and paper bags; and she took them all.

Everybody knew where to come when they found something helpless, something that had bounced off the front of the car or had been abandoned.

They nearly always die because they don't, like us, imagine the future or any other alternative reality. So they don't co-operate. Mostly they die, and that's hard to get used to. Neither of us liked that, but she handled it better than I did; she didn't struggle like me after it was over. She always smiled sadly and then moved on to the next case while I walked around in circles and suffered.

One day she went away.

She said goodbye to me with the certain air of someone who knew they'd done a really good job, had taken some potential and turned it into a perfect crop. She knew that I would be her. And so I became her, except for the crying part when animals died.

Gradually I set up shop in my parents' small conservatory at the back of their small house on Tannsfeld Road (number 58). When I pass it now, it doesn't look anything like a freelance animal hospital run by an under-age doctor! But then it was. The people came, and they came with their boxes and rags just like before. Most of the cases were hopeless, and that didn't change; but a few of them were not, and that didn't change either.

My parents were embattled, like all the rest, with mortgages and work and the thieving drudgery of all that. So they didn't have a lot of energy for the exotic. But with the animals they knew it was right. It was extreme and often it was very sad, but it was right and it was clear. And they could see in me the golden light of pure conviction.

They stepped aside for it, they gave it its true space and they respected it. When I was too tired to service the situation I had got myself into, it was my mother or my father who stayed up to keep the animals warm and to feed them.

The people kept knocking. I would take in the sparrow, feed it a little crushed aspirin. I'd put it at the end of a woollen sock and then hang it on the nail in the room, black and quiet under the stairs just like she showed me. The next day I would take it out, fix its wing and feed it. I felt as if I was connected to everything. Later on, when I became a painter of paintings, I tried to fill my paintings with love and with this refusal to give up that I learned from the wounded animals. That, I learned through her.

New York, November 2001

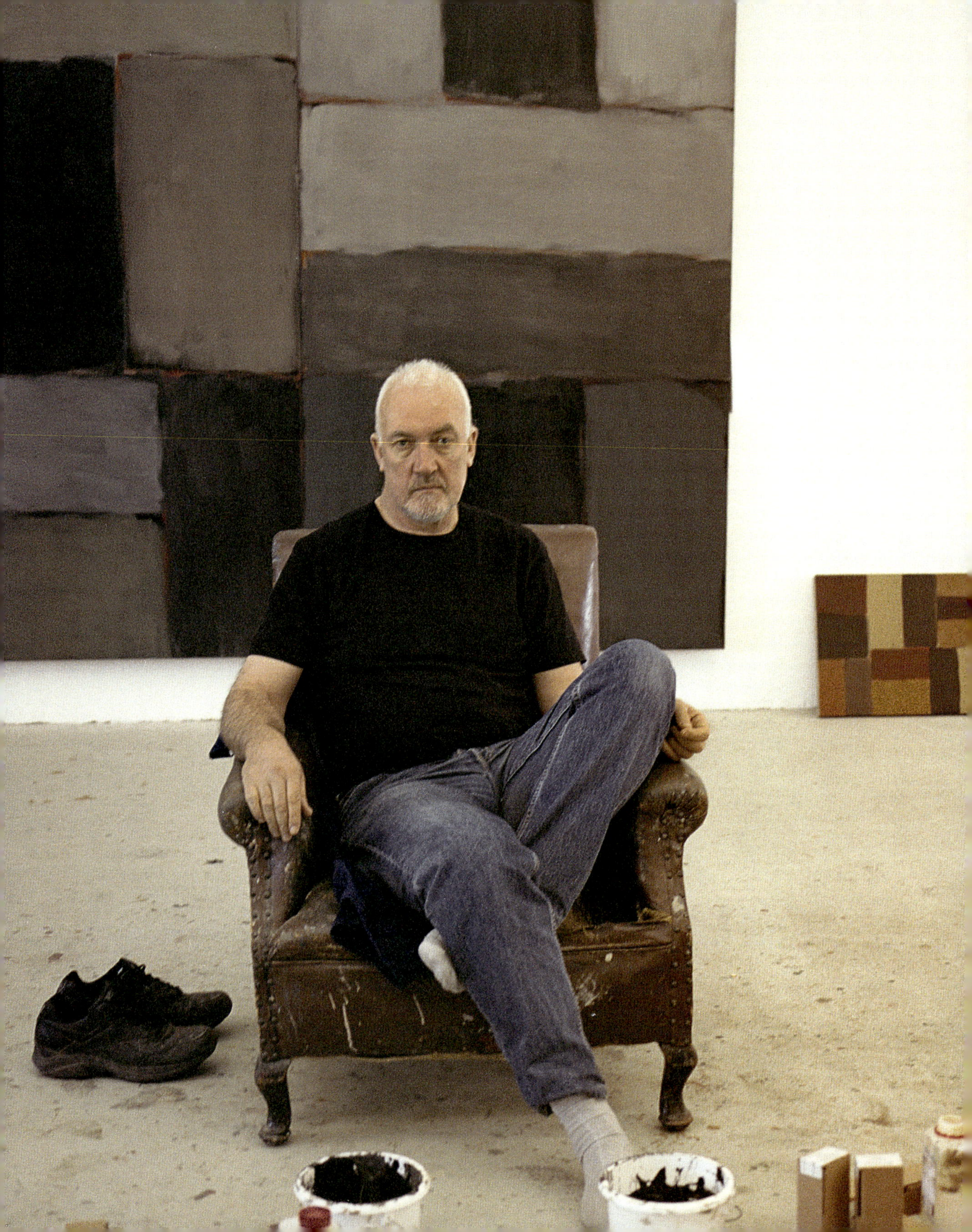

DAVIS: Why do you make art?

SCULLY: I think that I wanted to do something in my life that wasn't ordinary, that wasn't normal. I couldn't bear to live my life as a normal person – put another way, conventionally. So if I had a choice between living in suburbia and being dead, I would rather be dead. That implies I am going to do something with my life that is not ordinary. Then it is only a question of what that is. I could have gone into a number of different things.

When I was young, I was extremely political. I don't think there is such a thing as effective political art. There is only art that is politicized. You either do politics or you do not. I wasn't interested in pretending to be political while I was an artist. There is another aspect to it. I came from an Irish background and started out life as an immigrant. I went to a convent school, and I was yanked out because my parents had a big argument with them and I was put into a state school, which was full of emptiness and violence. In other words, I moved from something very exotic and difficult – but rich and full of mystery and the belief in another reality, in a reality that we couldn't see, that we could only imagine – into something that dealt with just what you could see. What you could imagine did not even seem to be a question. I found the banality of it crushing and the shock profoundly disturbing. I think at that point, taking all of those things into account, at some early moment in my life I decided I was going to be an artist.

ED: It was the most abnormal thing you could do, or the most adventurous?

SS: It was the most adventurous, in a sense the most dangerous, the most insecure and, potentially, the most profound thing I could do.

ED: The most life-affirming?

SS: Yeah, the most life-affirming; that is a very good way of putting it. So my work is really based on a kind of idealism and romanticism with beauty and form and profundity all wrapped up.

ED: It seems beauty is pejorative in art right now. Over the last three centuries there have been varying ideas about beauty in art. At the end of the eighteenth century the concept of beauty was that it was a direct and personal response. At the end of the nineteenth century the belief was, more or less, that beauty was only related to beliefs and moral judgements and not independent of other values. Now, at the end of the twentieth century, it doesn't seem beauty matters. Is beauty still important? Does it stand a chance in this next century?

SS: Beauty is denoted by a word that we have invented. We have invented the word out of necessity. Therefore, I think it is logical to believe we will continue to need to use that word in the future. I don't really believe in these kinds of ruptures. I don't think things change that much. The difference between the eighteenth and nineteenth centuries is quite great in some ways, but there are many things that carry over between the classicism and order of the eighteenth century and the Romanticism, or what one might argue is the romantic order, of the nineteenth century. There are certain characteristics that run through art. At the end of the twentieth century we are going through a phase, in this decade, where form and beauty do not seem to sit very well together or with anything else for that matter. However, it is interesting to note that only ten years ago we were saturated with nothing but a certain kind of emotive painting. Look how it has changed. It can change back again; it can turn on a dime, and it does. I'm pretty sure it will.

I think coming to the end of the century has something to do with, perhaps, a certain kind of closing down, knocking down, maybe a kind of hysteria that accompanies the closing of something. It is almost as if the ship of the twentieth century is about to go down, and everybody is scrambling around trying to see what they want to take off and how they are going to get off. Pretty soon the twenty-first century will start, and then we will want to start building up again; that is what I am interested in. I am interested in making something very affirmative. In times of crisis, and we are in a certain crisis now in relation to the kind of art I am interested in, it always comes down to a few people. Especially in art it comes down to a few people who are prepared to fight for something and prove a point. It is, of course, difficult to say in advance what is going to happen, what the outcome of this debate will be. I simply cannot think that human beings will be able to discard their desire and need for something that is sublime, something that transports them, takes them out of time, takes them out of the banality of the everyday world. I just can't see it happening with the virtual, because to make something is tremendously powerful in and of itself. Even before we get to the point where we judge its value, the fact that someone has gone to all the trouble to make something is very moving.

ED: At what point does something become beautiful? Does it only occur when 'true art' emerges, or is it simply an effect of creation, the process of creation?

SS: I think it is very difficult to decide, to quantify what goes into it. There was a period where people thought a certain shape in relation to the 'S' made beauty. The Serpentine river in London is based on that principle, and you would find this shape occurring in paintings, or people talking about paintings and looking for this shape. I don't believe you can do it like that. I am not sure I believe in 'schools' either. I am really an individualist. The question for me is whether or not something moves me and engages me. If I am moved and engaged by something, I find it beautiful. For me the term 'beautiful' is not pejorative; it is always affirmative. If I say I find it very convincing, even though it is ugly, the fact it is done with such authenticity and conviction makes it finally persuasive; it becomes beautiful. In other words, I don't think beauty is simply a question of appearances. It can come out of left field and redefine itself. It can be something you've never seen before, or it can be something you think you have seen before, like my work, that presents itself with another life.

ED: So there is no real standard for beauty.

SS: No, there is no standard any more. There is no way of formulizing it any more. There is no way of making a treatise to say in advance what beauty is; that is not the age we are in. I think we are in an age where there are many different options open. More or less everything is possible in art. There aren't really any barriers any more. There aren't really many barriers in socio-sexual behaviour any more. This all goes together, of course, as part of a cultural parcel. The only thing for me that distinguishes whether or not I think something is moving or profound or necessary or beautiful – they are all more or less the same thing to me – is whether it is convincing. And this in the end comes down to the character of the person making it, not the style in which it is made. I don't think that works any more.

    I can be convinced by a painting by Lucian Freud and very unconvinced by a painting by Eric Fischl, but they are both kind of expressionistic figurative paintings. One has a kind of force behind it, a moral fury, and a resistance I find interesting. The other is just full of acquiescence and complicity. Even though they look superficially similar, they have an entirely different effect on me. I can say the same thing about many abstract painters.

ED: Yet beauty plays a role in determining the value of art.

SS: Certainly.

ED: Is it playing less of a role than it used to?

SS: No, I think it plays an extraordinarily important role. I think it plays a crucial role. When I look at, for example, Bill Viola's piece on death [*Nantes Triptych*, 1992; page 67], I find it extraordinarily beautiful. Of course, it is a sad subject, but it's dealt with very sensitively and it ennobles us. That in itself is beautiful. That's why I say it is not a question of appearances. It is a question of whether something is, to my mind, humanistically convincing. That to me is a very important factor. I think what we need is an extraordinary humanistic assertion made by individuals, and that is our great necessity at this point in time. The whole thing, as something that can be codified, as it was, let's say in the time of Clement Greenberg, has become unravelled. The only thing that can put it back together again is extreme individual action. That is why I am so comfortable in a time like this, because I am so much of an individualist. In a sense, it is my time. It's a perfect moment.

I think I'm a good person to have around in a shipwreck, in the sense that culture has run aground. The ship of culture has hit a sandbank, or crashed. The stuff that is coming out of London, for example ... I can put it very briefly – people who talk about the "Brit Pack" always say the name should simply be changed to "Shit Pack", because it's a pack of shit. It is exploitive, superficial, opportunistic, hip, laconic, sarcastic, sardonic: everything I don't like. It's full of cynicism and opportunism. They work in a gang, which is another thing I don't like. So I am happy to stand against that as an individual without feeling outnumbered.

ED: There is no individual identity in that work because of the cohesiveness of them as a group?

SS: Precisely. It is a marketed package.

ED: In that case, have the artists gone too far?

SS: When you say "too far", I'm not sure what you mean.

ED: With people like Damien Hirst, is what he is doing in the name of art, or does it take on some other identity?

SS: Well, a lot of these people learned their lesson from Andy Warhol. Andy Warhol is not an artist whose work I like. In a sense, Andy Warhol was the visual artist equivalent of the method actor who becomes the subject. I do the same thing. My work is based on immersion. I am immersed in a very different set of parameters and aspirations. I am taking on the history of art; I'm immersed in it, and I'm immersed in what I make. I am what I make, in other words; there is no difference. He was the same way, but he was really a television ad, or a billboard. He had as much depth as a billboard. To talk about him as a profound person is ridiculous.

It might be argued, however, that he was profound in his emptiness and he was profoundly attached to something in the culture that drives out all content and all hope. He was profoundly attached to the dehumanization of the culture and embraced it and really became a part of it. He is like a blinking sign that says nothing except "I want to be famous." The emptiness of it is stunning. It is that emptiness and the slickness of it that have appealed to so many other artists who followed him. In that sense he is like [Marcel] Duchamp. Duchamp made it possible for people who couldn't compete with the Van Goghs of this world, and the

Matisses, and the Brancusis and the other great masters, he made it possible for them to be in the game as spoilers. Andy Warhol paraphrased this possibility in the 1960s and made it possible for people who understand the mechanisms of the media and the advertising world, and whose only ambition is to be famous, to do that. He offered a model upon which they can base their actions. He made it possible for a whole generation, and many generations of artists who follow him, to be unburdened. To my mind, it is the burden of art making that is so interesting. So I am absolutely the polar opposite of Warhol.

ED: For Warhol and this current generation of British artists it is more about product than process, whereas for you it is both process and product.

SS: It is process and product in relation to the weight and continuum of history. That's a huge burden to take on, but it's a burden that is interesting and can make our culture so interesting. To try to make a culture where people are detached from history is not only unrewarding but also potentially dangerous. It is like knowing nothing about the Parthenon, nothing about the birth of democracy, knowing nothing about the Age of Reason, knowing nothing about the Industrial Revolution, knowing nothing about the Holocaust. It makes for an empty life and for an empty culture. I think they are not even particularly concerned with product. What they're concerned with is the effect that something can have, and only that. It is a pure and unbridled form of capitalism. It is pure exploitation. To give one example, it is exactly the equivalent, in the political sense, of taking out as much as possible from the rainforest. Without any idea of what happened before and what could happen afterwards, it is like making art that has no sense of consequentiality. It is not only a question of its relation to history; I'm talking about history as something that is going to be in the future too. We're going to have more history in the future. What these guys are doing is trying to make five-year careers. It is pure capitalism.

ED: Whom should we fault for this? Should we fault the artist for doing this and getting away with it, or the viewer and collector for propagating a myth?

SS: I think one of the problems with democracy, which is generally good, I think we would all agree, is that you need more art to reach more people more easily. Now, if you take more art, to more people, more easily, that points towards the impossibility of maintaining its extraordinary place and position. With a genuine democratization of art, you cannot just have incredibly authentic artworks because the demand is so enormous and the machinery for it is so great. There are so many *Kunsthalles* in the world now, and there are so many people running around trying to fill them up with stuff that is attention-grabbing, without any thought about whether they are going to be interesting in six months let alone sixty years. So what you've got is a dangerous axis developing between the popularization of culture, which is called Pop culture, and how that can get into the art world and get into the whole art structure.

If that happens, as it has happened in England for very good reasons, to take a particular example, there is no true support for art. There is none. There aren't any collections being made in England. There aren't any museums being built. It's an image. It's like a confidence trick; it's an advertising campaign. There's nothing behind it. It's like having a mail-order catalogue or an image on a TV screen, but when you go to order it, there isn't anything there, because there's nothing behind it. That is one of the main reasons art has gone the way it has gone in England. In a sense, that is the only way it can go. If you have no museum structure, real authentic museum structure in a national sense, that energy has to go somewhere. It has to become simply an image of art and of an art culture. It is actually virtual over there. London is a great city that is a giant billboard for the country. London is bigger than England.

I think you have different problems in different countries. I travel a lot, so I have a lot of experience in this. It seems to me that in Germany, Spain and Italy it is a very different situation from England, or from London and New York. I see a great correspondence between London and New York, but I don't see a great correspondence between London and the USA. I think the USA has within it a lot of resistance, because the culture is different and is based on a more authentic fabric that can actually back up and support financially, and physically, a place like New York. The USA is a country with a much greater resource base for a start, a much greater industrial base, a much greater nature base, and it can back it up and support it. There are museums being built here, as we know; we're sitting in one that's being expanded. There is a belief in art. There are enough people to support that. It is a very different situation.

ED: Have these younger artists become oppressors, within the public at large, by creating art that is so highly personal and eventually impersonal and nonsensical? It seems they are foiling themselves by becoming rather élitist and that it defeats art and continues a fear of art.

SS: I certainly agree they are defeating themselves. I certainly agree that they represent, to a degree, the death of art. Not just the death of painting or sculpture, but the death of art as I understand it. And this has a strong relationship to all the things being said by Peter Plagens in the recent conference. [Peter Plagens, artist and critic, was a speaker at the 24th Annual Ruth K. Shartle Memorial Symposium, 'Writing About Art: A Closer Look at Art Criticism', held at the Museum of Fine Arts, Houston, on 31 October 1998. Other speakers were Arthur C. Danto, Libby Lumpkin and Frances Colpitt.] What has happened in one branch of culture is that you have a debasement of what I would call quality and authenticity. The success of that debasement sets an example for other people who follow to look at. It is a salutary lesson for them. They have to ask themselves a very tough question: do I want to be an artist?

When you have, for example, the blues singers in the United States being shamelessly ripped off by British rock-and-roll stars, like Elton John and the Rolling Stones, and watching these guys become zillionaires, and not only zillionaires but cultural icons, then you have got to ask yourself what is going on and what is it that the culture really wants. In the visual arts they borrowed a lot from the theatricality of movie sets and they've tried to make art into '*Kunsthalle* as adult fun house' so people can walk around and get a hit.

I saw an ad on TV in New York that impressed me greatly. A woman comes out of a show called 'The New York Experience'. I think it is a series of images and light effects and strobe lights and sounds. She comes out with a dazed, and ecstatically bedazzled, expression on her face saying, "It was fantastic. It was all those lights and sounds and everything." However, when you have all those lights and sounds and everything, serving nothing except the desire to impact on another human being, what you have is a series of empty experiences. This is the same as advertising, which is a deadening accumulation of information, sound bites and visual bites that, in a sense, disenfranchises and immobilizes and pacifies the population that leaves the television on all day. But they like it because it impacts on them. They don't make any judgement at all about what it does, whether it transforms their life, whether it enriches their life, whether it is three-dimensional, and whether it is humanistic, whether it calls to us or moves us in some way. That is not of importance; it is simply a question of whether it impacts. These are what I would call publicity bites. They want to be famous for a short while. They frankly don't care about making a body of work that they leave behind. I think that concept is under tremendous threat, but so is the concept of culture, unless we live in a world of TV culture.

To give you another example: if you see an early film by [Quentin] Tarantino – let's say *Pulp Fiction* – it is full of violence, and the violence is stylized. The violence is, in fact, emptied out of all its horror. It becomes amusing and entertaining. It's aestheticized. There's a certain kind of amoral pleasure, I guess, that can be gleaned from that. Not by me, I might add. But when he makes another film – *Jackie Brown* – without violence, you see what a load of crap it is. You see the characters in it are cardboard cut-outs. The acting in it is nothing; it is banal and flat. Without all the shock, the impacting part of it, it carries nothing. It's like a little piece of paper you could flick off the table and it's gone. And that is how substantial his films are without all the violence.

If you put shock into art, and you make shock the point, and you've gone to art school and have some kind of visual education, I imagine you will achieve shock. But that is the same as looking at ads all day. You go to the *Kunsthalle* in order to be impacted upon, not to be lit up as a human being, not to be engaged as a human being. It is extraordinarily short-sighted and hopelessly inadequate in relation to the subject of cultural history and how to add to it and make it better and bigger.

ED: It is like certain movies that are about the special effects and not telling a story.

SS: Right.

ED: How easy should art be? How much does one need to bring to it to gain an understanding? Do we need to know about its creation, its background? My feeling is that what we need now is much different than what we needed even ten years ago; that the viewer must be more sophisticated.

SS: I think that's correct. There is probably a lot more manipulation going on now, which is to the detriment of the viewer. The viewer, with the co-operation of the art establishment, is being assaulted and in a sense disenfranchised. The viewer is being bombarded and turned into a kind of passive target. As a viewer you have to be more aggressive and you have to fight back. You have in fact to fight for your own ground in an area where formerly you did not. The viewer cannot come to the museum with as much trust as they could formerly.

The values of the advertising world, the virtual media world, the world that assaults, have infiltrated the quality of the human personality. It is colluding with that. It is borrowing the same techniques and using those techniques, because they have been proven to be successful in the world of advertising or motion pictures, of a certain kind, where special effects and violence are the order of the day; squeezing out everything else that is more reflective and thoughtful. These films, the ones that are more reflective and thoughtful and beautiful at times, generally win the awards, but hardly anyone goes to see them any more. So the viewer now has to fight for his own humanism in an area where formerly it wasn't as necessary, which is quite a devastating thing to have to admit. Art no longer offers the sanctuary that it once did. It can, but you have to fight for it more because the enemy is already inside the walls.

ED: The viewer's response is even more important now than it ever was.

SS: With the advent of the avant-garde, the stakes were raised. That happened, obviously as we all know, at the beginning of the twentieth century, with André Breton making poems by throwing words up in the air; putting it all on you. Or Ad Reinhardt saying, "Well, what are you?" Now, the mechanisms of the world of greed and exploitation in art have polluted art. This is why Warhol is such an interestingly negative figure.

ED: Did Warhol ruin art?

SS: No, I don't think Warhol ruined art, because I don't find Warhol that important. You have to be very important to be able to ruin art.

ED: Even though he was so set on bringing the everyday, the commercial, into the realm of art that we now seemingly judge things only as being relevant by an immediate audience response? I feel such art is tied to a sense of commercialism and immediacy. It is all snippets and sound bites and special effects. It has become this very commercial thing.

SS: Well, it has all come out of advertising and the techniques of advertising.

ED: Which is something he took and ran with.

SS: Yeah, but before him we had the Dada artists, who were all spoilers. This isn't just Duchamp. André Breton was a huge influence. They certainly tried to bring down the house of art. To be perfectly frank, there's no way in the world that any of those people could live with Picasso, Matisse, Miró; they couldn't be in the same room with them. They had to invent another game. They had to become spoilers. They invented a way to be purely famous. That's the key issue – to be purely famous, devoid of work. The name André Breton is enormous in relation to what he gave us. It's as big as the name Brancusi, who left a magnificent body of work. That's the mechanism at work already, you can see it. One left something quite minor; the other left something unreservedly major. But they're almost as famous as each other as names. That's very interesting. It's kind of like the difference between something that is solid and something that is inflated, and they are both the same size. But one has density and the other one has not.

ED: The difference between one of Brancusi's stone columns and Warhol's floating pillows. One has substance and one is full of hot air.

SS: Yeah, yeah, it's just full of air.

ED: Does art have an obligation to inform about social issues? A moral or social responsibility?

SS: No, not in that way. If you want to inform about social issues, you should fight for those issues on a social issue platform. That's the medium, and I don't think that has anything to do with art. That's not the job of art. But one could say, for example, that some art has in it a moral character, a kind of morality. But that's not talking about specific moral issues. It's just full of rightness: not righteousness, but rightness. Which could also be called beauty, depending on how right it is.

ED: I am interested in the concept of what makes art powerful and successful. Sometimes art, as we've seen in the current generation of artists, can be very powerful in its immediate impact, but it is not necessarily successful art. Is successful, powerful art then simply a melding of what one desires with what one wants to see represented?

SS: That's an interesting way of putting it. The question is, is art something that meets your desire at some point in space and time?

ED: Is this current generation filling some unspoken desire?

SS: Without question. You see that begs the question, "What is the desire?" Culture is a very fragile thing. We could easily go into the dark ages where we don't have any art. Why not? It happened before. That's why you need to know about history. It can easily happen if people's horizons are so low and so flat, and become so pacified and desensitized, that they can't work any more for something deeper, they will end up with that kind of work masquerading as an art experience. That will be a very, very bad period in art.

      My own work has gained an audience as I've got older. I've become more able to take for granted that my work is going to be shown all over the place. This implies it meets the desire of a rather large number of people. So, of course, in the culture, in a true democracy, as is right, there are a large variety of desires out there. To give you a crude example, if the desire for pornography were to meet with an overwhelming and positive response, then the only films we would ever have would be pornographic films. The people that didn't make pornographic films would be people who subsidized themselves and found ways to do it and were offering the voice of resistance; and those films might never get distributed, but they would get made, I am sure. At least, that is what has happened so far in our history, except with the dark ages. I'm not saying that what I do will become the majority voice, but I'm not saying it won't either. I don't really know how the game is going to play out. I will do it anyway, because that is what I believe in and I will fight for what I believe in.

ED: You would then consider yourself one of the resistors to the latest generation's 'pornography'.

SS: Yeah, but they could also say they are resisting the kind of work I make, which supports a certain view of history that they don't agree with. So they could see themselves as the resistors.

ED: Is it the beginning of the Sixties all over again? Are you now the establishment?

SS: Well, it depends what you mean by "establishment", because we've all got our different ideas about it. I think they're the establishment.

ED: Because of the capitalism of it?

SS: Yeah, and the kind of tidiness of it, the way it is all marketed. That's a real conspiracy involving money, advertising techniques, the buying and selling of work, using auction houses in order to pump up prices, the bullying of minor institutions to show it. It seems like the establishment to me. What I do, I tend to do as an individual. I have friends and other artists that I admire, but then I'm supported by a lot of people, there's no question about that. And I'm supported by a lot of museums. So then they could say you're supported by all these museums, so you're the establishment. In the end, what really matter are the values you believe in or, to put it another way, the way you put it earlier, what is the desire? What is the desire searching for?

Now, to talk about something more positive, instead of talking about these negative influences, like Warhol, let's talk about Rothko. Rothko obviously satisfies another desire in the culture, a desire for beauty and a sense of spirituality and a sense of precariously tragic drama. And Ad Reinhardt satisfies another desire. Sam Hunter, the art historian, once told me he had been very supportive of the Abstract Expressionists, but when the Pop artists came along, he supported them. He was walking down the street one day and he met Rothko, and Rothko refused to be friendly with him and was angry with him and said he had betrayed everything they had been working for to transform American art.

ED: Transcendental ...

SS: Yes, transcendental ... that could stand alongside the Italian painters of the Quattrocento. Sam Hunter couldn't understand his anger, and he was talking to me when he said this. He said, "You know, you always have to go with the new thing." As a critic, there is an example of someone who, like Warhol, offers no resistance. You can just roll over him without consequence and he will collaborate. To me, this is a little bit like living in France in 1940 and saying, "OK, this is the way the situation is now, let's see what we can make out of it." I think resistance is a very important component of culture. Without this human capacity to resist, to have the mental strength to be in the minority, you can't bring it back again. It's always being brutalized. It's always being attacked, assaulted. The assault comes in many different forms, shapes, colours and sizes. It's often subtle.

ED: And say "I am an individual."

SS: It's not a question of being fashionable. As an artist you have got your whole life to work, and you can't worry about whether or not you're in fashion. Fashion is nothing – it's transitory. If I wanted to be in fashion, I would be designing clothes. Or I would be making a certain kind of art. Then, of course, there are other artists who have a problem with being ... let's say, older. As you go through life you're presented with different possibilities at different points in your life, and you have to realize what those possibilities are. When you're fifty, you don't have the possibility to be twenty, but you do have the possibility to be fifty and everything that that means; all the accumulated power that you have and the vitality that you still have. That's a pretty good time to put things together. And whether you're in fashion or out of fashion is not so important.

ED: You mentioned Rothko and spirituality. You have said that art is a non-denominational religion ...

SS: It can be.

ED: Art has served religion, but when did art embody religion? Was there a certain point in modern history when art attained its own religious state?

SS: I think that point is [Kasimir] Malevich [1878–1935]. When he put a figure on a ground with all the severity of a Russian icon painting but with none of the descriptiveness and authoritarianism of one: in that moment it was liberated.

ED: It went to a higher level.

SS: It went to a level that could be, I'm not going to say higher, but it went to a level that was more inclusive. A painting by Malevich is not excluding anybody, whereas a Russian Orthodox icon painting is excluding a lot of people. It is excluding a Jew, for instance, or an American Indian or a gypsy. They are all excluded to one degree or another. They are included in other ways. They can appreciate the beauty of the line and the colours, and the shapes and the context of where it is, but they cannot indulge in a complete relationship with that artwork. With the advent of abstraction that became possible, and that moment is Malevich – a very important artist, of course.

ED: This created a worshipping of art in relation to the world in general, whereas the Russian icon stands alone and becomes exclusionary ...

SS: It's also very authoritarian and doctrinaire. But I don't think an abstract painting is something you worship. It is something that is part of the world. It is as if the spirituality in art stepped off a pedestal, or from behind a sheet of glass, and has joined the world of the living. That, of course, is the contradiction with it because many people find it more exclusionary than an icon painting. That is the contradiction with art. With intention and result there is very often conflict. That is one of the issues in abstraction I have tried to address; to use abstraction, I'm not fighting for abstraction. Those battles have already been fought. I'm using those victories to make an abstraction that is, in fact, more relaxed, more open and more confident. I take it for granted I don't need to abstract reality any more; that has already been done. That would be the equivalent of reinventing the wheel. What I am doing is using all the ground that has already been gained; I'm occupying it to try to make something that is more expressive and that relates to the world in which we live. In that sense my abstraction is quite figurative. It is not very remote.

ED: It is deeply connected to life.

SS: Yeah, it's deeply connected to life; many aspects of it connect it to life.

ED: For me, that guides your work and provides it with a broad humanity that isn't found in a lot of abstract painting.

SS: No, that marks it out, I think. That separates what I do and what is comfortable and uncomfortable for me. For example, I was in a show in New York called *New Abstract*

Painting. The show was written about by David Carrier. He talked about all of the work and then said, "Sean Scully's work separates itself. It has more in common with Richard Serra's weight and density of material than anything else in the exhibition." My work also does not dialogue with some of the concerns of the other abstractionists. With the show across the street I know that what those people are trying to do is dialogue with video art, with the kind of images, the kind of colour you see on the screens at the cinema. [Scully is referring to *Abstract Painting Once Removed*, held at the Contemporary Arts Museum, Houston, 3 October–6 December 1998.] I believe that is absolutely the wrong way to go about making a painting. The whole point of painting is that it has the potential to be so humanistic, so expressive. To give that up is a tremendous mistake, because then what you are doing is imitating forms of technological expression which can be manifested more directly, more efficiently and, frankly, more beautifully, in their original form. It's quite sad; artists who are trying to, let's say, de-express the brushstroke. It is the opposite of what I am trying to do. I want my brushstrokes to be full of feeling; material feeling manifested in form and colour.

ED: There again, your work is about the process and the end product, whereas the work in that show is quite often just about craft.

SS: You see, there you have hit the nail on the head. What has happened to painting, a lot of painting – I wouldn't say what has happened to painters, there are a lot of very good painters out there (Terry Winters is a very good painter) – is that it has been reduced to the level of craft. It has turned into craft. I see so many paintings around now where people are using this technique of overlapping transparency that the Italian wall painters use, that the house painters use and have been for the last hundred years. There is nothing special about it. The fact that you put it on canvas does not make it more interesting. There is a strange detachment in that, and it is very second-rate. And frankly, it is a form of cowardice. It is so lacking in any kind of guts to take the medium of painting and make it so limp, and to exchange feeling for irony is not a very interesting trade-off.

ED: Where must art first touch an individual – the intellect or the soul?

SS: For me it is very easy to say the soul. It is the attachment to the soul that we deeply need. It is what moves us. It is not simply a question of what makes sense; it is deeper than that. When that inner part of ourselves is engaged, we are truly alive.

ED: Are you religious?

SS: Religious? No. I would make a distinction between being religious and being spiritual. I think a person who is spiritual is somebody who is trying to exchange a religious belief for a spiritual search. I am against brand names basically. I think that is one of the most interesting things about going into the twenty-first century.

I really believe the twenty-first century will be a very spiritual century. A lot of things are going to be dealt with in a way that is very different; a lot of the struggles of the twentieth century are over. I also hope a lot of the violence that accompanied those struggles in the twentieth century is over. In the way that the twentieth century took for granted and used the battles and the ground that was won in the Industrial Revolution in the nineteenth century. I think we are going to do the same thing with a lot of the discoveries that were made in the twentieth century and use them differently. Take them for granted, and use them with a greater effectiveness and a greater sense of responsibility about where we are on the planet and what kind of world we want to live in and how open that is to everybody. I'm basically against anything that is exclusionary. I try to make my work accessible if I can, as open as I can or certainly as honest as I can. I try and speak about it as directly as possible without, of course, making it simplistic.

ED: Your paintings have a geometric centre, which implies a certain precision, rigidity and construction. Yet the shapes within your work tend to have soft edges. For me this lack of absolute precision and very clean lines suggests a sense of freedom, freedom from total authoritative order. This is something that seems to have held back a lot of the more formal abstract painters of our time. Does some of the humanity in your work stem from the basic tenet that, despite being considered abstract, it contains recognizable forms ... forms that everyone can see, has seen and therefore can, on some level, connect with more quickly?

SS: I recognize two questions in there. One of them is, I guess, you're asking me if I resist the closure of perfection, or do I associate perfection with some kind of authoritarianism? Which I do. One of the most interesting things I have ever heard was something that Albert Einstein said, which is, "When I know what something is, I don't have to think about it any more." I don't want to present that kind of closure. I'm not very fond, for example, of Donald Judd's work. It represents a certain closure to me. I know it has a certain kind of ambiguity about it in relation to other objects in the world, and I know how it operates, but still it is too much like a lump of furniture. It is too inert.

ED: Too finite.

SS: Yes, it's too finite. I try to make paintings that everybody can relate to in terms of their drawing, it's a very simple kind of counting. It's based on rhythm or simple architectural structures. You can also relate it to music, rhythmical musical structures or mathematical structures. I'm not making them complicated. They are very simple. Within that the painting of them can be quite emotive. So the emotive painting is, in effect, rendering something; it's attached to something that in fact takes the place of the object in figurative painting. That is why I believe people lock into my work so naturally. It has the same kind of dynamic in it as a Matisse painting. Matisse is painting a chair, and you see the way it is painted in relation to what is being painted and what colour it is.

What I am painting is a simple divisional structure, but you see the way it is painted, what colour it is painted, and how many times it is painted in relation to that simple structure. So, in fact, the dynamic is the same. I've re-established something that I think had been broken – the abstractionists kept building on abstraction, and I think they forgot what it was originally based on. What I did, basically, was I went back to what it was originally based on. Then I just had something that I could compose with. So in that sense my painting is completely open. That is why I can make so many different compositional forms. It comes very naturally out of the way I draw and work and paint; one thing leads to another, which leads to another. I'm not really, in that sense, in a corner, which is what happens to a lot of abstract painters – they end up in a corner. People can kind of look at it and enjoy it because it has a kind of open vitality. I'm very free to paint them the way I want to paint them, with many, many layers. The paintings, in that sense, are not absolute. There is nothing authoritarian about them.

As one critic said, which I thought was interesting, they are like intimate paintings on a giant scale. They maintain the connection with painting; they don't give that up. At the same time, the language I use is the language of the contemporary world you can find anywhere: on computer screens, things are arranged in rows and lines. It's simple numerical order. If I stand in the subway in New York and I look down, everything is repeated. That's how we put the world together now. And that is how I put my paintings together. In that sense they are in complete accord with the contemporary world, so people can enter them quite naturally.

ED: They're not formula paintings.

SS: No. No, they are abstract paintings and they are quite lyrical. But they remind you of things that exist in the world. They remind you of the way the world is ordered.

ED: Would you consider them traditional?

SS: They are traditional in the sense that they make a connection, certainly, with the history of painting. One can think about other painters when one is looking at my paintings. If you want to you can think about Velázquez and you can think about Rothko, but you can also think about Cimabue when you think about Rothko; that is part of Rothko's greatness.

ED: A few years ago, in his essay on the *Catherine* paintings, Carter Ratcliff said you want to be "a painter who proposes amendments to painting's constitution". ['Sean Scully: The Constitutive Stripe', *Sean Scully: The Catherine Paintings*. Modern Art Museum of Fort Worth, 1993, p. 23. Arthur C. Danto and Stephen Henry Madoff also wrote essays for the exhibition catalogue.] What is the state of that constitution now, almost four years later?

SS: At this moment in time – and one has to remember it is only a moment in time which will pass, and then it will be followed by another moment in time – and without in any way implying what the next moment will be like, I would say the constitution of painting is a little insecure. That is really because it has been told that it is insecure. It is like a rumour.

ED: Is that particular to the USA or the American and European art communities, which are generally considered the leaders?

SS: In Germany and Spain, and France perhaps, and Italy, it is a little bit different from the USA. There is a more balanced view at the moment between painting and sculpture and other forms of visual expression. But then they have a greater achievement in painting to refer to. So, of course, they are working from a very different cultural background; in fact, a stronger cultural background.

At the moment the question for painting is whether or not … it is a little bit like the question for painting at the end of the nineteenth century. At the end of the nineteenth century the question was, should all painting imitate photography? Should all painters paint like Georges Seurat? (And hundreds of them did, much to the disapproval of Seurat, who turns out to be a great painter, but not the greatest painter – the painter probably most in tune with the medium of photography, but not the greatest painter.) Now that is an interesting lesson that we can learn from, certainly a lesson I learned something from as a painter.

I would say the constitution of painting at the moment is fragile because a lot of painters believe they have to correspond with something that they see as inevitable – the demise of the authentic handmade surface that is representing the work of art made by a human being directly. I don't necessarily see that as the case … well, obviously, because I fight for it so emphatically. I see the constitution of painting as being somewhat re-jigged in favour of some kind of truce. It is a little like the American Indians having to give up a little more land, then a little more and a little more. I think the painters believe that they have to give up a little more land and then everything will be all right. But as we know from the history of the USA, that is not going to make it all right. Appeasement is a process that becomes a thing in itself; more appeasement requires, in fact, more appeasement, which is then followed by more appeasement, which is, of course, not what I'm doing. I would like to assert even more strongly than I did when I was showing at the time of that essay by Carter – the building aspect of it – that I'm going to try and emphasize more of the painting aspect of it. I think that is what is needed: for somebody to be able to make painting that is convincing and which sets an example. That cuts out a position, without having to collude with the virtual.

ED: Is there room in the realm of art for technology? You are fighting the good fight by keeping the human touch in painting, but is there room for technologically based art, whether it is purely about the technology or used to create the image?

SS: Is there room for technology in art? Yes, I'm sure there is. We had another age of technology in art in the 1960s, when we had all the kinetic art. There isn't that much of it around anymore is there? At the time it was red hot, it was almost impossible to say "art" without using the word "kinetic". It is a bit like saying "donut" without saying "Dunkin'", the correspondence was that close. But, yeah, sure, I made a reference to Bill Viola, whose work I like a lot. There are one or two other video artists I like a lot. If they can find a poetic language for what they are doing using that medium, that is fine. One of my favourite media in the world is film, so obviously I believe that you can use technology. If I wasn't a painter, I would definitely be a film-maker, but I would not be a video artist. To generalize, which I know is unfair, I think video is like stunted film. A fully rounded expression of what you can do with a camera and sound and people inside the little box is actually film. It's called film; we've had it around for quite some time. There have been some great films made, but can you use all this to make installation art? Yeah, I'm sure you can. I think Joseph Beuys, for example, is a great artist. I love Joseph Beuys's work. That's not technological, but it uses a lot of Duchampian ideas. But it is not necessary for me to do that. I think it is not interesting to do that if you are a painter.

To invoke Clement Greenberg's words again, what one has to do is realize the full potential of the medium within which one is working. It is not to the advantage of painting to imitate another art form. It's ridiculous. A painting is not plugged into the wall. It cannot compete on those terms. It's a little bit like black people trying to be like white people back in the 1950s. They were on a beating to nothing. They were using the wrong terms. They were all trying to straighten their hair. What is the point of trying to straighten your hair if your hair is not straight in the first place? You are working against yourself when you do that. There is room for everything. I'm not telling anyone else what to do; I'm not boss of the art world. But I believe that in order to make a case for painting, one has to use the natural advantages of painting and not confuse it with something else. You can't get hoodwinked into a position of weakness. You cannot be apologetic. If you are apologetic, you are lost before you start. If you are going to make installation art, then you have to do it without being sorry or having to apologize that you are not making a painting. But the converse also applies. You can do certain things with painting that are unique to painting that you cannot do with anything else. With a painting you can contain within borders a lot of experience, narrative, emotion, poetry, idea, thought, time, references and so on, all within a frame. You can't do that with installation art. But you can do something else. In other words, everything has its own set of rules and opportunities. Painting has a unique potential to stop time and compact feelings and experience.

You have to realize yourself where your own strengths are, where your own weaknesses are, what you can do and what you can't do. Picasso couldn't be an abstract painter; that wasn't his strength. His strength was that he was a great figurative painter. That is why he could never convert to abstraction. The fact that Picasso recognized that about himself and realized that and was prepared to be old-fashioned at a certain point in his life is a great power.

ED: It goes along with the line from the blues song we've talked about.

SS: "Whatever you is, be it." That is it, you have got to be that, and not be something else. You have to work to your own advantages, not disadvantages.

ED: It also goes back to the idea of resistance and not caving in.

SS: Greenberg generally is not a person I agreed with. But that doesn't matter, that isn't the point. Greenberg had the personal power to be in the minority and he ended up in the minority, but he still defended his position very eloquently. That is why he is a great critic, even though, in a certain sense, he was defeated in his own lifetime. In another sense, though, he is still greater than the people that defeated him are. It is not a question of being right or wrong; there isn't any right or wrong. That's a good point to end on.

Text copyright © 1999, Journal of Contemporary Art, Inc., and the authors

Liliane Tomasko
Sean Scully
Mooseurach, Germany, 2002

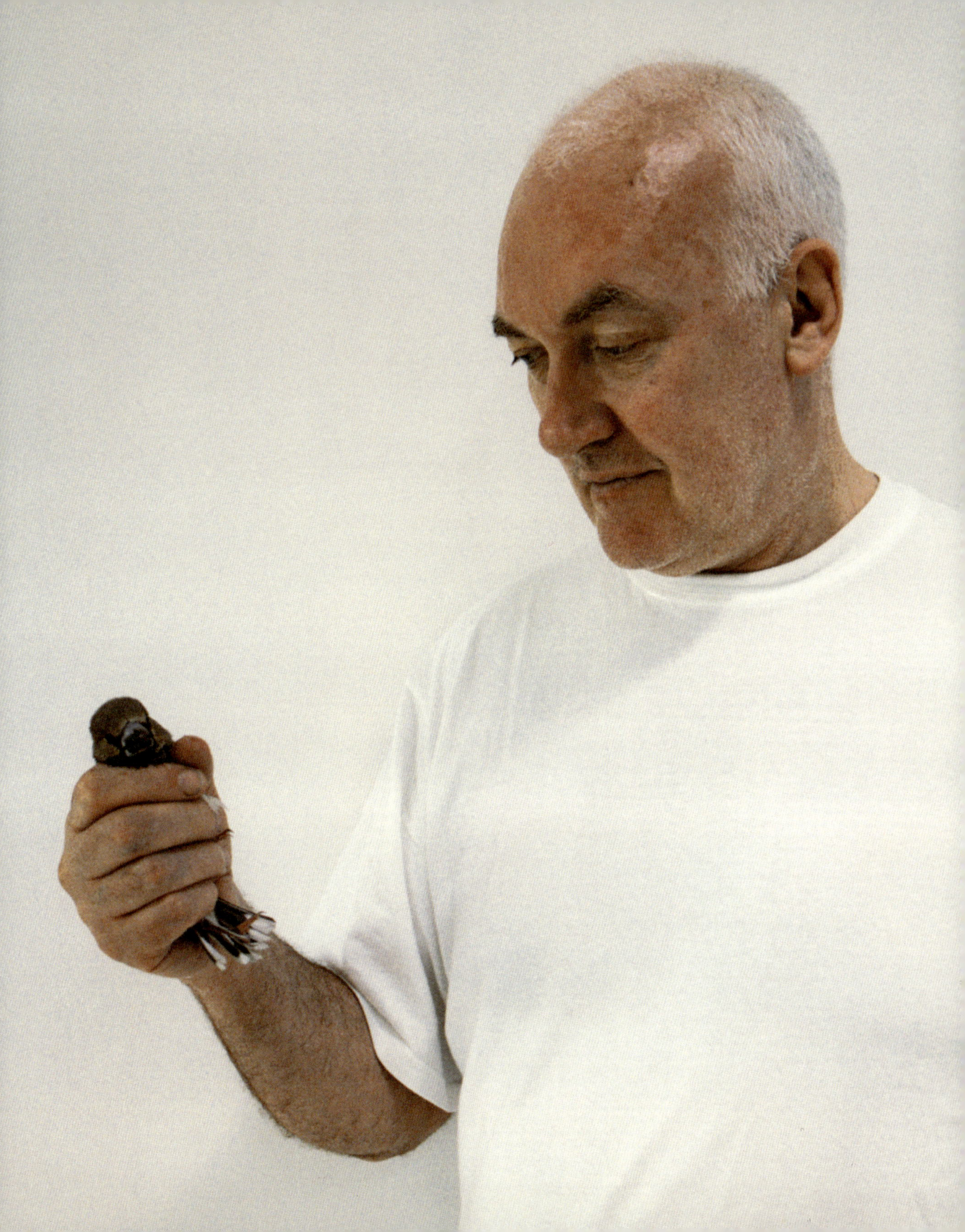

I spent much of my misguided adult life emulating my noble grandfather. A great Scully who hanged himself from the beam of the barracks building where he had been 'pressed' into the British Army. Rather than submit to this, he took his own life, as an act of utter disobedience. What they call now a "conscientious objector". The image of this filled me with power and pride. There was, in fact, another version of the same event which describes a mentally ill young man who was simply found hanged. Seeking ancestral inspiration, I, of course, preferred the first version. I myself intended never to be in the British Army, and indeed I never was. And although I had been brought up (or dragged up) in London, which wasn't so bad either, as far as inner cities go, I was descended from a wild and aristocratic past that was based in Tipperary. I was the issue of something mythic, and I was its heir. The one who would correct the wounds and insults of our tribal past. I would restore to us what we had lost. I would paint it into place. And place it into the present, as a picture of what should have been and now is.

It was only five years ago, after I had turned myself into the Irish warrior poet, that I discovered that my heroic grandfather was not my grandfather after all. And that my father, full of rage, had lived his life as the little prince of five older sisters, though he in fact was a bastard.

My grandmother, alone, tragically abandoned, and mourning the death of her three-year-old daughter who had died of an illness the way children did then, had fallen into the arms of her dead husband's best friend to be impregnated with my father. And his name wasn't Scully at all; he was Jimmy Myles. He wasn't an educated coach painter; he was a bookkeeper who was training to be a priest and a man of the cloth. An opportunistic numbers man who had slid his hand up the dress of a desperately grieving woman. And subsequently caused her in concert with her political views (she wasn't a radical republican) to be pushed out of Clonmel with my father as a three-year-old, stumbling toward the quayside with her five daughters and all their bits and pieces. Or, as she later said, I left in the clothes I stood up in and no more. There in 1924 they took the boat to England, where not everybody knew absolutely every facet, no matter how trivial, of everybody else's life, troubles, losses and secret pleasures. There in London this warrior woman rented a giant old house from a butcher on Holloway Road and worked eighteen hours a day cooking, cleaning and renting rooms.

Jimmy Myles later became a baker, which I suppose is a sculptor of sorts. I've made sculpture myself, so that must be the blood connection. However, recently I've developed an allergy to bread, which represents, I suppose, a negative dough connection. Either way, it all seems weird now. My father once met his father on the streets of Clonmel, where he went on holiday aged nine. Jimmy Myles tousled the hair of his son, said he was a sweet boy and moved on. An act of proto-minimalism.

In 1915 the British Liner RMS *Luisitania* left New York for Liverpool with 1,959 souls on board. The Germans saw her as a threat, as she had a small amount of ammunition on board. So Walter Schwieger, the commander of submarine U-20, sank her near Cork. Of the passengers on board only 764 were saved. My grandmother went down to the Port of Cork, and there she found a big sign offering rewards for the bodies of victims. Fifty pounds for an American, twenty pounds for an English one. And two pounds for an Irish one. She wasn't pleased to see relative worth so bluntly posted. However it occurred to me recently that by simply obtaining an American passport I'd become twenty-five times as valuable as I used to be. Dead of course. But nevertheless a definite step in the right direction.

All my life I'd been stealthily striding the inner city urban centres of Europe and America as a knight: defender of the weak. But now, of course, I understand I'm not El Cid, saviour of Spain. I am Don Quixote, who falls off his horse and lands on his ass. Though I can still be a defender of the weak; that remains an option.

It's easy to blame these things on the English. They ruined Ireland; they made all the men drunk. Though in this case it won't quite cover the problem. And anyway, all those English are dead and part of history, and we are living and part of the present. So one thing doesn't have much to do with the other. Well, it does, but who are we going to blame? We all have one thing in common: we're born into the present.

The English Army killed my would-have-been grandfather. Except that without Jimmy Myles and his amorous sympathies I wouldn't exist. Life is life, and the absence of life is nothing except that absence. Thus, even though there's been a tremendous misunderstanding, and I'd modelled myself on somebody who existed but was only connected to me existentially (so to speak), I am here. Don Quixote or not, I am here. So it only remains for me to thank Jimmy Myles.

New York , March 2005

We left Alice Springs in a four-wheel-drive Japanese jeep, and we bounced up the nearly endless flat red stripe that connected the bottom of Australia with the top. This is called Darwin. If you go too slow, the ridges that run from left to right on the dust road will slowly dismantle your vehicle through vibration, so you have to speed up until you are more or less land-surfing. It's kind of like driving a boat on dust. When the road trains (which are massive 50-metre trucks) come the other way, one is obliged to take note of the road because pretty soon it is a matter of working from memory. It seems that the red dust cloud you find yourself in will last for ever. But every time, eventually, the road reappears. There are dead kangaroos that couldn't get out the way lining the red road. They seem to be about every kilometre. And they lie sadly on the verge, with rigor mortis regularity. I said to Lily that the government was probably moving them around, in an even distribution to stop your enjoyment of the landscape, whilst marking off the distance for your convenience.

We got stopped by a cop car. They asked us if we'd seen a young aboriginal boy on the run. We said no. But even if we had, we would have said no. The cop said, "No worries". I was thinking that "no worries" would depend on where you were, and what you were doing. Anyway, I said I wasn't worried, and I was happy to be able to say it. After quite a few hours we turned off the red road, namely Stuart Highway, for Yuendumu.

The red road turned brown, but the dust level remained constant. At an intersection we stopped to ask a bunch of guys where the art centre was. It was actually situated diagonally north-west from the intersection. One guy said we should go straight on, and his friend said we should turn left. If you took these two instructions and put them in a bucket and stirred them up, you'd get north-west. But if you only took one guy's idea and dropped the other guy's idea, you'd go the wrong way, which implied to me that they really do everything together. They're communal. And they're not competitive either, because both guys were half-right and together they were completely right! So we went straight on and turned left.

When we got near the place, we asked an old lady where Mrs Alfonso's house was. And her answer was that she was painting. We asked her if Mrs Alfonso was painting. She said that Mrs Alfonso wasn't painting and that she was a white lady, and that she herself was painting. Since we could see clearly that she was walking down the street and therefore not painting, we deduced that this elderly dear was in the gang of painters that worked around the art centre. So we attempted the question again. This time the response was significantly different. She reaffirmed that she was painting. However, she told us she wanted to pick up her pension, and she'd like a ride to the Community Services office. So we politely asked her to join us in the Japanese four-wheeler, and she climbed in. Ten minutes later we were outside her destination, and she was saying goodbye and sliding out of the vehicle. She had about a hundred flies with her that mainly circled her head; where she went, they went. So they came in the truck with her, but they never left her. And there was no attempt on the part of the flies to strike up a friendship with us. As she left the truck so did the flies, as if they were unable to depart her force-field and she was somehow their human leader. We asked her once again if we were anywhere near Mrs Alfonso's house, and she said no. But she also said goodbye. And that was sweet.

It was 'sports day' in Yuendumu. I looked over at the basketball court in the main square, where there were four boys and a girl playing a game that was not

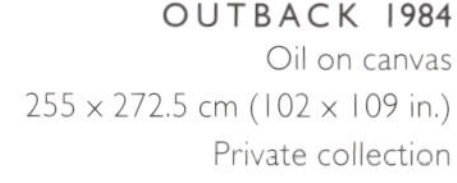

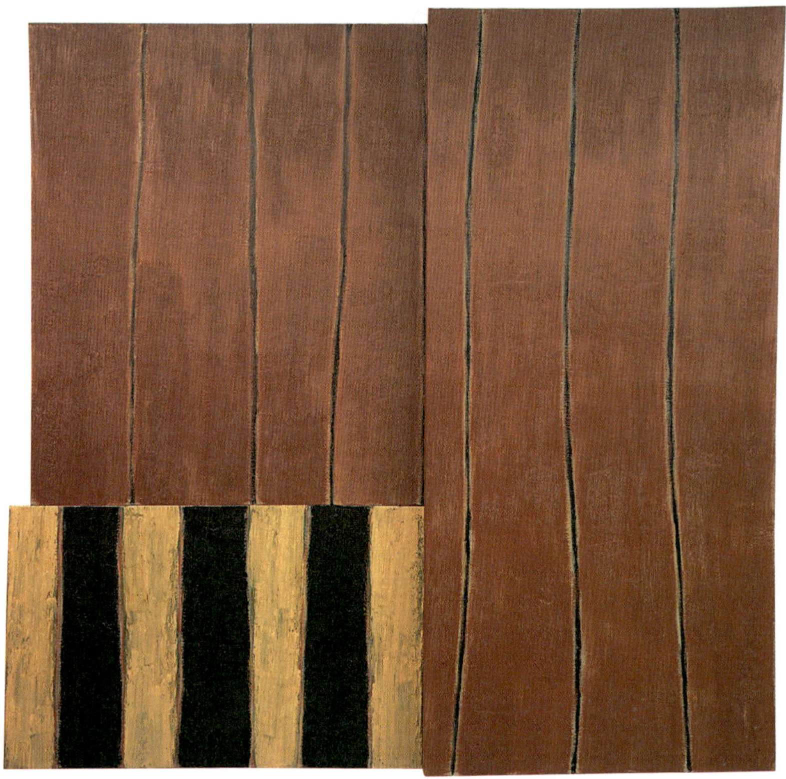

basketball. Plus, they all seemed to be playing on the same team, though I wasn't really sure. The game consisted of passing a rugby ball around a little bit, running, but not too much, and then kicking the ball so it went somewhere near the basketball hoop. I liked the game a lot, and I thought maybe it was an invention. Soon to be played in Ireland on national TV. Eventually, after a few detours, we found our way back to where we picked up our sweet old lady friend. There we parked the car because we were, in fact, right outside Mrs Alfonso's house.

We met Mrs Alfonso in her wooden house, where she was surrounded by young women, who were all twenty-five. I could see from her striking art collection that she had already stolen most of the painted treasures from the artists working at the art centre. This upset me quite a lot because, being an art expert, as I am, I

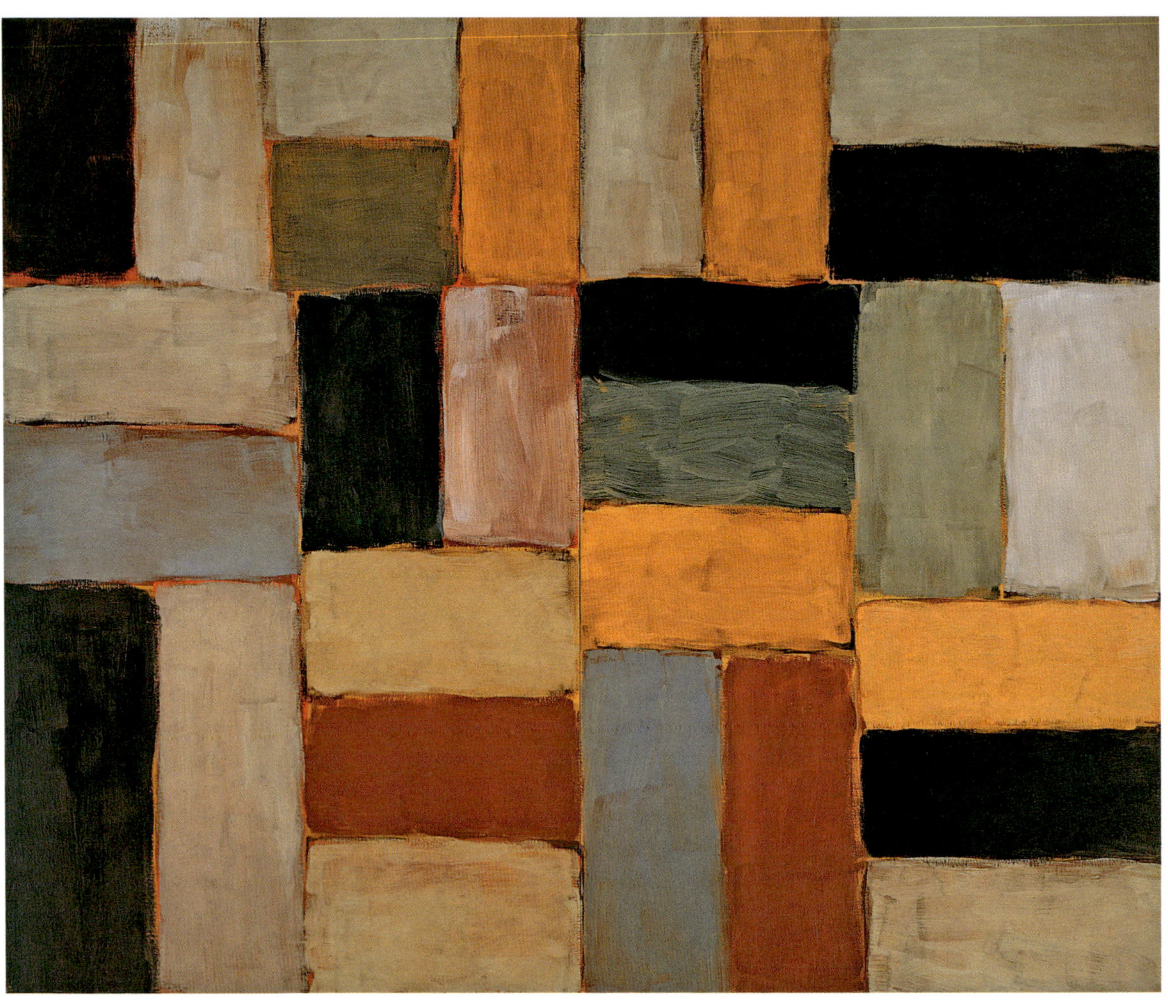

know it when I see it. So I was in dress rehearsal for what I assumed was soon to be the real thing: getting upset. However, I kept smiling, and since they really didn't know me, the ladies probably thought I was weird and not ready to be unhappy. Everything in the house, hung on the walls, was domestic-size and vibrantly beautiful. Made with a lot of red, as if Monet and Kandinsky were married and making paintings together. I decided to look on the bright side, just in case I was wrong about the paucity of what would be left after Mrs Alfonso had her way. So we had a cup of coffee, surrounded by the girls who had come to the centre to be slaves.

After the coffee break we were taken out to meet the artists, like all the other artists that visit. The first one was Paddy Stuart. Paddy sat on the floor finishing his almost finished eagle painting. The footprints of the eagle surrounding the nest, which was in the centre of the picture. Painted in, more or less, black and white, in the dot style, which has its mirror in Europe in Impressionism. Paddy sat with his legs crossed and his hips wide open, like the holy men in India and the dancers in New York, so that his knees rested effortlessly against the stone floor of the patio out back.

I was thinking about 'out back', because we were in the outback and we were out back. Out at the back of the main building. I painted a painting for Australia, I think, though I'm still not entirely sure. I called it Outback, because it went out and then it went back closer to the wall. Or it went back and then out, depending on what you like; whether you like going in or coming out. Personally I like it both ways. I painted it in the 1980s, when I was thinking about Australia and the idea of it and the colour of it and its markings. It was painted in dirt red that I imagined was like the ground in Australia, with deep black lines scored into it, left between the red paint of the regular rhythmical wide bands. I imagined back then that these would be like burnt sticks. Now it all seemed strangely accurate. The red they use in the outback is made from the ground. And so is the yellow. The yellow ochre and the red ochre are found as rocks in the ground, and then rubbed into existence against the stone floor. The black comes from burning. The burning of bones. So nothing is wasted. And everything they need comes out of the ground or has walked along its surface. At least, that's the way it was. Now they mostly use acrylic. But I don't mind that. And I don't suppose they do.

He was told by Mrs Alfonso that I was a very famous white artist from New York; well, I figured that Paddy could work out the white part for himself. I didn't want to come over all technical, but I did say that I considered myself as more a famous pink artist than a white one, especially under the Australian desert sun. Paddy looked up at me from his physically non-existent throne as if what I had just added to our introduction was imbued with veritas.

He raised his 75-year-old arm slowly, gently. My arm went out to meet his, and our hands embraced for quite a considerable time. I didn't know if I was empowering him or if he was empowering me, but anyway after a short eternity we mutually ended our tender, protracted handshake. It seemed like he'd already said what he needed to say in his eagle painting. The eagle marks the land with its prints, and Paddy sings it into existence with his painting. Me, I didn't say much either. And anyway Madame Alfonso was doing enough talking for all of us and a few more besides. So we looked at each other happily.

Madame Alfonso lifted up Paddy's painting, which she told me he'd just finished about six times, off the patio floor. She took it out of the shade, where Paddy worked in his special corner – the King Corner, I suggested to Lily – and put it in the sun so it would dry quicker. After so much repetition, of not the interesting kind, I think we were all relieved when she finally laid it to rest under the heat of the afternoon sun. Paddy didn't seem to notice her all that much, and he was sweetly polite to me. Giving me some credit maybe for being an artist, even though our worlds seemed slightly different. He had a beautiful, diffident spirit.

When we had moved to the other side of the patio to meet the lady artists, who were bunched up together in their own spot, we were out of Paddy's hair. His painting was finished, his day was done, and he began to sing his song. When he was finished, he got up quietly and left while we weren't watching, thus saving himself the further inconvenience of having to say goodbye. I loved Paddy. I was thinking in a way it would be nice if he was my dad. But I didn't buy the painting that he had just finished because I didn't like it all that much. I loved the story, but I didn't love the painting. Because the painting was too much of a story and not enough of a painting. But I didn't have to buy his painting to remember his kindness. And his indifference to that, I mean me not buying it, was painted in the air.

We went into the gallery, where we bought a painting by a woman working who we had met but had hardly met. She seemed to be somewhere else.

Her painting was red. We had wanted another one by her, but that was sold. Madame Alfonso told us this one was even better. I wanted to tell her to shut her gob, but I restrained myself. A momentary lapse in the free expression that she had been indulging in. Anyway, she kept up the barrage of words until my head was buzzing and I said, rather succinctly, "less words more look". Considering the frontality of my remark, she responded quite graciously, saying that she did "go on a bit" and that endeared her to me. Then we started looking at pictures.

Liddy's red painting with a black curve running through the middle of the painting's surface made me think of Kandinsky. There were other paintings around that looked like Kandinsky's. All jumbled up, painted in the desert, by people who weren't Kandinsky and had never heard of him. People who painted their own stories of the rhythm and the songs of the land. Where everything, all the world and the things in it are sung into existence.

Aboriginals are the heartbeat of Australia; without them it would be a land of white bread and sports. Their connection to the land and everything that is slumbering beneath it waiting to be sung into existence is profound. And their ancient and now contemporary invention of an abstraction grounded in the land, its rhythms and its myths is genius. I was thinking, driving through Australia, that it was like our invention of Cubism. And as radically brilliant – where we pushed all the images in our world through the improvised grid. We are all machine, and they are all ground.

Kandinsky was in Bavaria, where the land is also worshipped. His connection to it is also profound. He started out with dazzling landscapes in bright colour that painted the seething power of the mountains around Murnau, and then he made his abstracts. But then there weren't theoretical, despite his Olympian intellect. The abstracts that followed the landscapes were a sublime fusion of his spiritual ambitions for art that was still feeding off nature. Later on they got dried out. He was working with straight lines and hard edges. And the idea consumed the nature in his paintings, and they were no longer grounded in the earth.

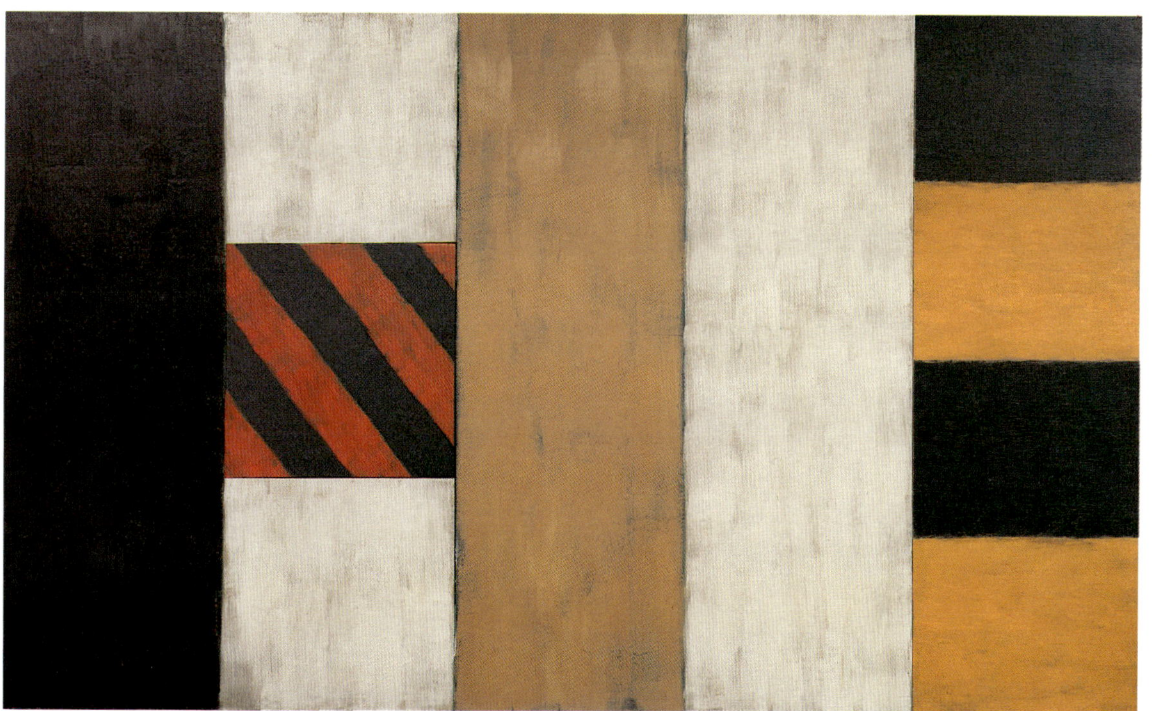

BIGLAND 1987–88
Oil on canvas
243.8 × 406.4 cm (96 × 160 in.)
Canberra, National Gallery of Australia

To return to Liddy. After we bought the painting, Madame Alfonso insisted we go out to meet her. Liddy sat on the floor surrounded by dogs that all looked vaguely related to dingos. There was one called the love dog. It was a female dog that went around adoring people. It would put its feet on your knees while you were sitting and look into your eyes adoringly. It adored everybody. But it seemed to adore Lily the most. So naturally I thought the only two people with real judgment in the whole place were me and the dog.

While we were buying the paintings, a youngish woman sat in the gallery watching like a bird of prey. She was, it transpired, making a film on the centre. One of those obligatory documentary efforts that cause further irritation to the aboriginals. She asked me, at just the wrong moment, which she thought was just the right moment, if I minded if she filmed us buying the paintings. And I said yes. She said yes again. And to save us further repetition with the over use of the word yes, I said that's right. I returned to my former position of merely saying yes. Then she said yes, you mind? I said yes. I mind.

Then she said, "what does the media do in Ireland?" And I said the media people in Ireland are very short with bandy legs. They smoke clay pipes and they have big noses with hair growing out of the end of them. And if you come back looking like that, I will let you film us buying these paintings. She then decided I was too weird to continue a dialogue with. And she just left me, abandoned to my own peculiar destiny. I got the idea she thought I was somehow lost.

Two minutes later I decided that I would like to have my picture taken with Liddy, who was working outside. It wasn't necessary for the documentary maker to state that she considered my position to be at the core of hypocrisy. I was very aware that it was. And so was Lily. But that's why we enjoyed it so much.

So we went outside followed by the documentary film-maker, who did not bring her camera. I asked Liddy if Lily could take a photo of us together. But I made the mistake of framing the question in similar style to our documentary maker. Did she mind? And Liddy said yes. So through my sense of mischievousness I had manoeuvred myself into the same position that the documentary film-maker had been obliged to suffer moments before. Needless to say, she was enjoying part two a lot better than part one. But to her credit she refrained from demonstrating her current amusement, not to say triumph, with a smile.

Liddy was leading me a merry old dance. Saying, more or less, that I could but she minded. Then later that she didn't mind. But I think it meant something more like she didn't care if I wanted to indulge in something so asinine. But she didn't want one. Lily and I were bathing in the mirth of it all afterwards. Saying that when we sell our art we are obliged to kiss ass. Though I understand I am not famous for that, and make a poor job of it, according to some people. And when we buy art we are also obliged to kiss ass. In a way it was beautifully symmetrical. Our destiny is to kiss ass. It doesn't seem to make the smallest difference whether we're buying or selling. Our obligations remain the same. Though I was considerably more prepared to follow my destiny with Liddy, than I am in New York, where I'm the painter. There I have my own special way of kissing ...

But eventually I settled down on the floor behind her with one of the dogs. The main thing was not to knock any paint over and not get on her nerves too much. So we did the photo. I had my hand on her back, which didn't seem to bother her too much. And as long as she could keep painting I could have what I wanted, and she could continue to have what she wanted. That moment might have been used as a model for the world. So in a sense we had the perfect human relationship. Where Liddy was able to oblige me and simultaneously give me the amount of attention that suited her, which was none.

Towards the end of our buying spree Madame began to become very amused – in between everything she said she was laughing, not at us especially but at everything. Everything started to get funny. Just like it should be when you're standing upside down. Though she wasn't of course, because she was from Australia: but we were. And when we left and said goodbye, good luck and enjoy your trip, she was still laughing. And when we drove away through the dusty streets of the town, we were laughing. And then pretty soon, we were laughing on the highway of red ochre dirt. The jeep was bouncing up and down and we were laughing and laughing. It was beautiful. The world is a wonderful place and so are the people in it.

In their art and their life exists the mythical beauty of belief. Like a magic stone in a river that stops the river from ever drying up. Life isn't a straight line. It's always folding back on itself. This makes it deeper and stronger. Nothing gets left behind; everything is continuously gathered up and remade in the folding rhythms of its song.

Yuendumu, Australia, August 2004

Beauty has not been integrated into our Western culture. It has been separated out. What's been integrated and absorbed is banality, because banality is already domesticated in a sense. We don't really have to think about it much, and it doesn't really bother us. It's simply inert and boring, even if it's in bright colours as image or loud music. (Except maybe in the case of rap or folk, which is more or less the same thing.) Because banality is banal, it doesn't start up a chain reaction in us, emotionally or intellectually. It's all around, like life's wallpaper, being there without the strength to radiate. Naturally this aspect of our culture has been absorbed. Thus, it is possible to say that Warhol is influential. But what is really influential is the supermarket, and to say that the supermarket is the future museum sounds amazing in the art world. Warhol certainly was a wag and a wit, but outside it's meaningless because the people behind the idea of the supermarket knew that in the first place. In Warholian terms, they are the real artists, and he is their decorator.

When art becomes like everything else (Duchamp), a flattening out occurs, a flattening of the difference, a general levelling. This has been turned into a capitalistic juggernaut in the West, with artists like Warhol imitating the idea of the factory, whilst maintaining their specialness in the market-place. In other words, to make art the same way that poster makers make posters, but charging more money for it.

So true integration of the ordinary and the banal and the mass culture was never achieved. Nor was it the objective. The objective was to use the previously established aesthetic of the banal, as in the items for sale in mass culture, but to charge more by involving the principle of the exalted brand name. As the market expanded and the moneyed middle class grew, the artist – like Warhol, for example – would be able to keep up with it, because he was using the concept of the factory: fast techniques and many assistants.

It's interesting that the flattening out of the difference between art and mass media coincided with the rise of communism; so everything is connected to everything else, though with entirely distinct consequences. In China, Mao's jacket was a philosophical fashion item, and I used to wear something identical when I was a student. Though the idea in China was that everyone would have one, the idea in the West was to create an image of the accessible by making it flat, poster-like, one that everybody could recognize, understand and want but would not be able to afford. This created desire and envy, the basis for capitalist paradise. The only artistic place where true availability and integration occurred is in the West, in music. Music now, shackled to big companies like Sony, is on the one hand triumphant, since it's blaring out its nothing message in taxis from Lima to Beijing. On the other hand, it is permanently enslaved, since it is made only for money. As an art form, popular music has gone flat.

Flat painting is somewhere in this argument, because it becomes a diagram of something. It might have some of its origins in map-making. You want to show one thing, not everything, or not many things, so you make a map: a diagram. That's what happened to painting as it tried to keep apace with the methods and the banality of the factory aesthetic. Paintings had to be made fast, they had to deliver their one-dimensional message, and then unfortunately they had to be thrown away.

The way things work out differently in different cultures is fascinating. The canvases are similar, but the result is opposite. But this is like saying it worked out this way in America, because Kansas City is not on the west coast.

Rio de Janeiro, September 2004

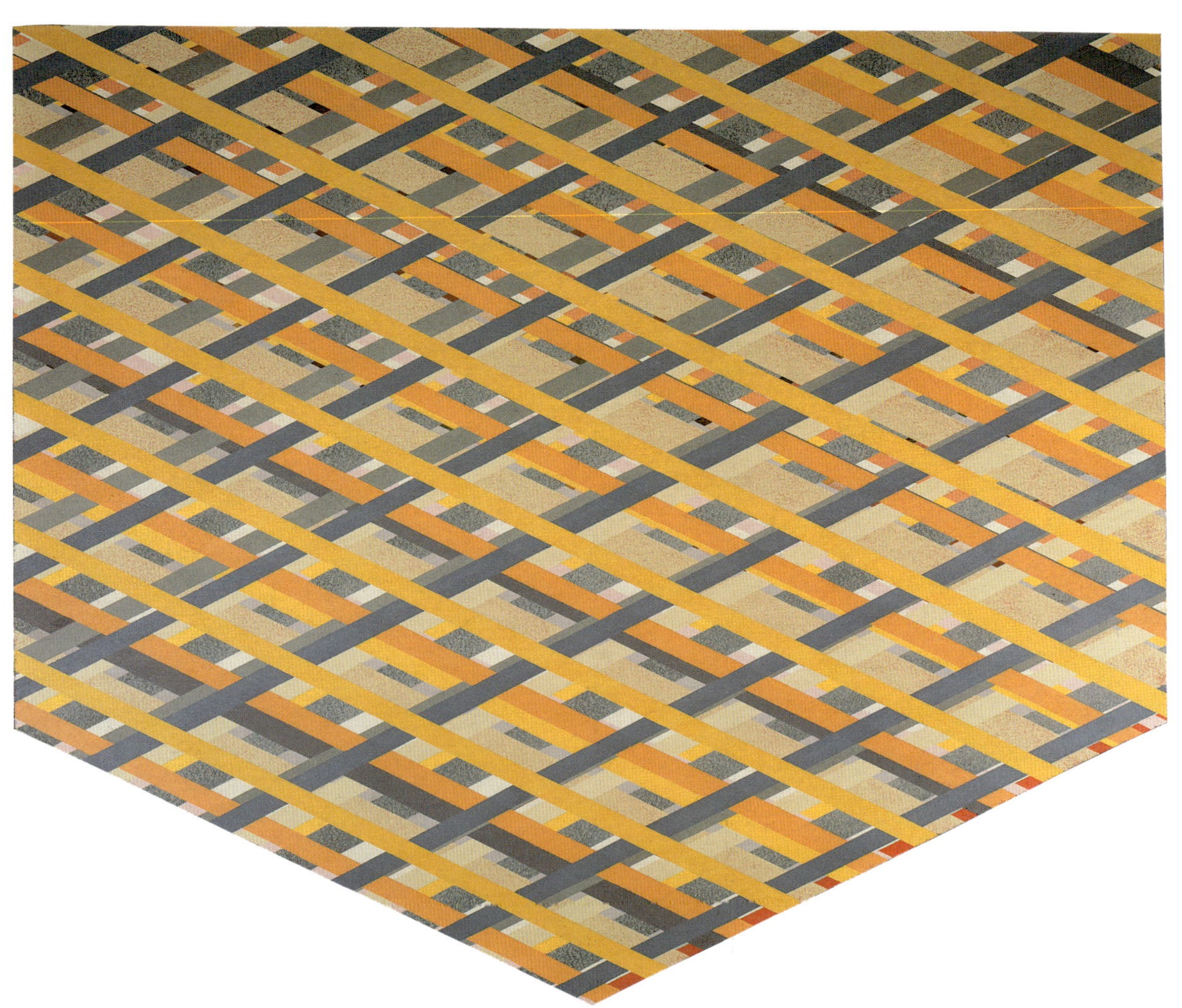

I will only talk for an hour. I will try to make it concise. Today I'm going to take you through a story of my work, how it evolved, a little bit about my life and how I got to make the paintings you will see in the Phillips Collection. On the second floor of the Phillips Collection there is a small retrospective to give you some background information. Today I'm going to try and cover the evolution of this early work and the crisis as I see it in abstraction, the fall of Modernism and what I did in response.

This painting (*Overlay 1*, 1973) was painted once I had returned to London after my first visit to the USA. The first time I came to the USA was on a fellowship, the Frank Knox fellowship. I went to Harvard University and worked in the Carpenter Center in a Corbusier building. I got $2500 a year to live on, which of course is far too much. I remember getting a bill for $8000 from the university, and when I went to the office the woman there told me it was all right I didn't have to pay it, so then I understood America. It's been working that way ever since. I wish someone had told me then that the more debt you were in, the more you money you had.

What I tried to do with the *Overlay* paintings was to do something in response to Cubism. I wanted to try to enliven abstraction by making it illusionistic: to put space into the painting and make the painting pictorial. Obviously if you have an abstract painting you've lost the possibility to tell stories, because you've lost the human figure, so as a compensating element I thought that perhaps I could make the painting so that it was systematically overlapping, and at the same time would give the pleasure of illusionism. This, I thought, would help to keep the visual interest going, the human need for narrative and representation. So, as I said, this was a painting I made after I had been in America, and what I used to do with these paintings was measure off grids, even but arbitrarily connected to each other. For example, this red edge was really an accident. What happened was the painting had a kind of inner tumbling space, so I would work on the painting until it was completely filled up, and when I got to the point when information that had already been put down was being taken away, then the painting would obviously be finished. Naturally it

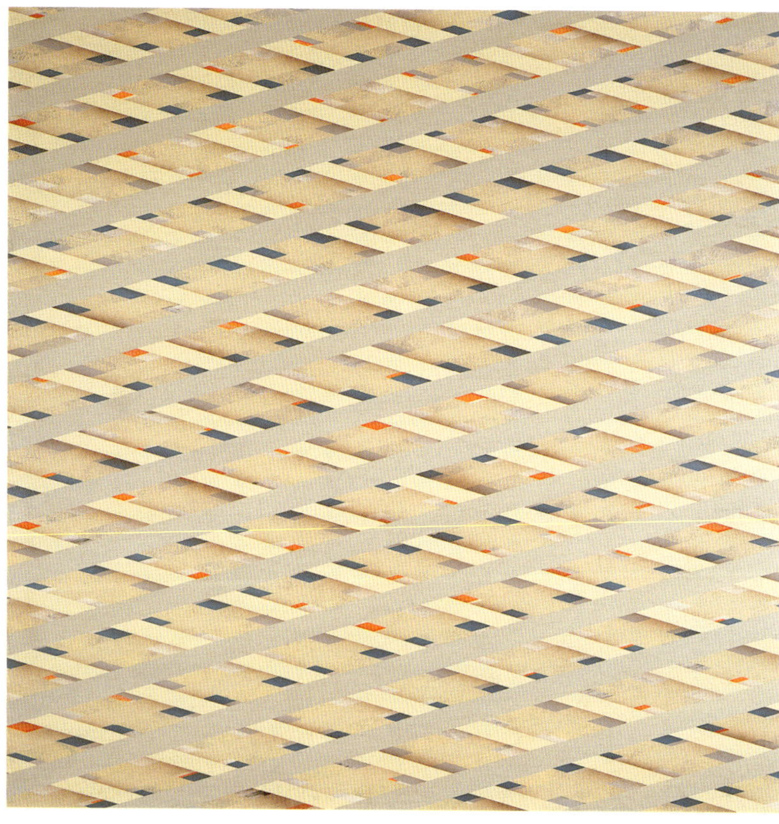

has a relationship to the space that one finds in Jackson Pollock's paintings, but it's far more systematized, I would say.

This painting (*Grey*, 1973) is in the show. It was painted around the same time immediately on my return from Boston. Again I began with primary colours and gradually worked over the painting until these were showing through from the back in chinks. So it's important once again to think of the relationship to Cubism where the object is broken down and the space becomes spread out and at the same time introverted; it's pushed into the painting in a way that's difficult to follow in terms of the narrative of the object, which represents the crisis of the object.

This (*Overlay 2*, 1974) is a very important painting in relation to what happened later. There was a period when I was in England and once again plotting my escape to the USA, and I was determined to come to the USA because I wanted to make free abstract painting, free-thinking abstract painting. These paintings were made in 1974, and they have never really been shown until now, and what I was doing with these paintings was questioning the idea of illusionism as a way of keeping

painting going. Now these open grid paintings represent my intent to return painting to the issue of surface, to make a very physical subjective surface cut through by a sense of structure. The paintings were all called *Overlay*, which is characteristic of my work from the very beginning, is still characteristic of it. In other words, there has always been an attempt by me to make a mystery or a compression of a surface. The paintings before were illusionistic, but they came out of a sense of layering, overlapping, a relentless sense of one thing on top of another thing to make a history of the making of the painting *within* the painting that can be followed. These are not narrative in the sense that the ones before are; these are paintings that have to be felt and are more mysterious, as the space of the painting is not explained. The lines in the painting were made with masking tape that was laid on the painting; it was painted again, and then another set of lines was laid on with masking tape and the painting was painted again with heavy rollers. Then the tape was pulled up and, if it wasn't what I wanted, I would start again and lay the paint down again with the rollers, to try and make a skin that was cut in the way that a wall has spaces between the bricks. So they are negative spaces, but in a sense they are holding the wall together. Here, then, you have the romantic and the structural, so I think these are crucial paintings and they are coming out now finally to see the light of the day. What is also interesting about these paintings for me in a personal sense is they haven't been shown for thirty-one years, since they were made. That's payback or, as Turner says, "painting is a rum business". If you decide to do it, you have to be ready to sit on your own work for thirty-one years.

This (*Brennus*, 1979) is kind of impossible to see, and these paintings were actually kind of impossible to sell, so there is a consistency there. These are the paintings I made when I came to America. When I came to America, I – metaphorically, of course – burned down my own house. I'd build up something that was based on the grid, as you can see, or the cross, the intersection of things, the one thing holding together another thing. There's a kind of binding in the early paintings – there's always a cross of one kind or another, a diagonal crossing, or weaving, or a vertical one, but there's always a cross – and what occurred to me recently is that when I came to the USA my cross became uncrossed, so in this painting, as you

can clearly see, there are only horizontal lines. All the paintings that I made after I came to the USA were made with horizontals only, so I stripped down the paintings to their utter minimum and the paintings became more connected to surface, and the history of surface-making, the subjective surface, as they developed.

Now naturally there is a relationship here with Minimalism. But I was a reluctant member, in the sense that this is a night painting. It is made with a kind of night light – red black, blue black, grey and brown – night colours that were set on top of one another and equally striped all the way down, so in a sense they are kind of Zen paintings. I was working like this for five years, marking my own time, holding a position. This was extremely important because I didn't come to the USA with the idea that I could just come to the USA. I think I understood the difficulty of being an immigrant, and there's more to being an immigrant than you would realize, at the outset. It is more difficult than one imagines it's going to be; places are more different than one might imagine, despite globalization. So I took out of my work the colour and the cross, that makes the sense of a prescribed shape – the drawing of a rectangle, or of a lozenge shape – and I only allowed myself to work with horizontal lines. And obviously I was very connected to the work of Agnes Martin at this time. These are, in a sense, burned paintings but relentlessly Zen, contemplative and meditative, and they gave me a chance to make my work, hold my position and be ready.

After working on these grey and black paintings for five years very consistently, with a tremendous amount of discipline, I decided in about 1980 to try to reintroduce the idea of relationship into painting. I was thinking, in other words, that if you take out a figure – house, tree, whatever – from a painting, then you take out representation, and you are creating an absence. But it is not possible to create the absence inside a human being. You are creating an absence of the satisfaction of the answer of a human being. But we can't alter the human need for narrative representation, a connection with the world, with sensuality and so on. All the things that we associate with content. I mean, you can't make monochromatic paintings and expect to save abstract painting. It's not going to fly because it doesn't have in it the things human beings need. So having taken out the space, taken out the geometry, the sense of divisions and the reference to architecture in these black paintings, having made a very intense but other-worldly body of work, I decided to put back relationships, proportion, zones, one thing against another in a kind of competition, a kind of dialogue. The painting on the next page is called *Araby*, painted in 1981. The areas in this painting start to become physical and painted. There is another dimension to it which is sculptural, the ability to make a relationship.

I got to *Backs and Fronts* (1981, page 47) from the black paintings you saw in about eighteen months. So, as you can see, I seriously changed my mind. It is

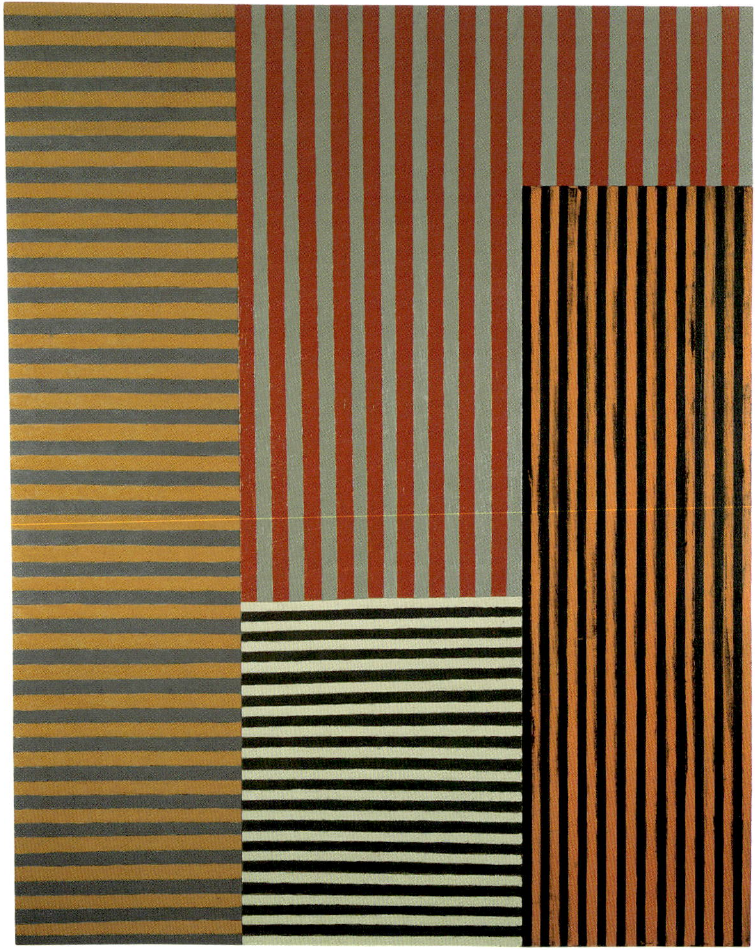

20 feet long, it was shown once in New York and has never been shown since. It is called *Backs and Fronts*, as I am making a reference to something figurative. It's not called *Untitled # 33* or whatever. It's a powerful reaction against Minimalism, and it involves proportion, colour, direction and surface. Some panels are casually painted, and others are less casually painted; some are quite tight, referring to the black paintings, some are really opened up; and the colour, of course, is exotic. So this is a form of declaration; it declares what I'm going to do thereafter.

This painting *(Red and Red,* 1986, opposite) is what I did thereafter, and here also is a painting called *The Fall* (page 172). This painting was bought by Gifford Phillips one lovely day when David McKee also came to the studio. At that time Gifford Phillips was about my age, so it's very interesting when you see these things after a time and you see what happens to them. This painting takes the notions that are in *Backs and Fronts*, and started in paintings such as *Araby*, to a more emphatically physically aggressive point. There is a huge lump of red divided physically and then somehow unified in a painterly sense. Unified to use the sense metaphorically, with the skin of culture, with handmade brushstrokes. Here in the right of this painting there's a shallow panel, a very heavy panel in the middle, and then the painting draws back and it's broken in two places on the left. So the paintings are structured yet painted; it's as though I'm trying to make the painting in pieces, to make something that is broken and put it back together again or hold it together with paint. So as a metaphor that's quite interesting. There's a psychological effort. What I'm trying to do, in a sense, is save abstract painting. One of the things about it psychologically is that I think of it as something that is broken, and I'm insisting that one can repair it with paint, bind it together with paint.

I'll tell you a little story that's quite interesting. There's a photograph of my studio on Duane Street, near where the World Trade Center was. When I moved into the studio, there were shelves because it had been a textile warehouse, and the entire inside of the space was a cavernous 4000 square feet that was filled with

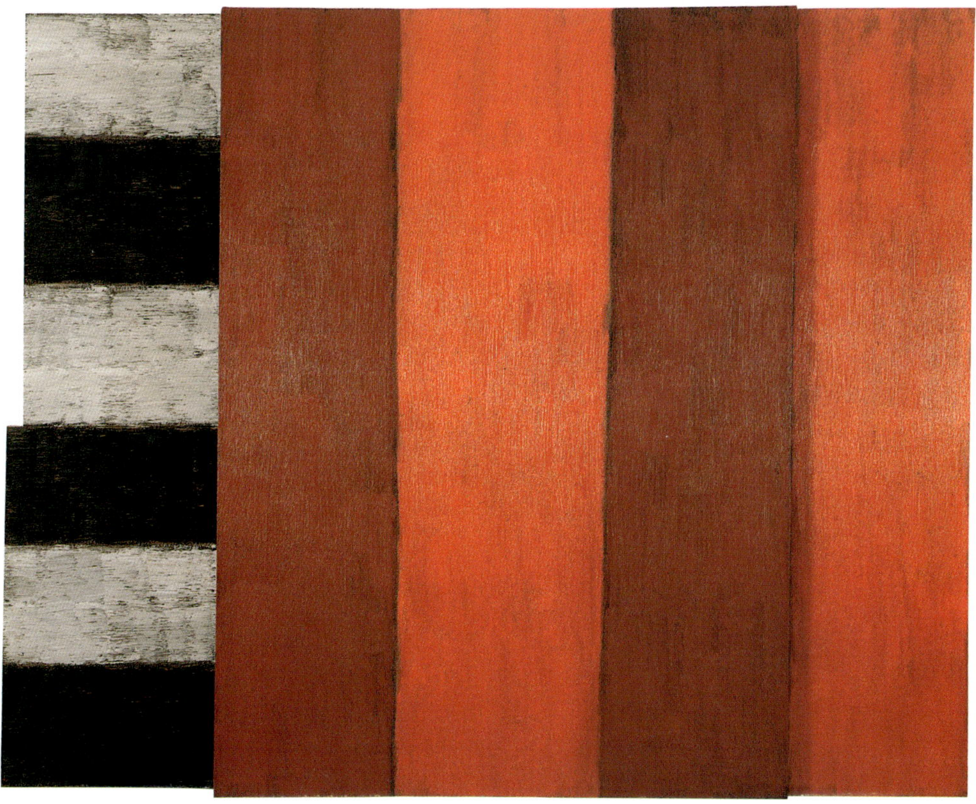

RED AND RED 1986
Oil on linen
190.5 × 215.9 cm (75 × 85 in.)
Washington, D.C., Phillips Collection

shelves that were all made of wood and the wood was beautiful because it had been there for thirty years. I dismantled all the shelves and used the verticals to build the loft so it was free, and then with the shelving I stacked it against the wall. I did that thing for a reason, I think, as it was like sculpture. The boards were as wide as a book and 3 metres long, and they were all stacked against the wall, so it looked really like a very physical minimal painting, a sculpture. Now the end of it projected from the wall, obviously, so it was a block against the wall that was very fascinating, and I'd pass this on a daily basis and, of course, I allowed myself to do this as self-manipulation. When I began later on to make little paintings out of lumps of wood that were found, I found that the wood, of course, was made of different thicknesses, so I was making steps in the paintings. And the little stretcher of this is built with the wood from the shelves that were in the loft when we moved in. So it's a very clear case of not only recycling but the suggestion of context, environment and how that can insert itself into your mind.

New York is a rough place; you can't really say you like it that much. You can say you like walking around Washington, D.C.; you like the lovely houses. But it's hard to love New York. However, its abrasiveness has something to do with inspiration, and art comes from discomfort or tragedy or difficulty, I think. So I see at this point, around 1984 or so, a tremendous crisis in abstract painting. At this point in history I'm working against all the neo-expressionists. So this represents in a sense the fall of the tower of Modernism; New York had been rolled over as the European painters started to come in. It's like watching a boxing match between a super-heavyweight and a flyweight. And the American artists in a sense were trying to paint like European artists, whereas only a decade before the European artists had been trying to paint like American artists, but by then the American idea had simply run out of gas.

So there I was, having thrown in my lot with the USA, but with an entirely personal history of European painting in my body and in my very being. So I was able to refer in a sense to both, and what I'm trying to do here; and what I have been doing ever since is trying to make something with tremendous feeling out of the very simple and obvious metaphor. It's also interesting to note that at this time I was also building lofts for other people.

Another painting is called *The Bather* (1983, page 53), and again it has a very strong attempt to reintroduce not the figure but the sense of the figure. It doesn't have a face or arms or legs, but it has a sense of being figural. It has the width of my hips and it is a landscape, and is a homage to my hero Matisse and a great painting in The Art Institute of Chicago. This painting has an orange bar running up the middle, and the stripes that are painted around it are painted as stripes, yes, but also like trees. They move and have broken edges; they have a complicated surface, and they have light within them. So the painting has a tension and a brutality, and this corresponds to a rather tender title, and a nostalgia for the figure, as I used to be a figure painter.

The Bather was painted in 1983, and this one is *No Neo* (1984), so you could say I'm always picking fights. At the time that this was painted in New York there was a lot of talk about 'Neo': 'Neo Geo', 'Neo' this and 'Neo' that. So in a sense there was a sense of turning history on its head, and I was reacting to the idea of regurgitation of the models already seen in the history of art, so I made this painting, which I called *No Neo*. I was making aggressive abstraction that had in it the ability to be relational. And this was very important then, as abstract painting had become arid and largely grey. There was a battle in the hearts and minds of the art world between the Minimalists and the Colour Field painters, and the Minimalists won, as the

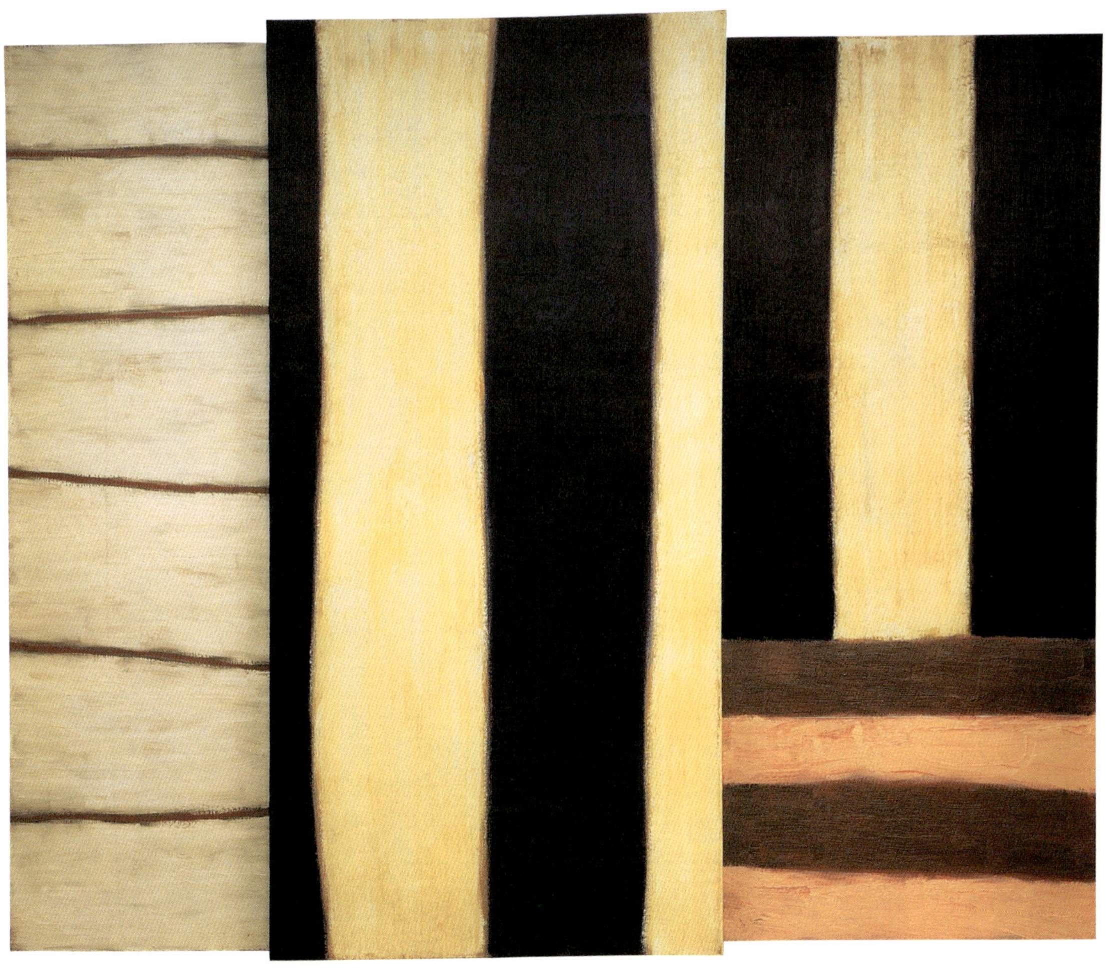

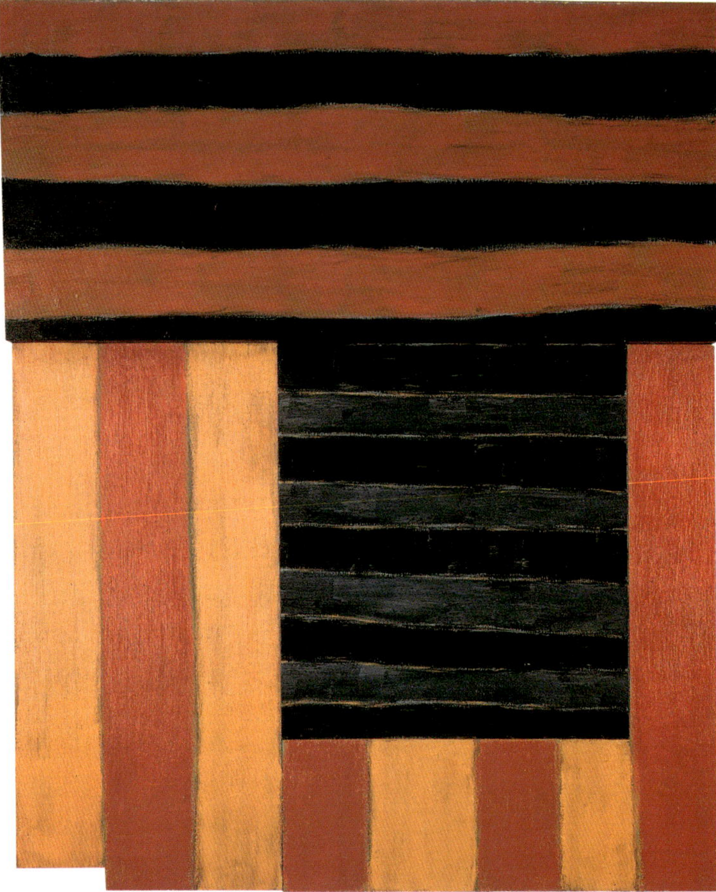

THE FALL 1983
Oil on canvas
274.3 x 243.8 cm (108 x 106 in.)
Private collection

Europeans jumped in on their side, so it wasn't a fair fight. What I was trying to do was to bring back the physical element of a painting you could feel you could walk into, and also the sense of weight. They would stick out of the wall; in fact, I would stand them up in the studio like sculptures. I almost made sculptures but I didn't, because if I had made sculptures they would have been literal, and I was only interested in saving painting. So I was flirting with sculpture, but making paintings that referred to the history of painting. I was mixing up the colours on the surface and paintings with a lot of feeling.

In *The Fall* (1983) there is a tremendous fight between falling and rising. Obviously the red and yellow are functioning like ascending columns, and the darkness of the painting, the doom of the painting, is that the top is falling into the bottom, and the bottom is holding it all up. I speak metaphorically, of course. Once again it has an inset in it. I added a piece on. It seemed that so far shaped painting in abstraction had been made by dividing inwardly, and what I did here was to make paintings by re-addition. I would add and then take off, put a bit here or there. This could be a horizontal painting or a vertical painting. It could be turned on its side and something could be added, so it was very free. Absolutely open. I had canvases that were mismatched, and I would put them together. The idea of falling apart and holding together in a dynamic contest for survival was rampant at the time that I was making these paintings, in the mid-1980s.

This is called *Empty Heart* (1987, page 57). Towards the end of the 1980s I started to flatten out my paintings and became more interested in the idea of windows. The idea of a double experience within a painting. This was painted for my son who died, so it is a painting of emotion and devastation. Based on two blacks and two whites, lightness and darkness. There is a frame, which in a sense is protective but also gives a sense of incarceration, which is prohibitive. Here are basically two paintings: the painting of a hole and a painting of what fills that hole. Once again, trying to put something into the painting that gives it a human figurative, figural aspect as a metaphor. In these paintings that follow I am dealing with the figure in the window.

This is *Why and What (Yellow)*, painted in 1988 (page 35). It has a metal panel and a red-blue panel in a kind of woven field. It is very aggressive in the way that it has been painted: the paint has been put on very heavily. The idea is that the surface is sensual, referring to the history of painting, and somewhat violated by this metal panel. I was doing this quite a lot in the late 1980s – breaking the romance of the painting, the narrative of the painting with a metal panel or with another painted panel. So one is looking all the time at near and far. I find it quite interesting too that there is sense of bigness and smallness, but it is the same stuff that is being recycled and twisted, and reintroduced in another way into the painting to keep it alive and to keep these relationships open and strange. One is looking at relationships that are not necessarily understandable but that have a force.

So this is called *Secret Sharer* (1989, page 174); I was reacting to a short story by Joseph Conrad. When I'm working, sometimes I think about things, but I'm not painting them deliberately but allowing them to influence the activity atmospherically. *The Secret Sharer* is the story of somebody who is carried secretly on a ship, a stowaway. Here there is a dark, almost hidden window on the left; on the right there is a red short band. It's a painting that has golden yellow running right through it. It is based very much on dark and light. This particular painting is extremely human, and there is a sense of collision on the right as it bangs up against another form of drawing and another colour.

There is also a painting called *Dakar* (1989). At the time I made this, I was playing a lot of music by John Coltrane and thinking about Dakar (not that I have

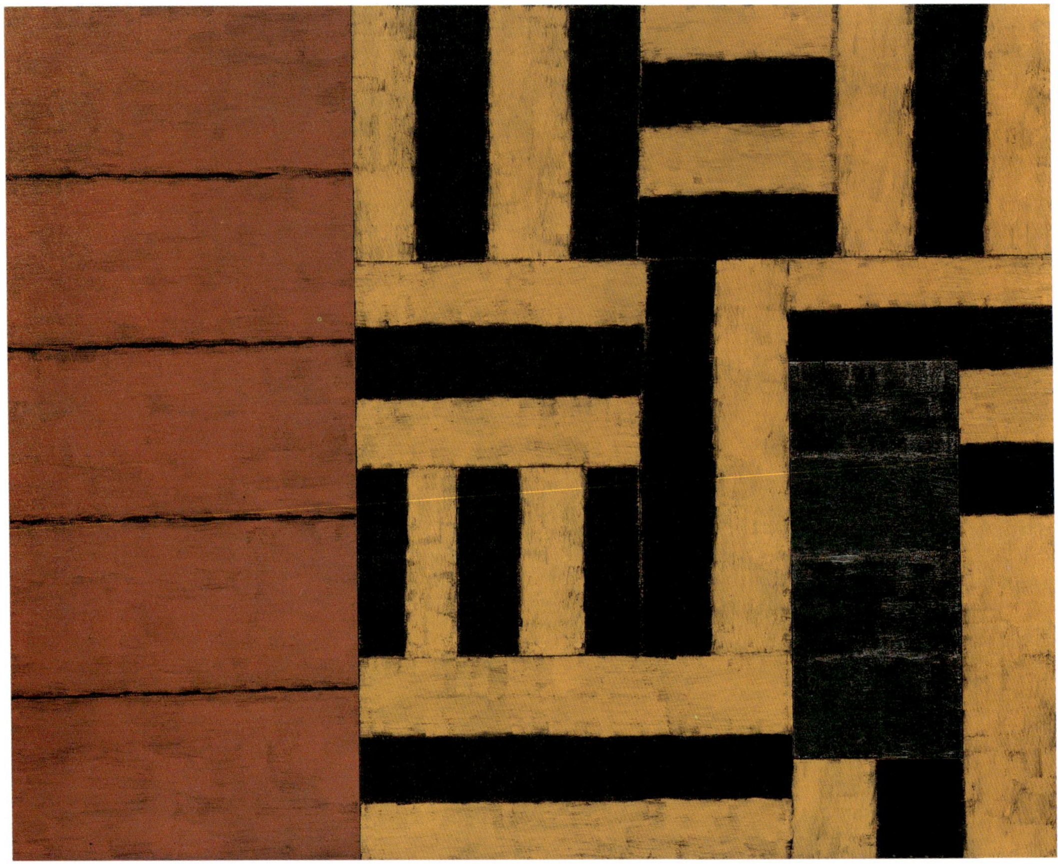

ever been to Dakar, but I was thinking about it), and the painting has a tremendously brooding quality, as do a lot of my paintings. They are very dark and romantic but unsettling – the relationships are unsettling, at least. So once again there is a heavy shelf that is hanging over and down on something that is working like architectural foundations, working like short, fat bars that are pushing it up. So these paintings are all working in relation to gravity: the idea of the figure, weight, body, mass, buildings, wall, the metaphor of holding, not holding etc. As you can see, the top is painted with a really devastating black and grey, which you might view as beautiful or extremely ugly, depending on how you react to the painting. I think that my paintings are concerned in a way with beauty because beauty is moving, but they are not sentimental. I appeal to sentiment as a human being, but I am making paintings that are always highly structured, so there is always a contest between the drawing and the way the thing is painted. This is one of the last of the sculptural paintings I made.

Tiree (1993) is another painting around the idea of the metal, also concerned with making again a relationship or a broken relationship, a separated relationship. So here you have the inverse of the relationship of *Why and What (Yellow)* (page 35). This little panel on the right is stranded. It is pulled away from the bigger painting on the bigger panel on the left, and what I was doing here was setting up the sense of distance. It is a relationship, and a relationship of distance; so one can see two things at the same time and they are not touching. The painted surface is no longer touching, and there is a steel column that is holding it in place like a form of incarceration.

There is *Ukbar* (1994), and another one called *Okbar* (1994; both page 63) and indeed another called *Ookbar*. I was responding in these paintings to a place in a short story by Borges, where nobody knows quite whether it is Okbar or Ukbar, or what this place is called. So nobody knows how to get there. When I started to paint these paintings I only did two, because they caused so much trouble as no one knew which painting was being referred to, but eventually I added another. It is very interesting, and it is also on a profound level connected to the notion of place in abstract painting. The notion of place in abstract painting is free. It is indistinct. One doesn't know quite where it is, and one has to find it for oneself within the painting. And this is why I like abstraction so much, because one gets to think out of context, and this is one of the few moments in life, or few that I can think of, where one can think freely as a human. All other thought seems to be burdened by context, historical context, historical prejudice; you don't get to think free ever. There is always information in front of you, and here, in abstraction, I try to make the space a place that is free of context and is liberated.

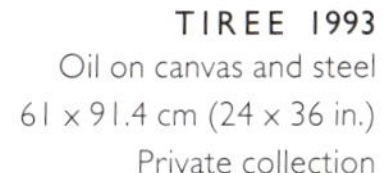

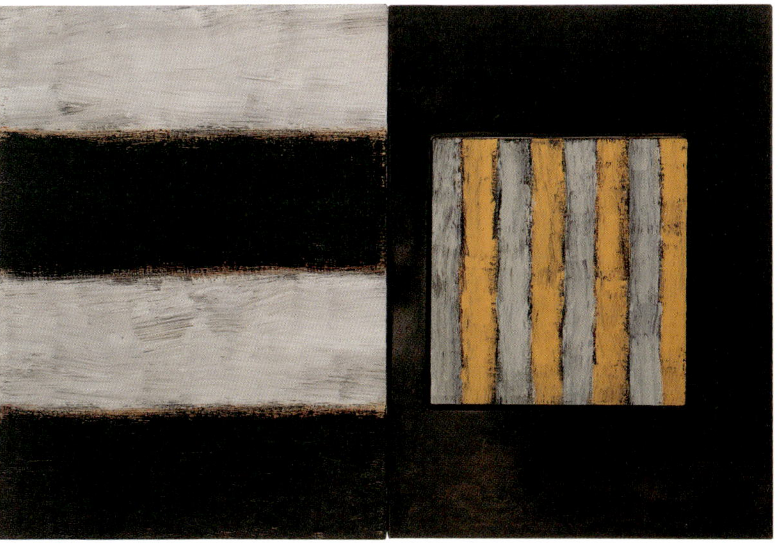

This little painting is called *Scarp* (1994). This painting is doing two things at once, and here I am breaking up the certainty of what you are looking at. Of course, the way I paint does that too, because the colours I am using are infuriatingly complex and made on the painting. The surface of the painting is very strong, and the geometry of the painting is painted out as struggle between the idea and the experience. The painting is simple but experiential.

The painting opposite is called *Because of the Other* (1997), because the things in the painting are where they are because of where the other bits are. In other words, one is the way one is in a relationship because of the other. I was going to make another painting before I made this, and I started to break up the surface one Sunday afternoon in London, in my studio, and when I finished the painting I realized that it was like a *Wall of Light* watercolour that I had made in Mexico in 1983. *Because of the Other* was made in 1997, and this says something about my whole endeavour. Clearly there is something wrong with a person who forgets to do something for fourteen years – we'll set that aside for a moment – however, things have to be made at the right time, and I am not working in competition with other people in my generation. I am utterly non-competitive. I am only working with things that are interesting to

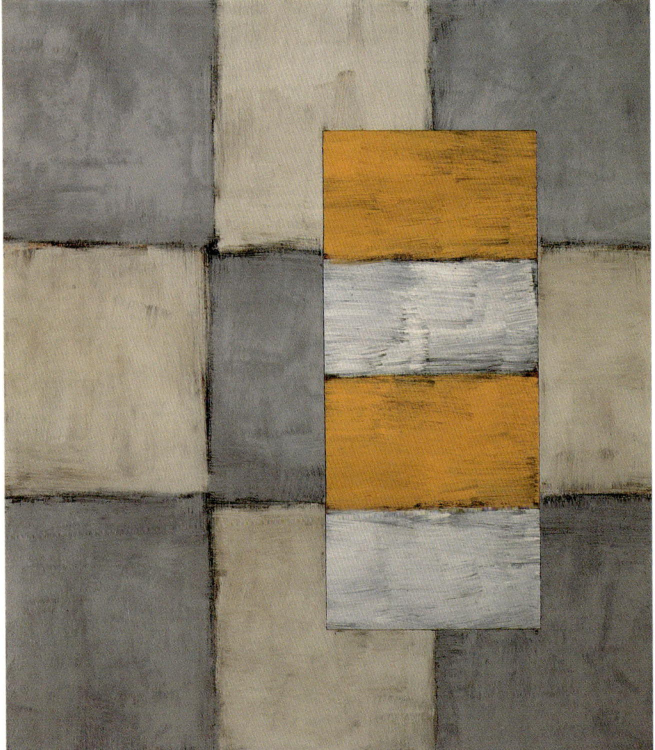

me and are holding my attention. I take my references from various points in art history – like Masaccio, who is very important to me, and Cimabue too. These are the artists I refer to in terms of colour, they use this dead light, a falling light. In Italian Quattrocento painting there is a beautiful sense of restrained exuberance – a lamentable exuberance would perhaps be a way to say it, or an exuberance of regret – and this is running through my paintings all the time. There is always a sense of subdued sensuality. So I made this painting later, because I had the idea for the painting in Mexico on the beach, in a moment of inspiration, after looking at the ruins there and seeing how the light changed the walls from orange, to blue, to black, to pink in the morning. I am very fond of running all over the ruins in Mexico. So after visiting them I made this little watercolour, with all these little zones in the work, reflecting the possibility of different times of day, and the way the stone structure can be brought to life with light, and the environment, which is fundamental to culture. But I had to make all the other paintings that I made first. In other words, it is first things first. And this means I am prepared to park something for fourteen years and come back to it. My work is not based on invention; it is really based on evolution, and there

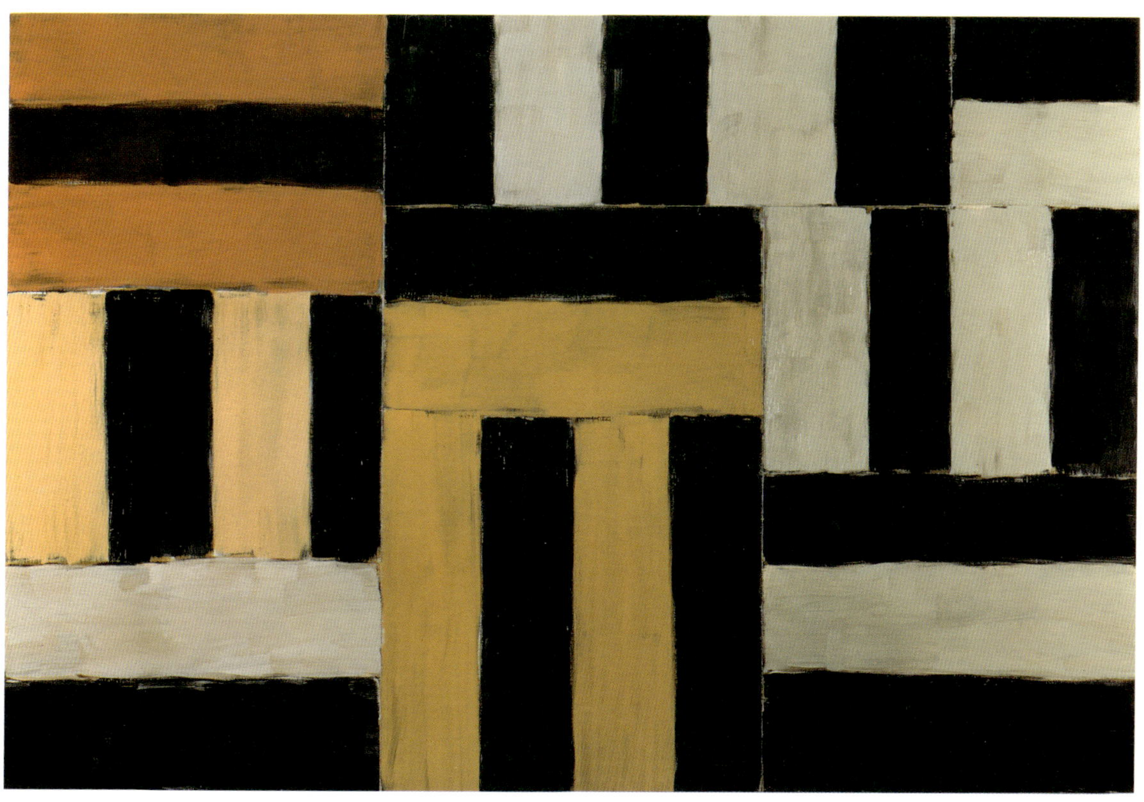

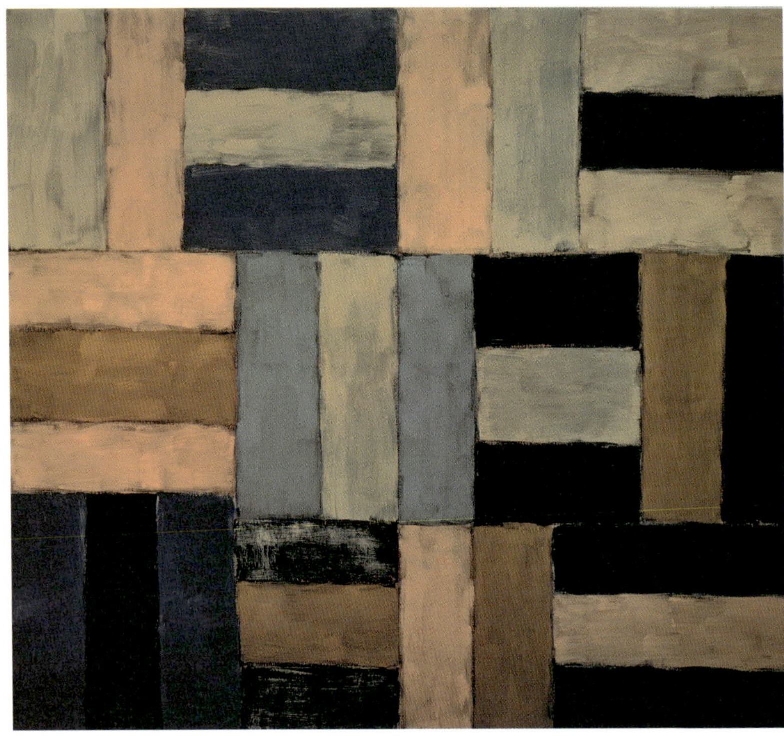

has to be an authentic gestation for it to be moving and to affect another human being. It cannot be made at the wrong time, out of fear that someone else might have the same idea. I actually don't care if someone else has the idea. I'm still going to do it when I am ready. I am not in competition in that way.

Wall of Light paintings. I got the inspiration for the colour from a De Kooning poster, and I was also thinking about Picasso, so I have made a painting with pink and blue, cream black and yellow. Part of the painting is scraped away. You will see that the way this has been painted is much rougher than some of the paintings that follow. *Wall of Light Pink* is from 1998, more or less at the beginning of this group of paintings. One thing I should also mention is that when I worked on this series, the *Wall of Light* series, I always worked on other things too. I always keep windows open and think this is very important.

Wall of Light Desert Night (1999) has an interesting narrative to it. Liliane and I were invited to go to Las Vegas to watch the boxing. And when I got there, I really flipped out. I was really upset by it. The architecture of all the hotels is like a wheel, and everything leads you to the casino. So it is a kind of trap, and you can't get out and you keep passing the same place. I have a tendency to get hopelessly lost anyway, so imagine a person who gets hopelessly lost two blocks from his own house; it is desperate in Las Vegas, as there is no sense of proportion. It is disorientating and the opposite of everything I do in my work, which is very much about a bodily sense of proportion. And here I was in a floating reality. One minute I was in Egypt and the next in medieval England. It was a desperate situation, so we hired a car and went out to the desert. We went to the Valley of Fire, where the colours were extraordinary. We were driving back towards dusk and all the rocks were turning different colours, and I held this within me. When I got back to New York, there was a giant canvas conveniently waiting, and I painted that painting the very next day. And this is something I do a lot. I see something, and have a feeling of something – it might be the light, or the heat, they are very specific in that sense – and I unload the painting. Anyway this one came out like this, first time, because it was ready. You can't do something when you're not ready. Painting doesn't need to be a

WALL OF LIGHT
DESERT NIGHT 1999
Oil on linen
274 × 335.3 cm (108 × 132 in.)
Fort Worth, TX, Modern Art Museum

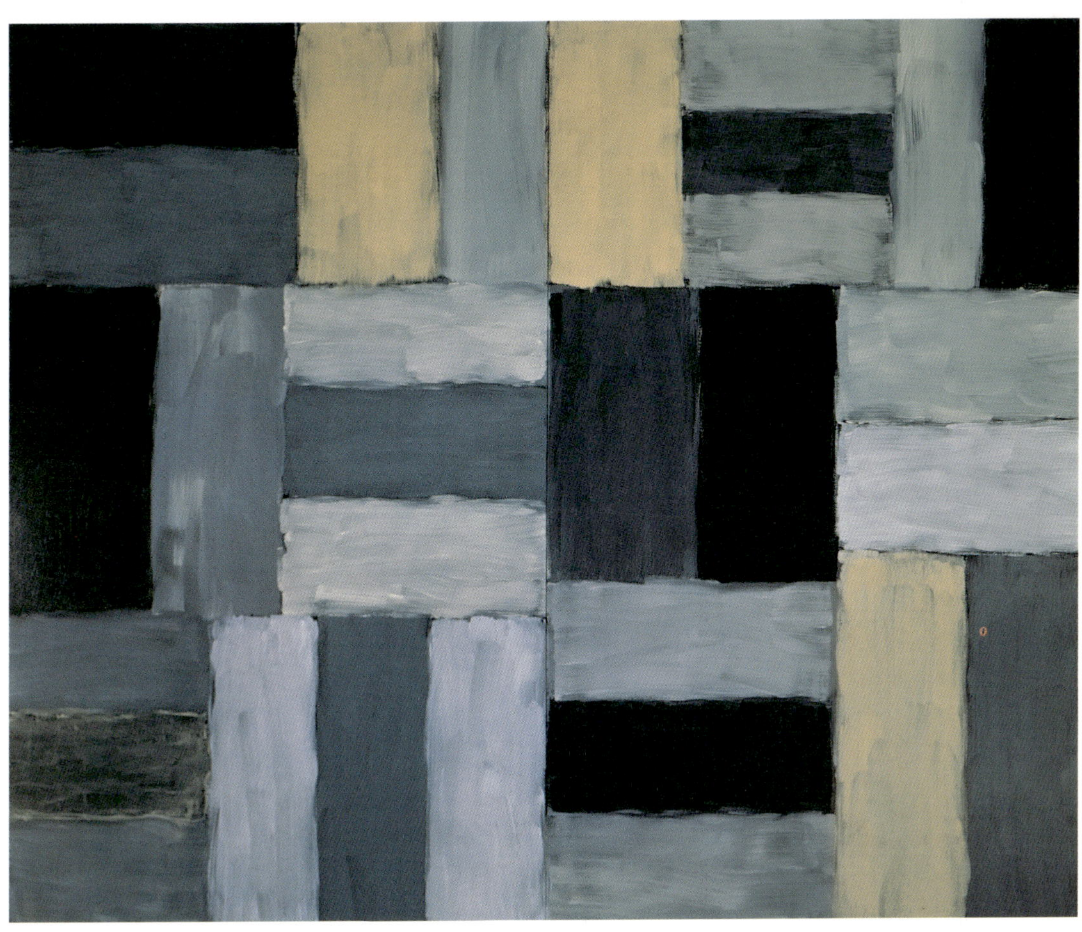

struggle. I agree with Woody Allen, when he said, "the best things come easy"; some of the best paintings that I have shown you were made in an afternoon. I always remember a story by Picasso. He was on a beach with his grandchildren all day, playing on the beach, and then they went up to the house to have dinner, and between 5 and 7 p.m. he made a painting, because he was ready to make that painting.

This is *Coyote* (2000). Of course, I named it *Coyote* because I love coyotes. They are survivors. It is quite arctic and I have used very reduced colour, but even so it has colour in it. I use a lot of grey in my paintings and am making reference to Manet, I suppose: the beautiful surface of Manet and the slow, noble hand. The hand says everything about a person, something that is disappearing from our culture. People used to have handwriting, but they send e-mail now. I think handwriting says a lot about a person. I have never seen it, but someone once described Adolf Hitler's handwriting to me and said it was virtually horizontal, as if it was flying off the end

COYOTE 2000
Oil on linen
274.3 × 304.8 cm (108 × 120 in.)
London, Tate

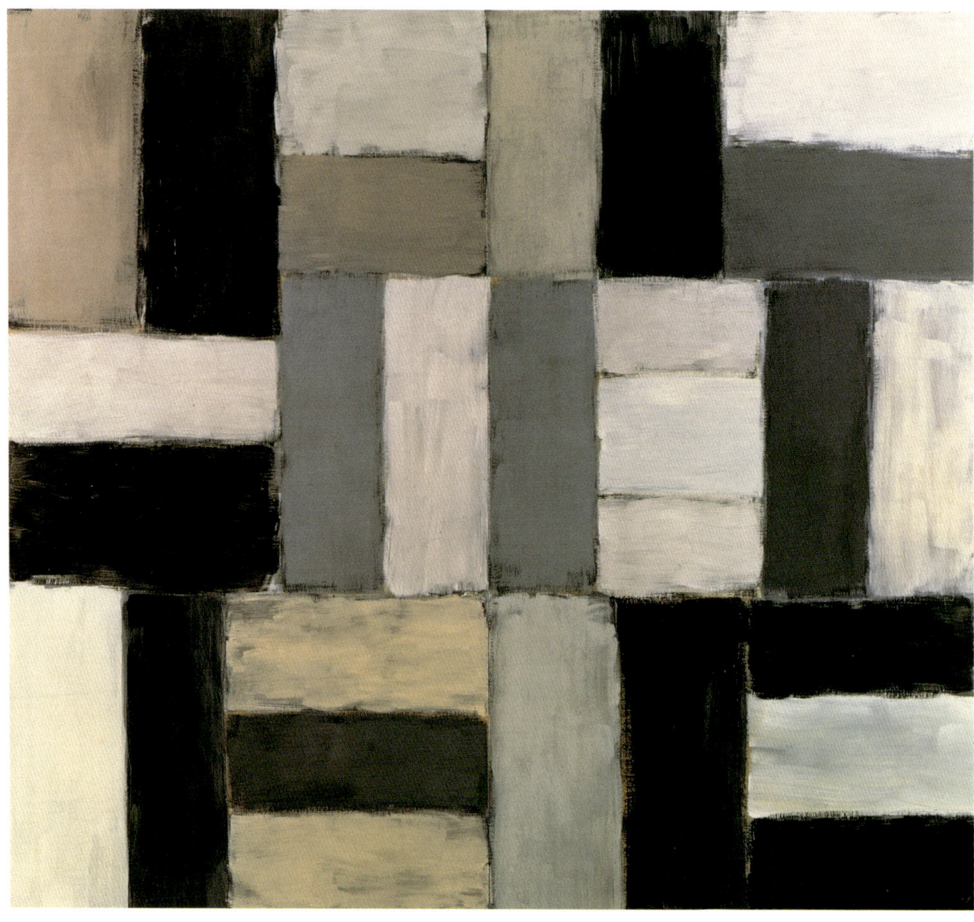

of the paper. Couldn't get from one end of the road to the other quick enough. A rather overly developed sense of ambition. But that is just a vulgar example of how handwriting reveals a person's nature.

Wall of Light Dark Orange (2001). This is in the Met. It is more monumental, thinner; some areas are taken out, some colour taken out. I do a lot of putting it on, taking it off, putting it on, taking it off, and there are a lot of seams in the back of the painting that give information, which has something to do with Vuillard. Vuillard's paintings are subversively controlled by what is at the back. Same with my photos, I guess. When you see a building, it is the front of the building you are meant to see, but I am more interested in the back of it, because that is what you are not meant to see. These paintings are being constantly emotionally unravelled by what is at the back. So here you are looking at a white painting that was an orange painting, which was a black painting, and has been converted to a white painting over time.

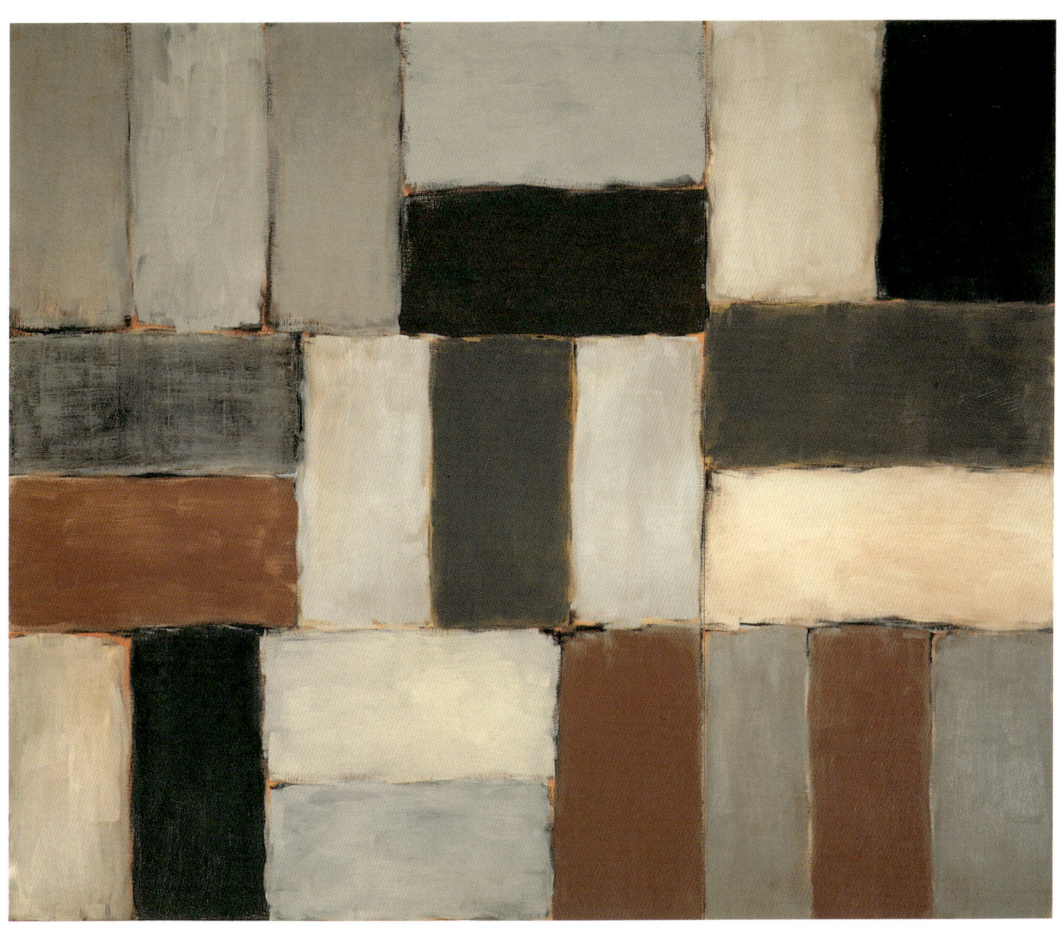

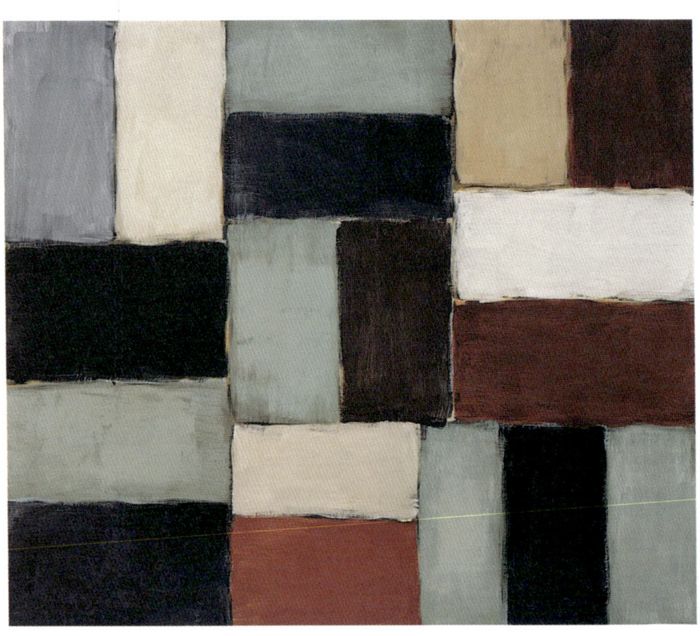

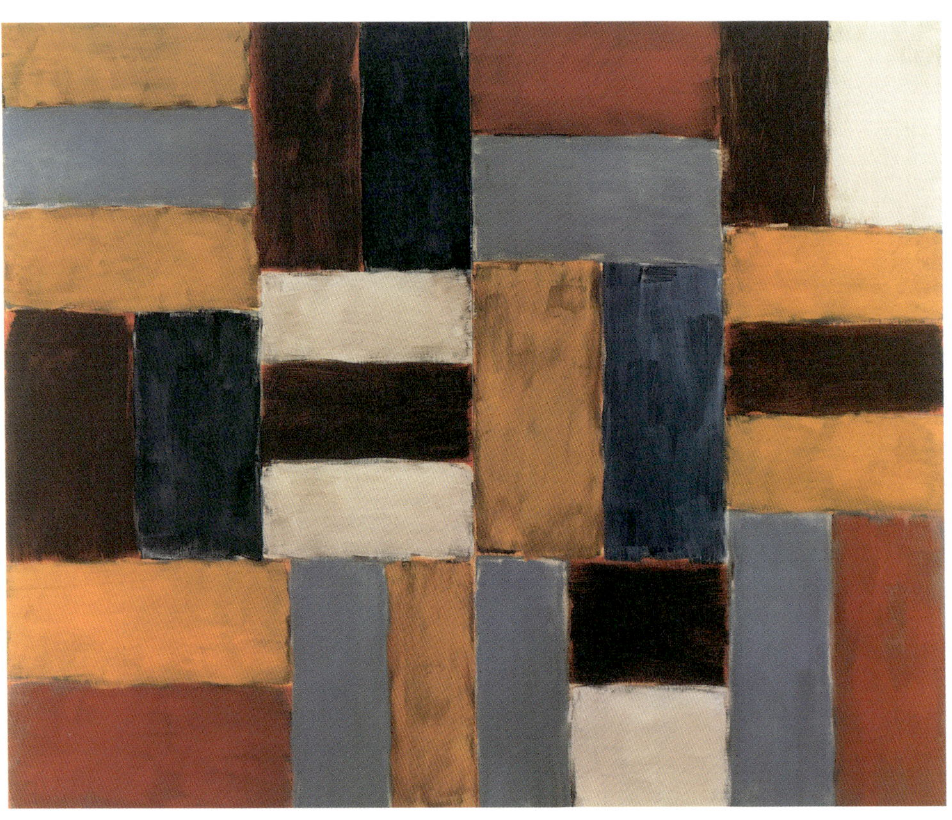

Opposite we have *Wall of Light Aran* and *Wall of Light Heat*. *Wall of Light Aran* is cool and melancholic, and gets its colour from three descending reds that light up as they fall to the bottom of the painting. *Wall of Light Heat* was painted in my bunker in London and is humid, made of rough brush strokes.

This (*Niels*, 2001) is a painting I made for a cousin of mine who was dying, and very ill at the time. So I made this painting with a lot of yellow. It isn't too big either; I can dominate it. I am trying here not to make something monumental, but something on a human scale: 2 metres by 2 metres. This brings me to an interesting point about proportion and scale, and the mystical relationship between people. I once went to see a De Kooning show, and I noticed that the canvases seem similar in size to mine. So I looked in a catalogue and they were all 75 by 80 inches, like this painting, which I found kind of funny. The other thing I should say about De Kooning is that I was a figurative painter, and when I make a drawing I am not counting or measuring, but feeling a drawing. So in a sense my work seems, perhaps, a lot less radical than the work of my American contemporaries, like Robert Ryman. And the same might be said for the relationships De Kooning had with his contemporaries. I have been thinking about this lately, in relation to Rothko and

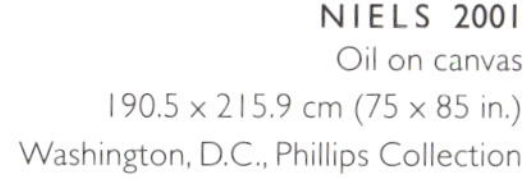

NIELS 2001
Oil on canvas
190.5 × 215.9 cm (75 × 85 in.)
Washington, D.C., Phillips Collection

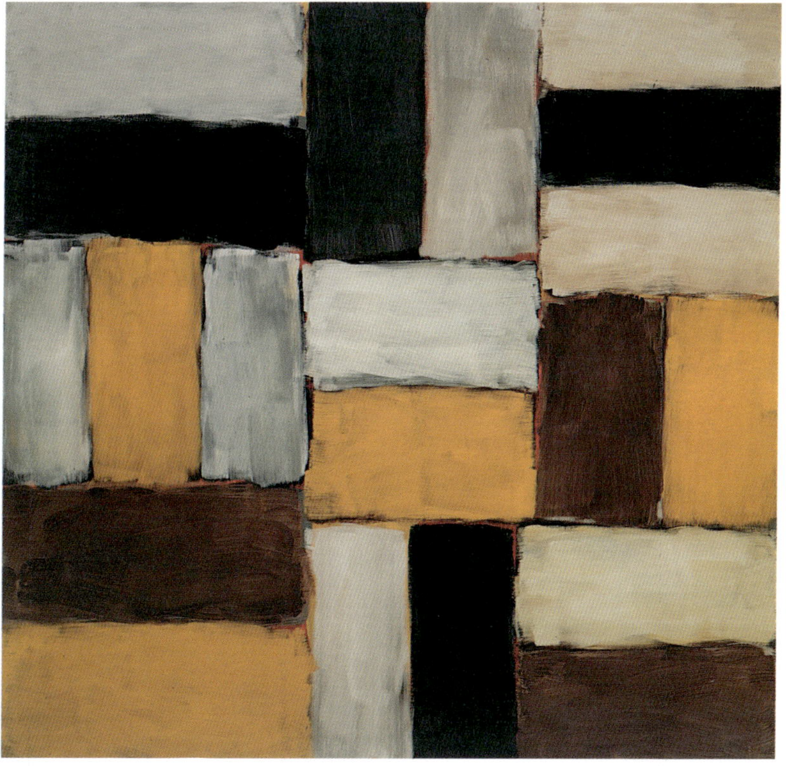

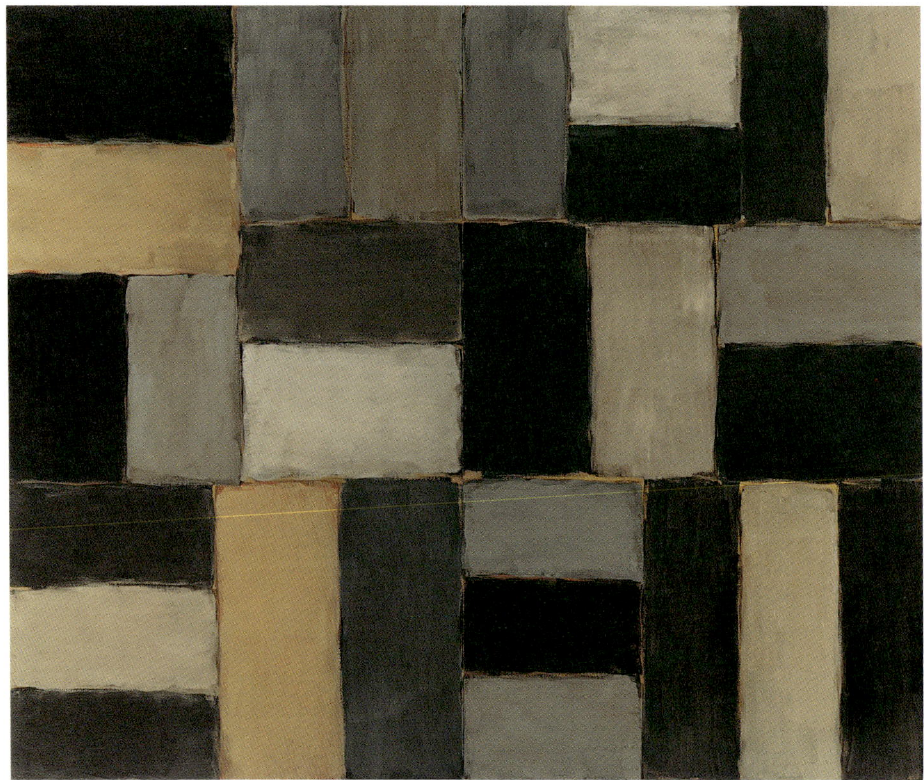

Pollock, for example. De Kooning seems less radical but over time he becomes more powerful, and it is this relationship that De Kooning had to the whole history of European art that is very similar to my own. The other thing is that the first time De Kooning came to the USA he was a very young man. The same is true in my case. I was twenty-six. So I was only partially made. I wasn't like I am now, but I had within me a reservoir on which I could draw, from Europe, which I had not discarded and which I could use in my moment of crisis within the paintings, and to get myself out of a Minimalist trap. And so I see myself configured in history in a similar way and I find this an interesting comparison, though of course one cannot design these things. Life has to be lived, and afterwards one sees what happens.

This one is called *Dorothy* (2003). I painted this for a friend of mine who died in Ireland. She was a wonderful woman and was instrumental in rebuilding my relationship with Ireland. I wanted to make a painting that was deep and sorrowful but also a painting that had some hold on life, that reached to life. So there are colours here that relate to the colours in nature; in other words, the natural world is not lost in this painting. It has its hand on the natural world. The painting is also

DOROTHY 2003
Oil on linen
274 × 355.5 cm (108 × 132 in.)
Dublin, Irish Museum of Modern Art

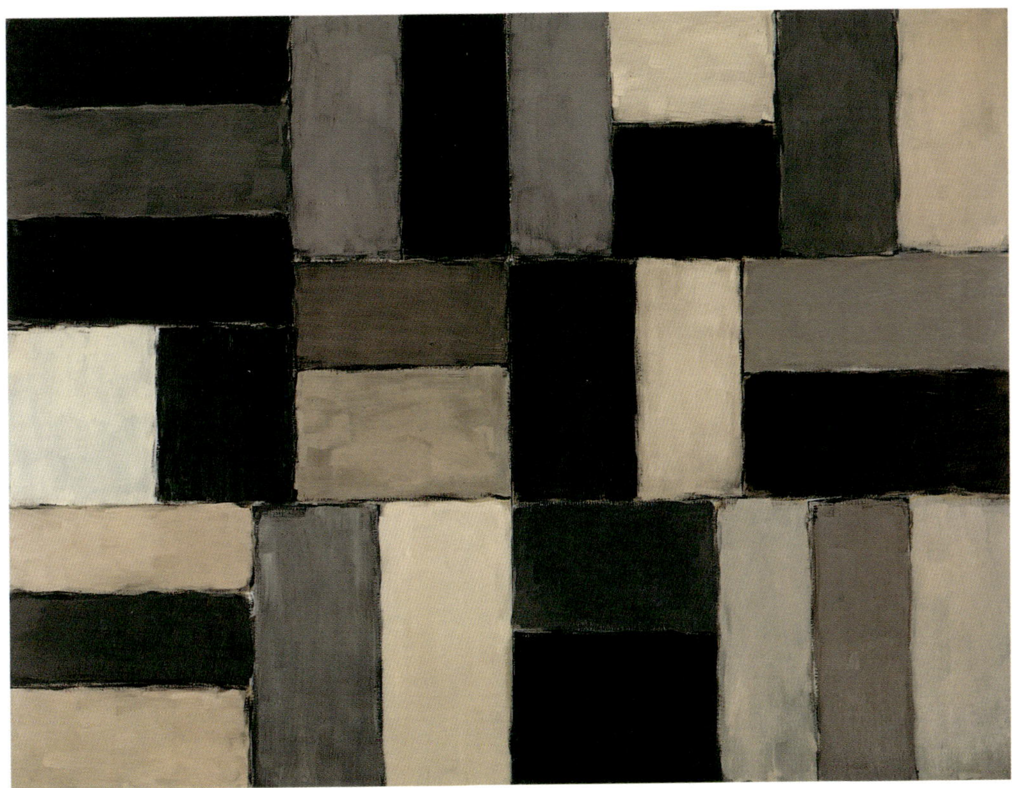

like stone, and it is awesome in a sense, but it is not unremitting. The argument isn't taken to an extreme where all colour is purged from the painting.

Raphael was made in New York, and in New York I am significantly more armoured than when I am in Europe. I feel that I have to be more rigorous in New York, and that makes New York interesting because it challenges me. This painting was made over a very long time. It has what Donald Kuspit called "human sedimentation". It is painted in layers, and as the layers are added over a long period of time so an experience is being made. Sometimes paintings are made in four hours, so one can't prescribe these things. But it is interesting for me to make this painting, to leave it, come back and make it again. Leave it, come back and make it again. So the issue of time, layering – not just a simple measure of time but time lived, is in this painting. But I called it Raphael because it has been classicized over time, and, as we all know, Raphael was the great conciliatory artist, as am I. A bridge builder. No, I am a warrior, but as a painter I am trying to build a bridge. Bridge builders are more important today than people who take hard positions in the world as it is now.

30 June 1945	Born in Dublin
1949	Family moves to London
1960–62	Works as a messenger in a graphic design studio, and as a plasterer's labourer. Apprenticed to a commercial printmaking shop and becomes a typesetter
1962–65	Attends evening classes at Central School of Art, London
1965–68	Croydon College of Art, London
1968–72	Newcastle University, England
1971	Prizewinner, 'John Moore's Liverpool Exhibition 8'. Awarded John Knox fellowship
1972–73	Harvard University, Cambridge, MA
1973	First exhibition, Rowan Gallery, London
1973–75	Teaches at Chelsea School of Art and Goldsmiths' School of Art, London
1975	Moves to the USA. Receives Harkness Fellowship
1978–82	Visiting Arts Professor at Princeton University, NJ
1981	Ten-year retrospective at Ikon Gallery, Birmingham
1981–84	Professor at Parsons School of Art, New York
1983	Receives Guggenheim Fellowship and the National Endowment for the Arts. Begins his first collaboration with a printer. Becomes an American citizen
1984	Receives Artist's Fellowship from the National Endowment for the Arts
1989	Exhibits at the Whitechapel Art Gallery, London. Nominated for the Turner Prize
1993	First exhibition of the Catherine Paintings, Modern Art Museum of Forth Worth, TX. Nominated for the Turner Prize
2000	Inducted as a Member into the London Institute of Art and Letters
2002	Part-time Professor for Painting at the Akademie der Bildenden Künste in Munich, Germany
2003	Honorary Doctor of Fine Arts, Massachusetts College of Art; Honorary Doctor of Fine Arts, National University of Ireland
2005	Dublin City Gallery The Hugh Lane, Dublin, builds an extension to house eight works donated by the artist

Sean Scully lives and works in New York, Barcelona and Munich.

An asterisk (*) indicates the publication of a related exhibition catalogue

2007 Retrospective exhibition, Fundació Miró, Barcelona, Spain;
  Museo d'Arte Contemporanea, Rome; Musée d'Art Moderne
  de St Etienne Metropole, France*
  Prints, Smithsonian American Art Museum, Washington, D.C.

2006 *Architecture of Colour*, Museum of Fine Arts Liechtenstein,
  Vaduz*
  Prints, Bibliothèque Nationale de France, Paris
  Opening of the Scully Room, Dublin City Gallery
  The Hugh Lane, Dublin
  Paintings, LA Louver Gallery, Los Angeles*

2006–07 Paintings, Timothy Taylor Gallery, London*

2005–07 *Wall of Light*, Phillips Collection, Washington, D.C.; Modern
  Art Museum of Fort Worth, TX; Cincinnati Art Museum;
  The Metropolitan Museum of Art, New York*

2005 Ingleby Gallery, Edinburgh*
  Galerie Lelong, New York
  Augustinerkloster, Erfurt, Germany
  Abbot Hall Art Gallery, Kendal, England*
  Staatliche Museum, Kassel, Germany*
  Centre de la Gravure et de l'Image Imprimée, La Louvière,
  Belgium
  Sala Alcala 31, Madrid

2004 *Winter Robe*, Galerie Lelong, Paris*
  Kerlin Gallery, Dublin
  Prints, Irish Cultural Centre, Paris
  Paintings from the 1970s, Timothy Taylor Gallery, London
  Etchings for Frederico García Lorca, Frederico García Lorca
  Foundation, Granada, Spain*

2003 Hôtel des Arts, Toulon, France*
  Wall of Light, Figures, Timothy Taylor Gallery, London*
  LA Louver Gallery, Los Angeles
  Sara Hildén Art Museum, Tampere, Finland; Stiftung Weimarer
  Klassik, Weimar, Germany; (2004) National Gallery
  of Australia, Canberra*
  Galería Carles Taché, Barcelona, Spain*

2002 Galerie Neue Meister, Staatliche Kunstsammlungen, Dresden,
  Germany*
  Centro de Arte Hélio Oiticica, Rio de Janeiro, Brazil*
  LA Louver Gallery, Los Angeles
  Gemäldegalerie Neue Meister, Staatliche Kunstsammlungen,
  Dresden, Germany
  Cámara de Comercio de Cantabria, Santander, Spain;
  Ayuntamiento de Pamplona, Spain*

2001 *Barcelona Etchings for Frederico García Lorca*, Instituto
  Cervantes, London
  Light and Gravity, Knoedler & Co., New York*
  New Works on Paper, Galerie Lelong, New York
  Paintings, Drawings, Photographs 1990–2001,
  Kunstsammlung Nordrhein-Westfalen, Düsseldorf, Germany;

  Haus der Kunst, Munich, Germany; Institut Valencià d'Art
  Modern, Spain*
  Work on Paper, Rex Irwin Gallery, Woollahra, Australia;
  Dickerson Gallery, Melbourne, Australia
  Galerie Lelong, Paris*
  Ingleby Gallery, Edinburgh
  Le Musée Jenisch, Vevey, Switzerland
  Walls/Windows/Horizons, David Winton Bell Gallery,
  Brown University, Providence
  Wall of Light, Museo de Arte Contemporáneo de Monterrey,
  Mexico; Museo de Arte Moderno, Mexico City*

2000 *Sean Scully on Paper*, The Metropolitan Museum of Art, New York
  Galería Carles Taché, Barcelona, Spain*
  Estampes 1983–99, Musée des Beaux-Arts de Caen, France*
  Photographies, Galerie de l'Ancien Collège, Châtellerault, France
  Graphics, Galleria d'Arte A+A, Venice, Italy

1999 Galerie Lelong, Paris*
  Print Retrospective, Graphische Sammlung Albertina, Vienna;
  Musée du Dessin et de l'Estampe Originale, Gravelines,
  France; Von der Heydt-Museum, Wuppertal, Germany*
  New Paintings and Works on Paper, Danese Gallery and
  Galerie Lelong, New York
  South London Gallery, London*
  Works from the Garner Tullis Workshop, Galerie Kornfeld,
  Zurich, Switzerland
  Ten Barcelona Paintings, Galerie Bernd Klüser, Munich, Germany
  Kerlin Gallery, Dublin

1998 *Paintings and Works on Paper*, Galerie Bernd Klüser, Munich,
  Germany*
  Mirror Images, Timothy Taylor Gallery, London
  Galerie Haas & Fuchs, Berlin
  Mira Goddard Gallery, Toronto, Canada
  BAWAG Foundation, Vienna*
  Galleri Weinberger, Copenhagen
  Galería Antonia Puyó, Saragossa, Spain
  Galerie Le Triangle Bleu, Stavelot, Belgium
  Denver Art Museum

1997 *1987–97*, Sala de Exposiciones Rekalde, Bilbao, Spain;
  Salas del Palacio Episcopal, Málaga, Spain; Fundació La Caixa,
  Palma de Mallorca, Spain*
  1982–96, Manchester City Art Gallery, England*
  Recent Paintings, Galerie Lelong, Paris*
  Kerlin Gallery, Dublin
  Floating Paintings and Photographs, Galerie Lelong, New York
  Galería El Diario Vasco, San Sebastián, Spain*
  Mary Boone Gallery, New York
  Paintings and Works on Paper, Galerie Jamileh Weber,
  Zurich, Switzerland
  Prints and Watercolours, John Berggruen Gallery, San Francisco

1996   *The Catherine Paintings*, Casino Luxembourg, Forum d'Art
            Contemporain, Luxembourg*
        Ediciones T, Barcelona, Spain*
        Floating Paintings and Work on Paper, Galerie National du Jeu
            de Paume, Paris; Neue Galerie der Stadt Linz, Austria;
            (1997) Culturgest, Lisbon*
        Paintings and Works on Paper, Galleria d'Arte Moderna,
            Villa delle Rose, Bologna, Italy*
        Galería Carles Taché, Barcelona, Spain*
        Pastels, Galerie Lelong, New York
        Prints, Galerie Angelika Harthan, Stuttgart, Germany
        Works on Paper 1975–96, Graphische Sammlung, Munich,
            Germany; Museum Folkwang, Essen, Germany; Henie Onstad
            Kunstsenter, Høvikodden, Norway; (1997) Whitworth Art
            Gallery, Manchester, England; Hugh Lane Municipal Gallery
            of Art, Dublin; (1998) Herning Kunstmuseum, Herning,
            Denmark; Milwaukee Art Museum; Denver Art Museum;
            Carpenter Center for the Visual Arts, Harvard University,
            Cambridge, MA; (2000) Albright-Knox Art Gallery, Buffalo*
1995   Galería El Diario Vasco, San Sebastián, Spain*
        Galerie de L'Ancien Collège, Châtellerault, France*
        Waddington Galleries, London
        Mary Boone Gallery, New York
        Galerie Bernd Klüser, Munich, Germany*
        Twenty Years, Hirshhorn Museum and Sculpture Garden,
            Washington, D.C.; High Museum of Art, Atlanta; La Caixa
            des Pensiones, Barcelona, Spain; (1996) Museum of Modern
            Art, Dublin; (1996) Schirn Kunsthalle, Frankfurt, Germany*
        The Catherine Paintings, Kunsthalle Bielefeld, Germany;
            Palais des Beaux-Arts, Charleroi, Belgium*
1994   *The Light in the Darkness*, Fuji Television Gallery, Tokyo*
        Works on Paper, Knoedler & Co., New York
        Butler Gallery, Kilkenny Castle, Kilkenny, Ireland
        Kerlin Gallery, Dublin
        Galleria Gian Ferrari Arte Contemporanea, Milan, Italy*
1993   Mary Boone Gallery, New York
        The Catherine Paintings, Modern Art Museum of Fort Worth, TX*
        Waddington Galleries, London*
        Paintings and Works on Paper, Galerie Bernd Klüser, Munich,
            Germany*
1992   *Prints*, Weinberger Gallery, Copenhagen
        Woodcuts, Pamela Auchincloss Gallery, New York
        Prints and Related Work, Brooke Alexander Editions, New York
        Woodcuts, Bobbie Greenfield Gallery, Los Angeles
        Woodcuts, Stephen Solovy Fine Art, Chicago
        Daniel Weinberg Gallery, Santa Monica, CA
        Paintings 1973–91, Sert Gallery, Carpenter Center for the Visual
            Arts, Harvard University, Cambridge, MA
        Woodcuts, Stephen Solovy Fine Art, Chicago
        Waddington Galleries, London
1991   *Paintings and Works on Paper*, Galerie Jamileh Weber,
            Zurich, Switzerland*
1990   Karsten Greve Gallery, Cologne, Germany
        Galerie de France, Paris*

1989   David McKee Gallery, New York*
1989   The Whitechapel Art Gallery, London; Palacio de Velázquez
            del Retiro, Madrid; Städtische Galerie im Lenbachhaus,
            Munich, Germany*
        Pastel Drawings, Grob Gallery, London
        David McKee Gallery, New York*
1988   *Four Paintings*, The Art Institute of Chicago
        Matrix/University Art Museum, University of California,
            Berkeley, CA*
        Fuji Television Gallery, Tokyo*
        Prints, Crown Point Press, New York and San Francisco
1987   *Monotypes from the Garner Tullis Workshop*, Pamela
            Auchincloss Gallery, Santa Barbara, CA*
        Monotypes, David McKee Gallery, New York
        Monotypes, Douglas Flanders Contemporary Art,
            Minneapolis*
        Mayor Rowan Gallery, London*
        Galerie Schmela, Düsseldorf, Germany*
1986   *Paintings 1985–86*, David McKee Gallery, New York*
1985   David McKee Gallery, New York
        Museum of Art, Carnegie Institute, Pittsburgh
        Museum of Fine Arts, Boston*
        Drawings, Barbara Krakow Gallery, Boston
        Neue Arbeiten, Galerie Schmela, Düsseldorf, Germany
1984   Juda Rowan Gallery, London
        Galerie S65, Aalst, Belgium
1983   David McKee Gallery, New York
1982   William Beadleston Gallery, New York
1981   Rowan Gallery, London
        Museum für (Sub)Kultur, Berlin
        Paintings 1971–81, Ikon Gallery, Birmingham, England;
            Sunderland Arts Centre, England; Douglas Hyde Gallery,
            Dublin; Arts Council of Northern Ireland, Belfast;
            Warwick Arts Trust, London*
1980   Susan Caldwell Gallery, New York
1979   *Painting for One Place* (installation), Nadin Gallery, New York
        Rowan Gallery, London
        The Clocktower, New York
1977   Duffy-Gibbs Gallery, New York
        Rowan Gallery, London
1976   Tortue Gallery, Santa Monica, CA
1975   Rowan Gallery, London
        Tortue Gallery, Santa Monica, CA
1973   Rowan Gallery, London

FURTHER READING

See also exhibitions marked with an asterisk (*) on pp. 187–88

BOOKS

David Carrier, *Sean Scully*, London and New York 2004
— *Sean Scully: Monotypes from the Garner Tullis Workshop*, New York 1990
Danilo Eccher, *Sean Scully*, Milan 1996
Galería El Diario Vasco, *Sean Scully: Obra Gráfica 1991–94*, San Sebastián 1994
Helsinki Festival, *Harvey Quaytman and Sean Scully*, Helsinki 1987
Bernd Klüser and John Ormrod (eds.), *Sean Scully: The Beauty of the Real*, Munich 1995
Michelle Meyers, *Sean Scully/Donald Sultan: Paintings, Drawings and Prints from the Anderson Collection*, Stanford CA 1990
Michael Peppiatt, *Espace et Lumière: Conversation avec Richard Meier et Sean Scully*, Paris 1999
Maurice Poirier, *Sean Scully*, New York 1990
Ned Rifkin, *Sean Scully: Twenty Years 1976–95*, London 1995
Sean Scully, Chicago 1987

ARTICLES

Brooks Adams, 'The Stripe Strikes Back', *Art in America*, October 1985, pp. 118–23
Anastasia Aukeman, 'Sean Scully at Bernd Klüser', *ARTnews*, April 1994
Kenneth Baker, 'Abstract Gestures', *Artforum International*, September 1989, pp. 135–38
Cyril Barrett, 'Exhibitions: ROSC, 84', *Art Monthly*, October 1984, pp. 11–14
Felicity Barringer, 'Matisse: He's Kind of Cast a Spell on Me', *ARTnews*, April 1993
Ruth Bass, 'Sean Scully', *ARTnews*, March 1991
David Batchelor, 'Sean Scully', *Artscribe International*, September–October 1989, p. 72
Tiffany Bell, 'Responses to Neo-Expressionism', *Flash Art*, May 1983, pp. 40–46
Ian Bennett, 'Sean Scully', *Flash Art*, January–February 1980, p. 53
— 'Modern Painting and Modern Criticism in England', *Flash Art*, March/April 1980, pp. 24–26
— 'Sean Scully', *Tema Celeste*, January–March 1992, p. 104
Larry Berryman, 'Abstraction of Opposites', *Arts Review*, December 1992
Roger Bevan, 'Scully's Decade', *Antique and New Art*, Winter 1990
— 'Controversy over the Turner Prize', *The Art Newspaper*, November 1991
Paul Bonaventura, 'Sean Scully: Hay que ligar la abstracción a la vida', *RS*, October 1989, pp. 26–34
Craig Bromberg, 'The Untitled Orbit', *Art and Auction*, October 1991
— 'Gefühl ist wieder angesagt. Die Renaissance der abstrakten Malerei in New York', *Artis*, February 1992, pp. 44–49
James Burr, 'Round the Galleries – People and Patterns', *Apollo*, November 1984, p. 354
— 'Sean Scully at the Whitechapel', *Apollo*, June 1989, p. 432

Rachel Campbell-Johnson, 'A Mere Stripe of a Thing', *The Times* (London), 16 June 1999
David Carrier, 'Spatial Relations', *Art International*, Autumn 1989, p. 81
— 'Art Criticism and its Beguiling Fictions', *Art International*, Winter 1989, pp. 36–41
— 'Afterlight: Exhibiting Abstract Painting in the Era of its Belatedness', *Arts Magazine*, March 1992, p. 60
— 'Sean Scully: New York and Fort Worth', *The Burlington Magazine*, July 1993
— 'Italia/America: L'Astrazione ridefinita', *Segno*, Autumn 1993
Victor de Circasia, 'Fade into Paint: Sean Scully speaks with critic and curator Victor de Circasia', *Label Magazine*, VII, Autumn 2002
Lynne Cooke, 'Sean Scully', *Galeries Magazine*, August–September 1989, pp. 60–63
Holland Cotter, 'Sean Scully', *Flash Art*, April–May 1985, p. 40
Fenella Crichton, 'Sean Scully at the Rowan', *Art International*, 15 June 1975, p. 58
— 'London', *Art and Artists*, October 1979, pp. 41–48
Peggy Cyphers, 'Sean Scully', *Tema Celeste*, March–April 1991, p. 92
Adrian Dannatt, 'Sean Scully: An Interview', *Flash Art*, May–June 1992, pp. 103–105
Arthur C. Danto, 'Painting Earns its Stripes', *The Nation*, 21 February 2000
Joshua Decter, 'Sean Scully', *Arts Magazine*, December 1986, pp. 123ff.
Toni Del Renzio, 'London', *Art and Artists*, December 1974, pp. 33–35
Bernard Denvir and William Packer, 'A Slice of Late Seventies Art', *Art Monthly*, March 1980, pp. 3–5
Francis Draper, 'Sean Scully', *Arts Review*, 25 November 1977, p. 714
Aidan Dunne, 'The Painter's Painter; Defender of the Faith', *The Irish Times*, 3 August 2002
Régis Durand, 'Sean Scully: Une abstraction ancrée dans le monde', *Art Press*, February 1991
James Faure-Walker, 'Sean Scully', *Studio International*, May–June 1975, p. 238
William Feaver, 'London Letter: Summer', *Art International*, November 1972, p. 39
— 'Sean Scully', *Art International*, November 1973, pp. 26, 32, 75
— 'Sean Scully', *ARTnews*, January 1978, p. 133
— 'Sean Scully', *ARTnews*, September 1989, p. 191
Susan Fisher, 'Catherine Lee/Sean Scully', *New Art Examiner*, June 1986, p. 52
Peter Frank, 'Sean Scully at LA Louver', *ARTNews*, February 2003
Paul Gardner, 'Waking Up and Warming Up', *ARTnews*, October 1992, p. 116
Margaret Garlake, 'Double Scully', *Gallery Magazine*, November 1987
— 'Sean Scully', *Art Monthly*, no. 127, June 1989, p. 23
Mark Glazebrook, 'The Star of the Stripes', *Royal Academy Magazine*, June 1999
— 'Positive Approach', *The Spectator*, 24 July 1999

Michael Glover, 'A Glimpse of the Light Fantastic', *The Independent*,
29 June 1999

Sharon Gold, 'Sean Scully', *Artforum International*, Summer 1977, p. 9

Mel Gooding, 'Scully. Startup. Leverett', *Art Monthly*,
December 1987 – January 1988, pp. 21–23

John Goodrich, 'Sean Scully', *Review*, 15 May 1999

John Griefen, 'Sean Scully', *Arts Magazine*, February 1980, p. 35

Scott Gutterman, 'Sean Scully', *Journal of Art*, January 1991

Charles Hagen, '40th Biennial Exhibition of Contemporary American
Paintings', *Artforum International*, October 1987, p. 135

Marianne Hartigan, 'Scully in the Extreme', *Sunday Tribune*, 24 October
1999

Eleanor Heartney, 'Sean Scully at Danese and Lelong', *Art in America*,
November 1999, p. 136

Judith Higgins, 'Sean Scully and the Metamorphosis of the Stripe', *ARTnews*,
November 1985, pp. 104–12

Andrea Hill, 'Sean Scully', *Artscribe International*, September 1979, p. 60

Thomas Hubert, 'Irish Abroad', *Roland Garros Correspondence*,
13 June 2001

Robert Hughes, 'Earning his Stripes', *Time Magazine*, 14 August
1989, p. 47

Sam Hunter, 'Sean Scully's Absolute Paintings', *Artforum*, November 1979,
pp. 30–34

Richard Huntington, 'Sean Scully: Works on Paper, 1975–96', *The Buffalo
News*, 28 January 2000

Waldemar Januszczak, 'A Star Earns His Stripes', *The Sunday Times*
(London), 18 July 1999

Françoise Jaunin, 'Une Héraldique Sensuelle', *Vaud-Région 24 Heures*,
23 September 2001, p. 33

William Jeffett, 'Sean Scully: Reinventing Abstraction', *Artefactum*, Summer
1989, pp. 2–6

Heinz-Norbert Jocks, 'Sean Scully: Kunst setzt voraus, daß man nackt ist
und dadurch offener wird' (interview), *Kunstforum International*, CXLI,
July–September 1998, p. 268–81

Ben Jones and Peter Rippon, 'An Interview with Sean Scully', *Artscribe
International*, June 1978, pp. 27–29

Enrique Juncosa, 'Las Estrategias de Apolo', *Lapiz*, VI, no. 60, 1989,
pp. 26–32

— 'Sean Scully', *Tema Celeste* (Italy), October–December 1993

Petra Kipphoff, 'Kritiker-Umfrage', *Art Journal*, January 1985, pp. 8ff.

Joyce B. Korotkin, 'Sean Scully', *The New York Art World*, 8 June 1999

Anne Krauter, 'Sean Scully: Galerie Jamileh Weber', *Artforum International*,
Summer 1992, p. 120

Donald Kuspit, 'Sean Scully: Galerie Lelong/Danese', *Artforum International*,
September 1999, p. 168

Franck K. Lehodey, 'La Griffe d'un Tigre', *Roland Garros Magazine*, May 2001,
pp. 80, 87–89

Valerie Le Parc, 'Abstraction et volupté des œuvres de Sean Scully',
Var-matin, May 2003

Mark Levy, 'The Permutations of the Stripe', *Shift*, I, no. 2, 1988, pp. 38–41

Constance Lewallen, 'Interview with Sean Scully', *View*, V, no. 4, Autumn
1988

Susanne Lingemann, 'Liebeserklärungen mit der Disziplin von Piet
Mondrian', *Art: Das Kunstmagazin*, July 1995, pp. 74–77

John Loughery, 'Sean Scully', *Arts Magazine*, December 1986, p. 122

— 'Affirming Abstraction: The Corcoran Biennial', *Arts Magazine*,
September 1987, pp. 76–78

— '17 Years at the Barn', *Arts Magazine*, April 1988, p. 110

Barbara A. MacAdam, 'A Stripe Day/La Metafisica della luce', *ARTnews*,
February 1992

John McCarron, 'Conversation: John McCarron with Sean Scully', *Shift*, II,
no. 3, 1988, pp. 14–19

Steven Henry Madoff, 'A New Generation of Abstract Painters', *ARTnews*,
November 1983, pp. 78–84

— 'An Inevitable Gathering', *ARTnews*, September 1987, p. 183

Angela Molina, 'Sean Scully: Una pintura hecha con amor puede cambiar el
mundo', *ABC Cataluña*, 17 March 2000

Robert C. Morgan, 'Physicality and Metaphor: The Paintings of Sean Scully',
Art Journal, Spring 1991, pp. 64–66

Mario Naves, 'Heroic Art is Bravura Only', *The New York Observer*,
31 May 1999

Michael Newman, 'Sean Scully', *Art Monthly*, October 1981, p. 17

— 'New York Reviews', *Flash Art*, June–July 1979, p. 52

Georgina Oliver, 'Sean Scully', *Connaisseur*, December 1973, p. 302

Saul Ostrow, 'Sean Scully at Mary Boone', *Flash Art*, December 1993,
p. 113

David Pagel, 'Monumental paintings done with a light touch', *Los Angeles
Times*, 22 November 2002

Demetrio Paparoni, 'L'Astrazione ridefinita', *Tema Celeste* (Italy),
October–December 1994

Maurice Poirier, 'Sean Scully', *ARTnews*, January 1987, p. 160

— 'Sean Scully sobre la geometira', *El Mundo: El Cultural*, 8–14 May 2002,
pp. 25–27

Nancy Princenthal, 'Irrepressible Vigor: Printmaking Expands', *ARTnews*,
September 1990

Renate Puvogel, 'Sean Scully: Neue Arbeiten', *Kunstwerk*, February 1986,
pp. 84ff.

Elena di Raddo, 'Sean Scully: Intervista al l'Artiste Irlandese', *Segno*,
Autumn 1994

Carter Ratcliff, 'Artist's Dialogue: Sean Scully, A Language of Materials',
Architectural Digest, February 1988, pp. 54, 62ff.

John Roberts, 'Patterns and Patterns: Sean Scully and Tony Sherman',
Art Monthly, September 1979, pp. 11ff.

Adrienne Rosenthal, 'Painting by Sean Scully', *Artweek*, 29 March 1975

Medb Ruane, 'Tales of Scully Duggery', *The Irish Sunday Times*,
24 October 1999

Meyer Raphael Rubenstein, 'Books: Sean Scully', *Arts*, March 1991

Jerry Saltz, 'Mayday, Mayday, Mayday', *Art in America*, September 1993, p. 44

Wolfgang Sauré, 'Sean Scully', *Weltkunst*, January 1994, p. 141

Frieder Schnock, 'Sean Scully: Bilder und Zeichnungen', *Nike*,
January 1986, p. 42

Barry Schwabsky, 'Sean Scully: Mary Boone Gallery', *Artforum International*,
December 1993, p. 78

Arturo Schwarz, 'Italia/America: L'Astrazione ridefinita', *Segno*,
Autumn 1993

Sean Scully, 'Bodies of Light', *The Times Literary Supplement*, no. 4988,
6 November 1998, and *Art in America*, July 1999, pp. 67ff.; reprinted
as 'Against the Dying of his own Light: Mystery and Sadness in Rothko's
Work', *Sean Scully: Barcelona Paintings and Recent Editions*, Munich 1999,
pp. 11, 63ff.

Sean Scully and Mimmo Paladino, '"In at the Deep End" (A Conversation by Telephone)', *Modern Painters*, Summer 1993

'Sean Scully at LA Louver', *The Art Newspaper*, no. 130, November 2002

Adrian Searle, 'Recent British Painting: Future Space', *Flash Art*, March–April 1980, pp. 28ff.

— 'The British Art Show', *Artforum International*, April 1980, pp. 87ff.

Richard Shone, 'Sean Scully', *The Burlington Magazine*, January 1963

Andrea Silverman, 'Sean Scully', *ARTnews*, October 1986, pp. 98ff.

Alistair Smith, 'Sean Scully', *Irish Arts Review Yearbook*, 1994

Ken Sofer, 'Monotypes from the Garner Tullis Workshop', *ARTnews*, November 1987, p. 210

Frances Spalding, 'Unequal Halves', *Arts Review*, September 1993

Hugh Stoddart, 'Sean Scully', *Contemporary Visual Arts*, no. 23, May 1999, pp. 30–35

Valentin Tatransky, 'Sean Scully', *Arts Magazine*, February 1980, pp. 35ff.

Judith Trepp, 'Five One-Man Shows: Jamileh Weber', *ARTnews*, January 1994

Martin Tschechne, 'Sean Scully: Strenge Form, große Gefühle', *Art: Das Kunstmagazin*, July 1998, pp. 16–27

Marie-Claire Uberquoi, 'Los Juegos de Luz de Sean Scully', *El Mundo*, 17 March 2000

— 'Reviews', *The Art Newspaper*, April 2001

— 'El Instituto Cervantes de Londres un Ciclo Sobre García-Lorca', *Granada*, 2 June 2001, p. 44

Dorothy Walker, 'The Ten Masters of Abstract Art', *The Irish Sunday Times*, 18 March 1999

Lily Wei, 'Sean Scully at Knoedler and Galerie Lelong', *Art in America*, January 2002

Marjorie Welish, 'Abstraction, Advocacy of', *Tema Celeste*, January–March 1992, pp. 74–79

Stephen Westfall, 'Recent Aspects of All-Over', *Arts Magazine*, December 1982, p. 40

— 'Sean Scully', *Arts Magazine*, November 1983, p. 35

— 'Sean Scully', *Arts Magazine*, September 1985, p. 40

— 'Sean Scully', *Art in America*, September 1989, pp. 208, 210

Peter Winter, 'Shape is not Abstract', *Art International*, Summer 1990, pp. 79–81

John Yau, 'Sean Scully: McKee Gallery/Pamela Auchincloss Gallery', *Artforum International*, April 1991, pp. 124ff.

Robert Yoskowitz, 'Sean Scully/Martha Alf', *Arts Magazine*, April 1980, p. 24

William Zimmer, 'Heart of Darkness: New Stripe Paintings by and an Interview with Sean Scully', *Arts Magazine*, December 1982, pp. 82ff.

— 'Sean Scully', *ARTnews*, May 1989, pp. 159ff.

INDEX

Titles and page numbers in *italics* refer to illustrations